Creative Crochet in a Day

Contents

Sunday

Monday

Tuesday

Chapter One
- 7   On The Double Shawl
- 8   Padded Hangers
- 10   Heirloom Tablecloth
- 12   Flower Girl Basket
- 14   Country Dining
- 16   Victorian Snuggler
- 18   Pineapple Doily
- 21   Serenade Doily
- 23   Earring Jackets
- 24   Little Sweetie
- 26   Lacy Bib and Bottle

Chapter Two
- 31   Floral Doily
- 32   Scrubby Pad
- 35   Pixie Christmas Stocking
- 36   Sewing Helper
- 38   Lacy Bookmarks
- 40   Fans & Lace
- 42   Foot Warmers
- 44   Diagonal Dishcloth
- 47   Lace Tissue Holder
- 48   Ponytail Ruffles

Chapter Three
- 51   Christmas Shell Afghan
- 52   Teapot Tidee
- 53   Doily Sachet
- 54   Kitchen Extras
- 56   Photo Album
- 57   Puppy Poncho
- 58   Headband and Mittens
- 62   Cotton Candy
- 64   Cro-Tat™ Jar Topper
- 66   Cool Water Bottle Holder
- 68   Sweet Baby Hat

Chapter Four
- 70   Doily & Bowl Cover
- 73   Present Pillow
- 75   Hooded Scarf
- 76   Bright Basics
- 79   Elegant Pastels
- 81   Pillow Toppers
- 84   Helpful Holders
- 86   Simply Beautiful Bibs
- 88   Floor Doily
- 90   Autumn Doily

Chapter Six
119 Striped Wave Afghan
120 Glass Slippers
123 Toe Cozies
125 Doily Hat & Doily
127 Quick Stitch Stocking
128 Playtime Puppets
131 Puff Stitch Pillow
133 Homespun Hat & Scarf
134 Dolly Backpack
136 Sports Carrier

Friday

6

Chapter Five
95 Black & White Afghan
96 Striped Chair Pad
98 Bath Duo
101 Peach Parfait
103 Pastel Bookmarks
105 Cro-Tat™ Snowflakes
110 Lacy Towel Edgings
112 Wild Rose Doily
114 Colorful Carryall
116 Baby Night Cap

Thursday

5

Wednesday

Chapter Seven
139 Bridal Set
142 Puttin' on the Ritz
144 Mini Angels
147 Cool Crochet Poncho
148 Hat Pincushion
151 Li'l Cowpokes
153 Currents Afghan
154 Centerpieces

Saturday

7

157 General Instructions
158 Stitch Guide
160 Index

4

Product Development Manager	CAROLYN CHRISTMAS
Publishing Services Manager	ANGE VAN ARMAN
Crochet Product Manager	DEBORAH LEVY-HAMBURG
Editor	DONNA SCOTT
Product Development Staff	DARLA HASSELL
	ALICE MITCHELL
Assistant Editor	SHARON LOTHROP
Copy Editor	SHIRLEY PATRICK
Book Design	GREG SMITH
Production Artist	JOANNE GONZALEZ
Photography Supervisor	SCOTT CAMPBELL
Photographer	ANDY J. BURNFIELD
Photo Stylist	MARTHA COQUAT
Photo Assistant	CRYSTAL KEY
Production Assistant	GLENDA CHAMBERLAIN
Chief Executive Officer	JOHN ROBINSON
Product Development Director	VIVIAN ROTHE
Marketing Director	DAVID MCKEE
Customer Service	1-800-449-0440
Pattern Services	(903) 636-5140

CREDITS

Sincerest thanks to all the designers,
manufacturers and other professionals
whose dedication has made this book possible.

Special thanks to
Quebecor Printing Book Group, Kingsport, Tenn.

Library of Congress Cataloging-in-Publication Data
ISBN: 1-57367-121-5
First Printing: 2001
Library of Congress Catalog Card Number:
2001098751
Published and Distributed by
The Needlecraft Shop, Big Sandy, Texas 75755
Printed in the United States of America.

Visit us at **NeedlecraftShop.com**

Within the pages of this book I want to share my love and passion for the art of crochet. It is as much a part of my life, professionally and personally, each and every day, as eating or sleeping. You can walk up to me at any given time, any day of the week, and ask me to show you what I have in my project bag. I take it with me everywhere I go. Sometimes the bag is small, and sometimes it's practically a suitcase!

I'm the person you see happily crocheting while sitting in the grandstands at a ball game or at the races. I'm the person you see stitching away the minutes while sitting in the waiting room at the doctor's office. Yes, I'm even the person you see with hook and yarn in hand while parked in the drive-thru lane waiting for my bank transaction to be completed. And I can't truly enjoy television without something in my hands.

However, I have found that I cannot stitch and hold on to my husband while riding on the back of a motorcycle. Oh well, sometimes one must suffer an inconvenience.

Donna

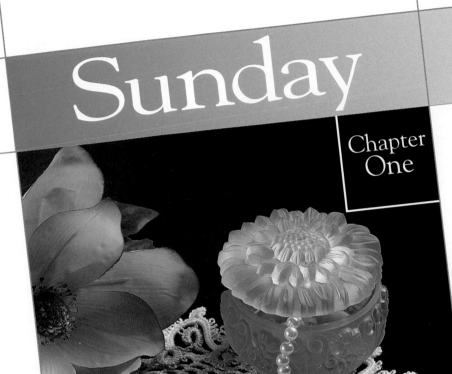

Chapter
One

7   On The Double Shawl
8   Padded Hangers
10 Heirloom Tablecloth
12 Flower Girl Basket
14 Country Dining
16 Victorian Snuggler
18 Pineapple Doily
21 Serenade Doily
23 Earring Jackets
24 Little Sweetie
26 Lacy Bib and Bottle

1

The warm ball of light in the sky during the day was given the name by Europeans of dies solis, Latin for "day of the sun."

On The Double Shawl

DESIGNED BY DARLA SIMS

Create this airy, elegant shawl using a double-quick technique with a double-ended hook.
It's great for a gift for yourself or a special daughter, mother or grandmother.
This lighter-than-air creation is perfect for both casual and dressy occasions.

FINISHED SIZE: 81" across top x 31" long not including Tassel.

MATERIALS: Worsted fluffy mohair blend yarn — 2½ oz. each gold and fisherman; tapestry needle; P crochet hook and Q double-ended hook or hooks needed to obtain gauges.

GAUGES: With **P hook,** 7 sc = 4". With **Q double-end hook,** 2 shells = 5"; 8 shell rows = 9".

BASIC STITCHES: Ch, sl st, sc.

SPECIAL STITCHES: For **beginning shell** *(beg shell),* yo, draw through first 5 lps on hook.

For **shell,** yo, draw through next 6 lps on hook.

GENERAL INSTRUCTIONS

To **draw up a lp,** insert hook in designated lp, bar or st, yo, draw lp through and leave on hook.

When **using a color already in use,** pick up color from row below, yo, draw through one lp on hook, (yo, draw through 2 lps on hook) across leaving last lp at end of row on hook (this is first vertical bar of next row).

To **work lps off with new color,** place slip knot on hook, draw slip knot through one lp on hook, (yo, draw through 2 lps) across leaving last lp at end of row on hook (this is first vertical bar of next row).

When **turning,** always slide lps to opposite end of hook. **Do not** turn unless otherwise stated.

To **turn,** rotate hook 180 degrees and slide stitches to opposite end.

If you have difficulty keeping all the stitches on the double-end hook, cap the unused end of hook with either a knitting needle protector or a clean wine cork.

SHAWL

Note: Read General Instructions before beginning pattern.

Row 1: With double-end hook and fisherman, ch 135, draw up lp in second ch from hook, draw up lp in each ch across, turn. *(135 lps on hook)*

Row 2: With gold; **beg shell** (see Special Stitches), (ch 5, **shell** *(see Special Stitches)* across, **do not turn.** *(130 chs)*

Row 3: Skip first ch of first ch-5 sp, draw up lp in next 4 chs, (draw up lp in next 5 chs) across, ch 1, turn. *(130 lps on hook)*

Rows 4-5: With fisherman, repeat rows 2 and 3. *(125 lps on hook)*

Rows 6-51: Repeat rows 2-5 consecutively, ending with row 3 and *10 lps on hook.*

Row 52: With fisherman, draw through first 5 lps on hook, ch 5, draw through last 5 lps on hook, **do not turn.** *(5 chs)*

Row 53: Skip first ch of next ch-5 sp, draw up lp in last 4 chs, yo, draw through all 5 lps on hook. Fasten off.

EDGING

Working around outer edge, with P hook and fisherman; working in starting ch on opposite side of row 1, join with sc in first ch, sc in each ch across; working in ends of rows, 3 sc in each stripe across to point, sc in point, 3 sc in each stripe across, join with sl st in first sc. Fasten off.

continued on page 9

Padded Hangers

DESIGNED BY JAN HATFIELD

Give a touch of luxury to your favorite newlyweds, or to a friend or relative moving into a first home or apartment. A small touch of crochet can add just the right note of comfort, warmth and affection, and your special gift will bring long-lasting memories.

FINISHED SIZE: Fits 15½" padded hanger.

MATERIALS FOR ONE: Worsted yarn — small amount each main color *(MC)*, flower color *(FC)* and green *(optional for off-white cover, see photo)*; 15½" padded hanger; tapestry needle; G and H crochet hooks or sizes needed to obtain gauges.

GAUGES: With **G hook,** 4 sts = 1"; 2 dc rows = 2". With **H hook,** 7 sts = 2"; 3 dc rows = 2".

BASIC STITCHES: Ch, sl st, sc, hdc, dc, tr.

OFF-WHITE COVER

SIDE (make 2)

Rnd 1: With G hook and MC, ch 4, 11 dc in fourth ch from hook, join with sl st in top of ch-3. (12 dc made)

Rnd 2: Ch 3, dc in same st, ch 1, skip next st, (2 dc in next st, ch 1, skip next st) around, join with sl st in top of ch-3. *(12 dc, 6 ch-1 sps)*

Rnds 3-15: Ch 3, dc in next st, ch 1, skip next ch sp, (dc in each of next 2 sts, ch 1, skip next ch sp) around, join. At end of last rnd, fasten off.

FINISHING

For **flower,** with FC, ch 5, sl st in first ch to form ring, (ch 4, 2 tr, ch 4, sl st) 5 times in ring. Fasten off.

For **optional leaf (make 2),** with green, ch 8, sl st in second ch from hook, sc in next ch, hdc in next ch, dc in last 4 chs. Fasten off.

Place Sides over ends of hanger matching sts and chs, sew last rnds together. Tack flower and leaves to top of Cover.

BLUE COVER

Rnd 1: With H hook and MC, ch 4, 11 dc in fourth ch from hook, join with sl st in top of ch-3. *(12 dc made)*

Rnd 2: Ch 4, dc in same st, skip next st, *(dc, ch 1, dc) in next st, skip next st; repeat from * around, join with sl st in third ch of ch-4.

Rnds 3-13: Sl st in first ch-1 sp, ch 4, dc in same sp, (dc, ch 1, dc) in each ch-1 sp around, join. At end of last rnd, fasten off.

Place Sides over ends of hanger; matching sts and chs, sew last rnds together.

FLOWER

Rnd 1: With G hook and FC, ch 4, sl st in first ch to form ring, ch 1, (sc in ring, ch 2) 8 times, join with sl st in first sc. *(8 ch-2 sps made)*

Rnd 2: (Sl st, sc, 2 dc, sc, sl st) in each ch-2 sp around. Fasten off.

Slip center of Flower over hanger hook and tack to Cover to secure.

GREEN COVER

SIDE (make 2)

Rnd 1: Repeat same rnd of Off-white Cover.

Rnd 2: Ch 4, skip next st, (sc in next st, ch 4, skip next st) around, join with sl st in first ch-4 sp. *(6 ch sps)*

Rnds 3-18: Ch 4, (sc in next ch sp, ch 4) around, join with sc in first ch sp. At end of last rnd, fasten off.

Place Sides over ends of hanger; matching sts and chs, sew last rnds together.

FLOWER

Rnd 1: With G hook and FC, ch 2, 6 sc in second ch from hook, join with sl st in first sc. *(6 sc made)*

Rnd 2: (Sl st, ch 4, 2 tr, ch 4, sl st) in each sc around. Fasten off.

Slip center of Flower over hanger hook and tack to Cover to secure. ✿

OTD Shawl

continued from page 7

TASSEL

Cut 23 strands fisherman each 8" long. Tie separate strand fisherman tightly around middle of all strands; fold strands in half. Wrap separate piece of fisherman ½" from top of fold covering ¼". Trim ends.

Tie Tassel to point on Shawl. ✿

Heirloom Tablecloth

DESIGNED BY VIDA SUNDERMAN

Transform any occasional table with a pretty fabric tablecloth and this elegant lace topper.
This fresh combination will even give new life to the plainest of flea-market tables.
Reminiscent of pineapples, this topper is quick and easy to make.

FINISHED SIZE: 40" across

MATERIALS: Size 10 crochet cotton thread —2,025 yds. white; No. 9 steel hook or hook size needed to obtain gauge.

GAUGE: Rnds 1-6 = 4" across.

BASIC STITCHES: Ch, sl st, sc, dc, tr.

SPECIAL STITCHES: For **beginning cluster (beg cl),** ch 3, *yo 2 times, insert hook in same st, yo, draw through st, (yo, draw through 2 lps on hook) 2 times; repeat from *, yo, draw through all 3 lps on hook.

For **cluster (cl),** yo 2 times, insert hook in next st, yo, draw through st, (yo, draw through 2 lps on hook) 2 times; *yo 2 times, insert hook in same st, yo, draw through st, (yo, draw through 2 lps on hook) 2 times; repeat from *, yo, draw through all 4 lps on hook.

For **picot,** ch 3, sl st in last tr of cl.

TABLECLOTH

Rnd 1: Ch 6, sl st in first ch to form ring, ch 1, 12 sc in ring, join with sl st in first sc. *(12 sc made)*

Rnd 2: Beg cl *(see Special Stitches),* ch 3, *cl *(see Special Stitches),* ch 3; repeat from * around, join with sl st in top of first cl.

Rnd 3: Sl st in next ch sp, ch 8 *(counts as first dc and ch-5 sp),* (dc in next ch-3 sp, ch 5) around, join with sl st in third ch of ch-8.

Rnd 4: Sl st in next 3 chs, ch 9, (dc in next ch lp, ch 6) around, join with sl st in third ch of ch-9.

Row 5: Ch 1, sc in first st, 7 sc in next ch sp, (sc in next dc, 7 sc in next ch sp) around, join with sl st in first sc.

Rnd 6: Sl st in next 2 sc, beg cl in same sc as last sl st, (ch 2, skip next sc, cl in next sc) 2 times, ch 3, skip next 3 sc, *cl in next sc, (ch 2, skip next sc, cl in next sc) 2 times, ch 3, skip next 3 sc; repeat from * around, join.

Rnd 7: Sl st in next ch sp, beg cl in same sp, ch 2, cl in next ch sp, ch 5, sc in next ch sp, ch 5, (cl in next ch sp, ch 2, cl in next ch sp, ch 5, sc in next ch sp, ch 5) around, join with sl st in top of beg cl.

Rnd 8: Sl st in first ch sp, beg cl in same sp, **picot** *(see Special Stitches),* ch 5, sc in next ch-5 sp, ch 7, sc in next ch-5 sp, (ch 5, cl in next ch-2 sp, picot, ch 5, sc in next ch sp, ch 7, sc in next ch sp) around, ch 3; to **join,** dc in top of first cl.

Rnd 9: Ch 8, (dc in next ch sp, ch 5) around, join with sl st in third ch of ch-8.

Rnd 10: Sl st in next 3 chs, ch 8, (dc in next ch sp, ch 5) around, join as before.

Rnd 11: Repeat rnd 4.

Rnd 12: Ch 1, 7 sc in each ch sp around, join.

Rnd 13: Sl st in next sc, beg cl in same st, (ch 2, skip next sc, cl in next sc) 2 times, ch 5, skip next 4 sc, sc in next sc, ch 5, skip next 4 sc, *cl in next sc, (ch 2, skip next sc, cl in next sc) 2 times, ch 5, skip next 4 sc, sc in next sc, ch 5, skip next 4 sc; repeat from * around, join.

Rnd 14: Sl st in first ch sp, beg cl in same sp, ch 2, cl in next ch-2 sp, ch 5, sc in next ch sp, ch 7, sc in next ch sp, ch 5, (cl in next ch sp, ch 2, cl in next ch-2 sp, ch 5, sc in next ch sp, ch 7, sc in next ch sp, ch 5) around, join.

Rnd 15: Sl st in first ch sp, beg cl in same sp, picot, ch 5, sc in next ch sp, (ch 7, sc in next ch sp) 2 times, *ch 5, cl in next ch sp, picot, ch 5, sc in next ch sp, (ch 7, sc in next ch sp) 2 times; repeat from * around, ch 3; to **join,** dc in top of first cl.

Rnd 16: Repeat rnd 9.

Rnds 17-18: Repeat rnd 10.

Rnd 19: Ch 1, 5 sc in each ch sp around, join.

Rnd 20: Beg cl in first st, (ch 2, skip next sc, cl in next sc) 2 times, ch 5, sc between fifth and sixth sc, ch 5, skip next 5 sc, *cl in next sc, (ch 2, skip next sc, cl in next sc) 2 times, ch 5, sc between fifth and sixth sc, ch 5, skip next 5 sc; repeat from * around, join.

Rnds 21-25: Repeat rnds 14-18.

Rnd 26: Ch 1, sc in first st, 5 sc in next ch sp, (sc in next dc, 5 sc in next ch sp) around, join.

Rnd 27: Beg cl in first st, (ch 2, skip next sc, cl in next sc) 2 times, ch 5, skip next 5 sc, sc in next sc, ch 5, skip next 5 sc, *cl in next sc, (ch 2, skip next sc, cl in next sc) 2 times, ch 5, skip next 5 sc, sc in next sc, ch 5, skip next 5 sc; repeat from * around, join.

Rnds 28-33: Repeat rnds 14-19.

Rnd 34: Repeat rnd 27.

Rnd 35-41: Repeat rnds 14-20.

continued on page 13

Flower Girl Basket

Designed by Katherine Eng

Create a beautiful keepsake basket for the next wedding in your family.
This beribboned basket serves as a reception table decoration, too.
Choose threads and ribbons in the colors selected for the ceremony and reception.

FINISHED SIZE: 7½" tall.

MATERIALS: Size 3 crochet cotton — 150 yds. ecru; 1 yd. each off-white and white ¼" satin ribbon; fabric stiffener; plastic wrap; tapestry needle; C hook or hook size needed to obtain gauge.

GAUGE: 11 sc = 2"; 11 sc rows = 2"; 4 dc rows = 1¼".

BASIC STITCHES: Ch, sl st, sc, dc.

BASKET

Rnd 1: Ch 4, sl st in first ch to form ring, ch 1, 8 sc in ring, join with sl st in first sc. *(8 sc made)*

Rnd 2: Ch 1, 2 sc in each st around, join. *(16)*

Rnd 3: Ch 1, (sc in next st, 2 sc in next st) around, join. *(24)*

Rnd 4: Ch 1, (sc in next 2 sts, 2 sc in next st) around, join. *(32)*

Row 5: Ch 1, (sc in next 3 sts, 2 sc in next st) around, join. *(40)*

Rnd 6: Ch 1, sc in each st around, join.

Rnd 7: Repeat rnd 3. *(60)*

Rnds 8-9: Ch 1, sc in each st around, join.

Rnd 10: Ch 1, (sc in next 4 sts, 2 sc in next st) around, join. *(72)*

Rnd 11: Ch 1, sc in each st around, join.

Rnd 12: Ch 3, dc in each st around, join with sl st in top of ch-3.

Rnd 13: Ch 3, dc in next 2 sts, **front post (fp,** *see page 159)* around next st, (dc in next 3 sts, fp around next st) around, join. *(54 dc, 18 fp)*

Rnds 14-17: Ch 3, dc in next 2 sts, fp around next fp, (dc in next 3 sts, fp around next fp) around, join.

Rnd 18: For **ruffle,** ch 1, (sc in next st, skip next 2 sts, 5 dc in next st, skip next 2 sts) around, join. *(60 dc, 12 sc)*

Rnd 19: Ch 3, 4 dc in same st, sc in center dc of next 5-dc group, (5 dc in next sc, sc in center dc of next 5-dc group) around, join.

Rnd 20: Sl st in next 2 sts, ch 1, sc in same st, ch 1, 5 dc in next sc, ch 1, (sc in center dc of next 5-dc group, ch 1, 5 dc in next sc, ch 1) around, join. *(60 dc, 12 sc, 24 ch-1 sps)*

Rnd 21: Ch 1, sc in each st and sc in each ch-1 sp around with (sc, ch 3, sc) in center dc of each 5-dc group, join. *(108 sc, 12 ch-3 sps)*

Rnd 22: Ch 1, *(sc, ch 3, sc) in next st, ch 2, (sc, ch 3, sc, ch 5, sc, ch 3, sc) in next ch-3 sp, ch 2, skip next 4 sts; repeat from * around, join. Fasten off.

HANDLE

For **side** (make 2), ch 89, sc in second ch from hook, sc in each ch across. Fasten off.

Holding sides wrong side together, matching sts, working through both thicknesses, join with sc in first st, (ch 2, skip next 2 sts, sc in next st) across; working on opposite side of starting ch, ch 5, sc in first ch, (ch 2, skip next 2 chs, sc in next ch) across, ch 5, join with sl st in first sc. Fasten off.

FINISHING

1: Apply fabric stiffener to Basket and Handle according to manufacturer's instructions. Let Handle dry flat. Place Basket over jar or straight-sided bowl covered with plastic wrap. Shape ruffle with fingers. Let dry.

2: Sew ends of Handle to inside of Basket on each side of rnd 18.

3: Cut white and off-white ribbon each into two equal pieces.

4: Holding one white piece ribbon and one off-white piece ribbon together, make 3½" bow leaving ends for streamers. Tack to outside of Basket where Handle is sewn on. Repeat with remaining pieces of ribbon on opposite side of Basket. ✿

Heirloom Tablecloth

continued from page 11

Rnds 42-46: Repeat rnds 14-18.

Note: To make larger, repeat rnds 20-32 until piece is desired measurement across.

Rnds 47-48: Repeat rnd 10.

Rnd 49: Sl st in next 2 chs, ch 3, 2 dc in same ch sp, (tr, ch 3, tr, ch 5, tr, ch 3, tr) in center ch of next ch sp, *3 dc in next ch sp, (tr, ch 3, tr, ch 5, tr, ch 3, tr) in center ch of next ch sp; repeat from * around, join. Fasten off. ✿

Country Dining

DESIGNED BY JENNIFER MCCLAIN

This table setting conjures up images of a warm country kitchen. You can almost smell the fresh bread baking! Arrange this place mat and napkin ring on a table with crocks of freshly-churned butter, home-canned jams and ears of corn fresh from the garden.

FINISHED SIZES: Place Mat is 11¾" x 19½". Napkin Ring is 2¾" wide.

MATERIALS FOR ONE OF EACH: Worsted yarn — 1½ oz. desired color; 1½ yds. of ¼" ribbon; H hook or hook size needed to obtain gauge.

GAUGE: 1 dc = ¾" tall; 1 med. shell = 1¾" across.

BASIC STITCHES: Ch, sl st, sc, hdc, dc.

SPECIAL STITCHES: For **small shell (sm shell),** (2 dc, ch 2, 2 dc) in next ch sp or st.

For **beginning medium shell (beg med shell),** ch 3, (2 dc, ch 2, 3 dc) in same ch sp.

For **medium shell (med shell),** (3 dc, ch 2, 3 dc) in next ch sp or st.

For **beginning large shell (beg lg shell),** ch 3, (2 dc, ch 3, 3 dc) in same ch sp.

For **large shell (lg shell),** (3 dc, ch 3, 3 dc) in next ch sp.

For **picot,** ch 3, sl st in top of last st made.

PLACE MAT

Foundation Loops: Ch 4, dc in fourth ch from hook, (turn, ch 3, dc in top of ch-3) 8 times, **do not turn.** *(9 Loops made)*

Rnd 1: Working around outer edge of Loops, ch 1, (sc, ch 2, sc) 2 times in first Loop, (sc, ch 2, sc) in each Loop across to last Loop, (sc, ch 2, sc) 3 times in last loop; working on opposite side of Loops, (sc, ch 2, sc) in each Loop across to last Loop, (sc, ch 2, sc) one more time in last Loop, join with sl st in first sc. *(20 ch-2 sps)*

Rnd 2: Sl st in first ch sp, ch 3, (dc, ch 2, 2 dc, ch 2, 2 dc) in same sp, [sc in next ch sp, *sm shell (see Special Stitches)* in next ch sp, sc in next ch sp; repeat from * 3 more times], (2 dc, ch 2, 2 dc, ch 2, 2 dc) in end ch sp; repeat between [ ], join with sl st in top of ch-3. *(10 sc, 8 sm shells, 4 ch sps)*

Rnd 3: Sl st in next st, sl st in next ch sp, ch 3, (dc, ch 2, 2 dc, ch 2, 2 dc) in same sp, *ch 2, (2 dc, ch 2, 2 dc, ch 2, 2 dc) in next ch sp, sm shell in next sc, (sc in ch sp of next sm shell, sm shell in next sc) 4 times*, (2 dc, ch 2, 2 dc, ch 2, 2 dc) in next ch sp; repeat between **, join.

Rnd 4: Sl st in next st, sl st in next ch sp, **beg med shell** *(see Special Stitches)*, sc in next ch sp, *med shell *(see Special Stitches)* in next ch sp, sc in next ch sp; repeat from *, (med shell in next sc, sc in next ch sp) 4 times, (med shell in next ch sp, sc in next ch sp) 3 times, (med shell in next sc, sc in next ch sp) 4 times, join. *(14 med shells, 14 sc)*

Rnd 5: Sl st in next 2 sts, sl st in next ch sp, ch 5 *(counts as first dc and ch-2 sp)*, (dc, ch 2, dc) in same sp, *ch 3, dc in next sc, ch 3, sc in ch sp of next med shell, ch 3, dc in next sc, ch 3, (dc, ch 2, dc, ch 2, dc) in ch sp of next med shell, (ch 3, dc in next sc, ch 3, sc in ch sp of next med shell) 4 times, ch 3, dc in next sc, ch 3*, (dc, ch 2, dc, ch 2, dc) in ch sp of next med shell; repeat between **, join.

Rnd 6: Sl st in first ch-2 sp, ch 1, sc in same sp, ch 3, (sc in next ch-2 or ch-3 sp, ch 3) around, join with sl st in first sc. *(36 ch-3 sps)*

Rnd 7: Sl st in first ch-3 sp, **beg lg shell** *(see Special Stitches)*, sc in next ch-3 sp, *lg shell (see Special Stitches)* in next ch-3 sp, sc in next ch-3 sp; repeat from * around, join with sl st in top of ch-3. *(18 lg shells, 18 sc)*

Rnd 8: Sl st in next dc, ch 1, sc in same st, [*ch 2, skip next dc, (sc, ch 2, sc) in next ch-3 sp, ch 2, skip next dc, sc in next dc, ch 2, skip next dc, dc in next st*, (ch 3, sc in ch sp of next lg shell, ch 3, dc in next sc) 2 times, ch 2, skip next dc, sc in next dc; repeat between **, (ch 3, sc in ch sp of next lg shell, ch 3, dc in next sc) 5 times, ch 2, skip next dc], sc in next dc; repeat between [ ], join with sl st in first sc.

Rnd 9: Sl st in first ch-2 sp, ch 6, [*(dc, ch 3, dc) in next ch-2 sp, ch 3, dc in next ch-2 sp, ch 3, hdc in next ch-2 sp, ch 3*, (sc in next ch-3 sp, ch 3) 4 times, hdc in next ch-2 sp, ch 3, dc in next ch 2 sp, ch 3; repeat between **, (sc in next ch-3 sp, ch 3) 10 times, hdc in next ch-2 sp, ch 3], dc in next ch-2 sp, ch 3; repeat between [ ], join with sl st in third ch of ch-6.

Rnd 10: Sl st in first ch-3 sp, ch 1, sc in same sp, ch 2, (sc, ch 2, sc) in next ch-3 sp, ch 2, *sc in next ch-3 sp, ch 2, (sc, ch 2, sc) in next ch-3 sp, ch 2; repeat from * around, join with sl st in first sc.

Rnd 11: Ch 1, sc in same st, skip next ch-2 sp, (4 dc, **picot**—*see Special Stitches,* 4 dc) in

continued on page 17

Victorian Snuggler

Designed by Maggie Weldon

Select the latest best-selling book, prepare a cup of fragrant spiced tea, put on your most comfortable lounging outfit. Then snuggle in this soft and cozy afghan for hours of contented reading. This warm afghan feels just like a hug.

FINISHED SIZE: 49½" x 56½" not including Fringe.

MATERIALS: Fuzzy worsted yarn — 31 oz. white, 19 oz. green and 15 oz. pink; size 50 broomstick lace pin; N hook or hook size needed to obtain gauge.

GAUGE: One row = 1½".

BASIC STITCHES: Ch, sc.

AFGHAN

Note: Work entire pattern with 2 stands same-color yarn held together unless otherwise stated.

Row 1: With green, ch 226, sc in second ch from hook, sc in each ch across, **do not turn.** *(225 sc made)*

Row 2: Slip last lp onto broomstick; working form left to right, holding broomstick in left hand, skip first st, (insert hook in next st, draw lp through, place on broomstick) across *(see illustration No. 1),* **do not turn;** ◊slip first 5 lps from broomstick onto hook, yo, draw lp through all 5 lps on hook *(see illustration No. 2),* ch 1, 5 sc *(see illustration No. 3)* in same 5-lp group, *slip next 5 lps from broomstick onto hook, yo, draw lp through all 5 lps, yo, draw lp through both lps on hook *(first sc made),* 4 more sc in same 5-lp group; repeat from * across changing to white *(see page 159)* in last st made◊, **do not turn.**

Rows 3-38: Working in color sequence of white, pink, white, green, repeat row 2. At end of last row, fasten off.

FRINGE

For **each Fringe,** cut 8 strands yarn each 18" long. Holding all strands together, fold in half, insert hook in end of row, draw fold through, draw all loose ends through fold, tighten. Trim ends.

Matching row colors, Fringe in end of each row across each short end of Afghan. ✿

Broomstick Lace

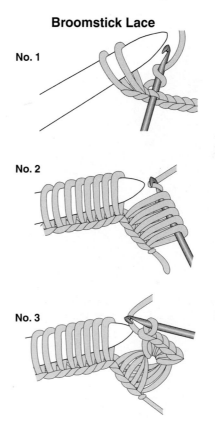

No. 1

No. 2

No. 3

Country Dining

continued from page 15

next ch-2 sp, *sc in next sc, skip next ch-2 sp, (4 dc, picot, 4 dc) in next ch-2 sp; repeat from * around, join. Fasten off.

Weave 36" piece of ribbon through ch-2 sps on rnd 10, tie ends into a bow at one corner.

NAPKIN RING

Rnd 1: Ch 18, sl st in first ch to form ring, ch 1, sc in same ch, ch 2, skip next 2 chs, (sc in next ch, ch 2, skip next 2 chs) around, join with sl st in first sc. *(6 ch sps made)*

Rnd 2: Sl st in first ch sp, ch 1, sc in same sp, (2 dc, picot, 2 dc) in next ch sp, *sc in next sp, (2 dc, picot, 2 dc) in next ch sp; repeat form * around, join with sl st in first sc. Fasten off.

Rnd 3: Working in ch sps on opposite side of rnd 1, join with sc in first ch sp, (2 dc, picot, 2 dc) in next ch sp, *sc in next ch sp, (2 dc, picot, 2 dc) in next ch sp; repeat from * around, join. Fasten off.

Weave remaining ribbon through ch sps of rnd 2, tie ends into a bow. ✿

Pineapple Doily
DESIGNED BY JUDY TEAGUE TREECE

The pineapple is a well-loved and time-honored symbol of greeting and hospitality. And nothing is more soothing to the eyes than a beautiful piece of needlework on a bedside table or dresser. This unique doily is perfect for a guest bedroom or bath.

FINISHED SIZE: 8" square.

MATERIALS: Size 10 crochet cotton thread — 150 yds. white, small amount each pink and orchid; No. 6 steel hook or hook size needed to obtain gauge.

GAUGE: Rnds 1-4 = 2" across.

BASIC STITCHES: Ch, sl st, sc, dc.

SPECIAL STITCHES: For **cluster (cl),** yo, insert hook in next ch sp, yo, draw lp through, yo, draw through 2 lps on hook, (yo, insert hook in same ch sp, yo, draw lp through, yo, draw through 2 lps on hook) 2 times, yo, draw through all 4 lps on hook.

For **picot,** ch 4, sl st in top of last st made.

DOILY

Rnd 1: With white, ch 4, sl st in first ch to form ring, ch 3, 11 dc in ring, join with sl st in top of ch-3. (12 dc made)

Rnd 2: Ch 3, 2 dc in same st, ch 5, skip next 2 sts, (3 dc in next st, ch 5, skip next 2 sts) around, join. *(12 dc, 4 ch sps)*

Rnd 3: Ch 3, dc in next 2 sts, ch 4, sc in next ch sp, ch 4, (dc in next 3 sts, ch 4, sc in next ch sp, ch 4) around, join. *(12 dc, 8 ch sps)*

Rnds 4-6: Ch 3, dc in next 2 sts, ch 4, (sc in next ch sp, ch 4) around to next dc, *dc in next 3 sts, ch 4, (sc in next ch sp, ch 4) around to next dc; repeat from * around, join, ending with 20 ch sps in last rnd.

Rnd 7: Ch 3, dc in next 2 sts, *[(ch 4, sc in next ch sp) 2 times, ch 2, dc in next ch sp, (ch 1, dc in same sp) 4 times, ch 2, (sc in next ch sp, ch 4) 2 times], dc in next 3 sts; repeat from * 2 more times; repeat between [ ], join. Fasten off.

Rnd 8: Join orchid with sl st in first st, ch 3, dc in next 2 sts, *[(ch 3, sc in next ch sp) 3 times, ch 2, (sc, ch 2, sc) in each of next 4 ch-1 sps, ch 2, (sc in next ch sp, ch 3) 3 times], dc in next 3 sts; repeat from * 2 more times; repeat between [ ], join. Fasten off.

Rnd 9: Join pink with sl st in first st, ch 3, dc in next 2 sts, ◊[ch 4, sc in next ch sp, (ch 3, sc in next ch sp) 3 times, ch 2, *cl *(see Special Stitches)* in next ch sp, ch 2; repeat from * 3 more times, sc in next ch sp, (ch 3, sc in next ch sp) 3 times, ch 4◊, dc in next 3 sts]; repeat

between [ ] 2 more times; repeat between ◊◊, join. Fasten off.

Rnd 10: Join white with sl st in first st, ch 3, dc in next 2 sts, *[ch 4, sc in next ch sp) 4 times, ch 2, sc in next ch sp, (ch 4, sc in next ch sp) 4 times, ch 2, (sc in next ch sp, ch 4) 4 times], dc in next 3 sts; repeat from * 2 more times; repeat between [ ], join.

Rnd 11: Ch 3, dc in next 2 sts, *[ch 4, sc in next ch sp) 5 times, ch 4, skip next ch sp, 2 dc in next ch sp, ch 3, 2 dc in next ch sp, ch 4, skip next ch sp, (sc in next ch sp, ch 4) 5 times], dc in next 3 sts; repeat from * 2 more times; repeat between [ ], join.

Rnd 12: Ch 3, dc in next 2 sts, *[ch 4, sc in next ch sp) 5 times, ch 4, skip next ch sp, dc in next ch sp, (ch 1, dc in same sp) 6 times, ch 4, skip next ch sp, (sc in next ch sp, ch 4) 5 times], dc in next 3 sts; repeat from * 2 more times; repeat between [ ], join.

Rnd 13: Ch 3, dc in next 2 sts, *[ch 4, sc in next ch sp) 5 times, ch 4, skip next ch sp, sc in next ch sp, (ch 2, sc in next ch sp) 5 times, ch 4, skip next ch sp, (sc in next ch sp, ch 4) 5 times], dc in next 3 sts; repeat from * 2 more times; repeat between [ ], join.

Rnd 14: Ch 3, dc in next 2 sts, *[ch 4, sc in next ch sp) 5 times, ch 5, skip next ch sp, sc in next ch sp, (ch 2, sc in next ch sp) 4 times, ch 5, skip next ch sp, (sc in next ch sp, ch 4) 5 times], dc in next 3 sts; repeat from * 2 more times; repeat between [ ], join.

Rnd 15: Ch 3, dc in next 2 sts, *[ch 4, sc in next ch sp) 5 times, ch 6, skip next ch sp, sc in next ch sp, (ch 2, sc in next ch sp) 3 times, ch 6, skip next ch sp, (sc in next ch sp, ch 4) 5 times], dc in next 3 sts; repeat from * 2 more times; repeat between [ ], join.

Rnd 16: Ch 3, dc in next 2 sts, *[ch 4, sc in next ch sp) 5 times, ch 7, skip next ch sp, sc in next ch sp, (ch 2, sc in next ch sp) 2 times, ch 7, skip next ch sp, (sc in next ch sp, ch 4) 5 times], dc in next 3 sts; repeat from * 2 more times; repeat between [ ], join.

Rnd 17: Ch 3, dc in next 2 sts, *[ch 4, sc in next ch sp) 5 times, ch 8, skip next ch sp, sc in next ch sp, ch 2, sc in next ch sp, ch 8, skip next

continued on page 22

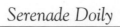

Serenade Doily

DESIGNED BY DOT DRAKE

A silent, but eloquent tune that only a crocheter can hear is woven through this stunning doily design. This lacy work of art is a symphony of basic crochet combined with the beauty of crochet tatting using a special tatting hook.

FINISHED SIZE: 12" across.

MATERIALS: Crochet cotton thread — 200 yds. white, 100 yds. peach, 50 yes turquoise; crochet tatting hook.

GAUGES: Rnd 1 of Doily is 2" across.

BASIC STITCHES: Ch, sl st, sc, dc.

SPECIAL STITCHES: For **double stitch (ds),** to make **first half,** hold the thread with the left hand and wrap clockwise around left index finger; scoop the hook under the thread from front to back toward the fingertip *(see photo a)* and lift the thread off your finger to form a loop on the hook, pull the thread snug. Move the right index finger over the last loop made to hold it in place. To make **second half** of stitch, wrap the thread counter-clockwise around left index finger; scoop the hook under the thread from the back toward the fingertip *(see photo b),* lifting the thread off your finger

to form a loop on the hook. Pull the thread snug against the last lp and hold in place with the right index finger.

For **picot (p),** with right index finger, hold the thread against the hook and make the next ds, approximately ¼" from the last ds (see photo c), slide the last ds made over to the previous ds forming a loop; the loop is the picot. Pull the picot to tighten the thread around the hook.

To **close ring,** make a loop a little longer than the stitches on hook, *(see photo d),* yo, above loop and pull through all lps on hook making sure not to lose first loop *(see photo e),* keeping loop made after pulling through sts on hook, insert hook into first loop, *(see photo f),* pull second loop to tighten first loop around hook, pull end of thread to tighten second loop around hook, continue pulling until both lps are snug on hook, yo, pull through both lps on

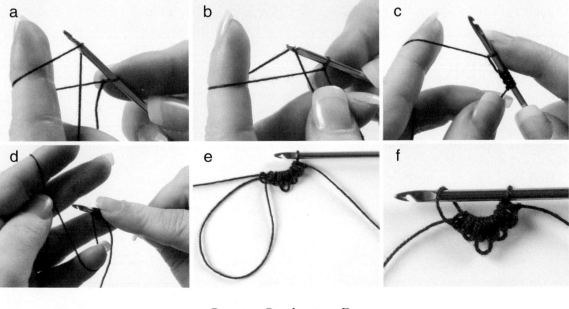

hook forming a ring.

For **joined picot (joined p),** insert hook in corresponding picot from front to back, yo, pull lp through picot and place on hook.

For **sc picot** *(sc p),* pull up ¼" loop, insert hook in top of last sc made, pull lp through.

DOILY

Rnd 1: With peach, *make ring of **6 ds** *(see Special Stitches),* **p** *(see Special Stitches),* (3 ds, p) 2 times, 6 ds, **close ring** *(see Special Stitches),* ch 1; repeat from * 5 more times, join with sl st in base of first ds. Fasten off. *(6 rings made)*

Rnd 2: Join white with sc in center picot of any ring, ch 12, (sc in center picot of next ring, ch 12) around, join with sl st in first sc.

Rnd 3: Ch 1, *5 sc in next ch sp, **sc p** *(see Special Stitches),* (sc in same ch sp, sc p) 6 times, 5 sc in same ch sp; repeat from * 5 more times, join. Fasten off.

Rnd 4: With turquoise, make ring of 16 ds, close ring, ch 12, make ring of 8 ds, **joined p** *(see Special Stitches)* in center sc picot of any 7-sc picot group, 8 ds, close ring, ch 12, (make ring of 16 ds, close ring, ch 12, make ring of 8 ds, joined p in center sc p of next 7-sc p group, 8 ds, close ring, ch 12) around, join with sl st in base of first ring. Fasten off.

Rnd 5: Join white with sc in any ch-12 sp, 4 sc in same sp, (sc p, sc in same sp) 7 times, 4 sc in same ch sp, *5 sc in next ch-12 sp, (sc p, sc in same sp) 7 times, 4 sc in same ch sp) around,

join with sl st in first sc. Fasten off.

Rnd 6: Join white with sc in first sc p of any 7-sc p group, (ch 5, skip next sc p, sc in next sc p) 3 times, ch 5, *sc in first sc p of next 7-sc p group (ch 5, skip next sc p, sc in next sc p) 3 times, ch 5; repeat from * around, join.

Rnd 7: Sl st in next 2 chs, ch 1, sc in same ch sp, (ch 5, sc in next ch sp) around, ch 2; to **join,** dc in first sc.

Rnds 8-11: Ch 1, sc around joining dc, (ch 5, sc in next ch sp) around, join as before.

Rnd 12: Ch 1, sc around joining dc, ch 5, (sc in next ch sp, ch 5) around, join with sl st in first sc.

Rnd 13: Ch 1, 6 sc in each ch sp around, join. Fasten off.

Rnd 14: With peach, *make ring of 6 ds, p, (4 ds, p) 2 times, 6 ds, close ring, ch 2, sc in fourth sc of next 6-sc group, ch 2, turn work, make ring of 6 ds, p, (4 ds, p) 2 times, ds, close ring, turn work, ch 2, sc in fourth sc of next 6 sc group, ch 2; repeat from * around, join with sl st in base of first ring. Fasten off.

Rnd 15: Join white with sc in center picot of first ring, ch 10, sc in base of next ring, ch 10, (sc in center picot of next ring, ch 10, sc in base of next ring, ch 10) around, join with sl st in first sc.

Rnd 16: [Make ring of 10 ds, close ring, *5 sc in next ch sp, (sc p, sc in same ch sp) 5 times, 4 sc in same ch sp; repeat from *]; repeat between [ ] around, join with sl st in base of first ring. Fasten off. ✿

Pineapple Doily
continued from page 19

ch sp, (sc in next ch sp, ch 4) 5 times], dc in next 3 sts; repeat from * 2 more times; repeat between [ ], join.

Rnd 18: Ch 3, dc in next 2 sts, *[(ch 4, sc in next ch sp) 6 times, ch 4, dc in next ch sp, (ch 1, dc in same sp) 4 times, ch 4, (sc in next ch sp,

ch 4) 6 times], dc in next 3 sts; repeat from * 2 more times; repeat between [ ], join.

Rnd 19: Ch 3, dc in next 2 sts, [◊ ch 4, *(sc, **picot**—*see Special Stitches on page 19,* sc) in next ch sp, ch 4*; repeat between ** 5 more times, skip next ch sp, (sc, picot) in each of next 4 ch sps, ch 4, skip next ch sp; repeat between ** 6 more times◊, dc in next 3 sts]; repeat between [ ] 2 more times; repeat between ◊◊, join. Fasten off. ✿

Earring Jackets
DESIGNED BY TERRI McCAUGHIN

A little bit of fashion is sometimes all that is needed to take a familiar favorite dress and turn it into a brand-new sensation. Add these earring jackets to a pair of simple studs and you'll feel your best whether dining out, going to a party or attending church service.

FINISHED SIZE: 1" across

MATERIALS: Size 10 crochet cotton thread —small amount each white and gold; No. 7 steel hook.

BASIC STITCHES: Ch, sl st, sc, hdc, dc.

EARRING JACKET (make 2)

Rnd 1: With white, ch 6, sl st in first ch to form ring, ch 1, 8 sc in ring, join with sl st in first sc. *(8 sc made)*

Rnd 2: Ch 1, sc in first st, (ch 3, skip next st, sc in next st) around to last st; to **join**, ch 1, hdc in first sc. *(4 ch-3 sps)*

Rnd 3: Ch 1, sc around joining hdc, ch 5, (sc in next ch-3 sp, ch 5) around, join with sl st in first sc. Fasten off. *(4 ch-5 sps)*

Rnd 4: Join gold with sc in any ch-5 sp, (hdc, 3 dc, ch 3, 3 dc, hdc, sc) in same sp, (sc, hdc, 3 dc, ch 3, 3 dc, hdc, sc) in each ch-5 sp around, join. Fasten off. ✿

Little Sweetie

DESIGNED BY SUE CHILDRESS

*It's usually impossible to hold back a coo of appreciation whenever a baby makes
her first appearance at family outings or church. Crochet a dainty new ensemble
your little debutante can wear for her first public outing or portrait.*

FINISHED SIZES: Instructions given fit 0-3 mos. Changes for 3-6 mos. are made by changing hook sizes to achieve gauges given below.

MATERIALS: Pompadour baby yarn — 8 oz. multicolor; six ¼" buttons; 1 yd. pink ⅛" satin ribbon; sewing thread; sewing and tapestry needles; E or F crochet hooks or sizes needed to obtain gauges.

GAUGES: For 0-3 mos., with **E hook,** 2 3-dc groups = 1"; rows 1-5 of Dress = 2½". For 3-6 mos., with **F hook,** 12 3-dc groups = 6¼"; rows 1-5 of Dress = 2¾".

BASIC STITCHES: Ch, sl st, sc, hdc, dc, tr.

DRESS

Row 1: Starting at **neckline,** ch 80, dc in sixth ch from hook, (ch 1, skip next ch, dc in next ch) across, turn. *(39 dc, 38 ch sps made)*

Row 2: Ch 4, dc in same st, ch 1, sc in next dc, *ch 1, (dc, ch 1, dc, ch 1, dc) in next dc, ch 1, sc in next dc; repeat from * across to ch-5, ch 1, (dc, ch 1, dc) in fourth ch of same ch-5, turn. *(58 dc, 58 ch sps, 19 sc) Front of row 2 is right side of work.*

Row 3: Ch 1, sc in same st, ch 2, skip next dc, dc in next sc, ch 2, *sc in center dc of next 3-dc group, ch 2, dc in next sc, ch 2; repeat from * across to last 2 dc, skip next dc, sc in third ch of ch-4, turn. *(38 ch-2 sps, 20 sc, 19 dc)*

Row 4: Ch 3, dc in same st, ch 1, sc in next dc, ch 1, *5 dc in next sc, ch 1, sc in next dc, ch 1; repeat from * across to last sc, 2 dc in last sc, turn.

Rows 5-6: Ch 3, dc in same st, ch 2, skip next dc, sc in next sc, ch 2, *5 dc in center st of next 5-dc group, ch 2, sc in next sc, ch 2; repeat from * across to last 2 dc, skip next dc, 2 dc in last dc, turn.

Row 7: Ch 3, dc in same st, ch 2, skip next dc, sc in next sc, ch 2, *7 dc in center st of next 5-dc group, ch 2, sc in next sc, ch 2; repeat from * across to last 2 dc, skip next dc, 2 dc in last dc, turn.

Row 8: Ch 3, dc in same st, ch 2, skip next dc, tr in next sc, ch 2, (dc in next 3 dc, 3 dc in next dc, dc in next 3 dc, ch 2, tr in next sc, ch 2) 3 times; [for **sleeve ruffle,** 3 dc in each of next 7 dc, *6 dc in next ch-2 sp, 3 dc in next sc, 6 dc in next ch-2 sp, 3 dc in each of next 7 dc; repeat from *; ch 2, tr in next sc, ch 2]; repeat between ( ) 6 more times; repeat between [ ]; repeat between ( ) 3 more times, skip next dc, 2 dc in last dc, turn.

Row 9: Ch 3, dc in same st, skip next dc, 3 dc in next tr, (dc in next 9 dc, 3 dc in next tr) 3 times; for **armhole,** ch 4, skip next sleeve ruffle; 3 dc in next tr, (dc in next 9 dc, 3 dc in next tr) 6 times; for **armhole,** ch 4, skip next sleeve ruffle; 3 dc in next tr, (dc in next 9 dc, 3 dc in next tr) 3 times, skip next dc, 2 dc in last dc, turn.

Row 10: Ch 3, dc in same st, skip next 2 dc, 3 dc in next dc, (skip next 3 dc, 3 dc in next dc, skip next 2 dc, 3 dc in next dc, skip next 2 dc, 3 dc in next dc, skip next dc, 3 dc in next dc) 3 times, 3 dc in second ch of next ch-4, skip next dc, 3 dc in next dc, (skip next 3 dc, 3 dc in next dc, skip next 2 dc, 3 dc in next dc, skip next 2 dc, 3 dc in next dc, skip next dc, 3 dc in next dc) 6 times, 3 dc in second ch of next ch-4, skip next dc, 3 dc in next dc, (skip next 3 dc, 3 dc in next dc, skip next 2 dc, 3 dc in next dc, skip next 2 dc, 3 dc in next dc, skip next dc, 3 dc in next dc) 3 times; skip next 2 dc, 2 dc in last dc, turn.

Rows 11-16: Ch 3, dc in same st, skip next dc, 3 dc in center st of each 3-dc group across to last 2 dc, skip next dc, 2 dc in last dc, turn.

Row 17: Ch 3, dc in same st, 3 dc in center st of next 3-dc group, (5 dc in center st of next 3-dc group, 3 dc in center st of next 3-dc group) across to last 2 dc, skip next dc, 2 dc in last dc, turn.

Rows 18-22: Ch 3, dc in same st, 3 dc in center st of each 3-dc group and 5 dc in center st of each 5-dc group across to last 2 dc, skip next dc, 2 dc in last dc, turn.

Row 23: Ch 3, dc in same st, sc in center st of next 3-dc group and 9 dc in center st of next 5-dc group across to last 2 dc, skip next dc, 2 dc in last dc, turn.

Row 24: Ch 3, dc in same st, skip next dc, sc in each sc and dc in each dc across to last 2 dc, skip next dc, 2 dc in last dc, **do not turn.**

Row 25: For **edging,** ch 1, evenly space 44 sc across to next corner, 3 sc in next corner, sc in

continued on page 28

Lacy Bib and Bottle

DESIGNED BY ELIZABETH ANN WHITE

Mealtime doesn't always have to be humdrum or messy.
Even the littlest one in the family should be treated to a fancy meal once
in a while, and what better way to treat baby than with lacy dining accessories.

FINISHED SIZES: Bottle Cover fits 8 oz. bottle. Bib is 9" wide.

MATERIALS FOR BOTH: 350 yds. white size 10 crochet cotton thread; 2½ yds. lt. blue ¼" satin ribbon; lt. blue sewing thread; sewing needle; No. 6 steel crochet hook or hook size needed to obtain gauge.

GAUGE: One shell and 3 dc = 1"; 7 shell rows = 2".

BASIC STITCHES: Ch, sl st, sc, dc.

SPECIAL STITCH: For **shell,** (2 dc, ch 2, 2 dc) in next st or ch sp.

BOTTLE COVER

Row 1: Ch 4, sl st in first ch to form ring, ch 3 *(counts as first dc),* 11 dc in ring, join with sl st in top of ch-3. *(12 dc made)*

Rnd 2: Ch 3, dc in same st, 2 dc in each st around, join. *(24)*

Rnd 3: Ch 3, dc in same st, dc in next st, (2 dc in next st, dc in next st) around, join. *(36)*

Rnd 4: Ch 3, dc in same st, dc in next 2 sts, (2 dc in next st, dc in next 2 sts) around, join. *(48)*

Rnd 5: Working this rnd in **back lps** only, ch 3, dc in each st around, join.

Rnd 6: Ch 3, dc in next 2 sts, skip next 2 sts, **shell** *(see Special Stitch)* in next st, skip next 2 sts, (dc in next 3 sts, skip next 2 sts, shell in next st, skip next 2 sts) around, join. *(18 dc, 6 shells)*

Rnds 7-22: Ch 3, dc in next 2 sts, shell in ch sp of next shell, skip next 2 sts of same shell, (dc in next 3 sts, shell in ch sp of next shell, skip next 2 sts of same shell) around, join.

Rnd 23: Ch 3, dc in next 2 sts, ch 2, sc in next ch sp, ch 2, skip next 2 sts, (dc in next 3 sts, ch 2, sc in next ch sp, ch 2, skip next 2 sts) around, join. *(18 dc, 12 ch-2 sps, 6 sc)*

Rnd 24: Ch 4 *(counts as first dc and ch-1 sp),* *[skip next st, (dc in next st, ch 1, dc in next ch sp, ch 1) 2 times], dc in next st, ch 1; repeat from * 4 more times; repeat between [ ], join with sl st in third ch of ch-4. *(30 dc, 30 ch-1 sps)*

Rnd 25: Sl st in first ch sp, ch 1, sc in same sp, (ch 3, sc in next ch sp) around; to **join,** ch 1, hdc in first sc.

Rnd 26: Ch 1, sc around joining hdc, (ch 3, sc in next ch sp) around, join as before.

Rnd 27: Ch 1, sc around joining hdc, ch 3, (sc in next ch sp, ch 3) around, join with sl st in first sc.

Rnd 28: Sl st in first ch sp, ch 1, (2 sc, ch 3, 2 sc) in same sp and in each ch sp around, join. Fasten off.

Weave 22" piece of ribbon through rnd 24. Place Cover over bottle. Tie ribbon into bow snugly around neck of bottle.

BIB

Row 1: Ch 65, dc in sixth ch from hook, (ch 1, skip next ch, dc in next ch) across, turn. *(32 dc, 31 ch-1 sps made)*

Row 2: Ch 4 *(counts as first dc and ch-1 sp),* dc in next dc, dc in next ch sp, dc in next dc, *skip next ch sp, **shell** (see Special Stitch) in next ch sp, skip next ch sp, dc in next dc, dc in next ch sp, dc in next dc; repeat from * 6 more times, ch 1, dc in fourth ch of ch-5, turn. *(26 dc, 7 shells, 2 ch-1 sps)*

Rows 3-20: Ch 4, dc in next 3 dc, (shell in ch sp of next shell, skip next 2 dc of same shell, dc in next 3 dc) across to last ch sp, ch 1, dc in third ch of ch-4, turn.

Row 21: Ch 4, dc in next 3 dc, shell in next shell, skip next 2 dc of same shell, dc in next 3 dc, (ch 2, sc in next shell, ch 2, skip next 2 dc of same shell, dc in next 3 dc) 4 times, shell in next shell, skip next 2 dc of same shell, dc in next 3 dc, ch 1, dc in third ch of last ch-4, turn. *(26 dc, 10 ch-2 sps, 5 sc, 2 shells, 2 ch-1 sps)*

Row 22: Ch 4, dc in next 3 dc, shell in next shell, skip next 2 dc of same shell, dc in next 3 dc, ch 1, (dc in next ch sp, ch 1) 2 times, *dc in next dc, ch 1, skip next dc, dc in next dc, ch 1, (dc in next ch sp, ch 1) 2 times; repeat from * 3 more times, dc in next 3 dc, shell in next shell, skip next 2 dc of same shell, ch 1, dc in third ch of ch-4, turn. *(32 dc, 21 ch-1 sps, 2 shells)*

Row 23: For **first side,** ch 4, dc in next 3 dc, shell in next shell, skip next 2 dc of same shell, dc in next 3 dc, ch 1, dc in next dc leaving remaining sts unworked, turn. *(8 dc, 2 ch-1 sps, one shell)*

Rows 24-29: Ch 4, dc in next 3 dc, shell in next shell, skip next 2 dc of same shell, dc in next 3 dc, ch 1, dc in third ch of ch-4, turn.

Row 30: Ch 4, dc in next 3 dc, ch 2, sc in next shell, ch 2, skip next 2 dc of same shell, dc in next 3 dc, ch 1, dc in third ch of ch-4, turn.

Row 31: Ch 4, dc in next dc, ch 1, skip next dc, dc in next dc, ch 1, (dc in next ch sp, ch 1) 2 times, dc in next dc, ch 1, skip next dc, dc in next dc, ch 1, dc in third ch of ch-4, **do not turn.** Fasten off.

Row 23: For **second side,** skip next 16 dc on row 22, join with sl st in next dc, ch 4, dc in next 3 dc, shell in next shell, skip next 2 dc of same shell, dc in next 3 dc, ch 1, dc in third ch of ch-4, turn. *(8 dc, 2 ch-1 sps, one shell)*

Rows 24-31: Repeat same rows of first side.

Border

Row 1: Join with sc in first ch sp on last row of second side, ch 3, (sc, ch 3) in each ch sp and in end of each row across to last ch sp on last row of first side, with (sc, ch 3, sc, ch 3) in each corner, sc in last ch sp, turn.

Rows 2-3: Sl st in first ch sp, ch 1, sc in same sp, ch 3, (sc, ch 3) in each ch sp and (sc, ch 3, sc, ch 3) in each corner ch sp across to last ch sp, sc in last ch sp, turn.

Row 4: Sl st in first ch sp, ch 1, (2 sc, ch 3, 2 sc) in same sp and in each ch sp across. Fasten off.

Weave one yd. of ribbon through ch sps across neck edge only, pull ends even.

Starting at inside edge of neckline, weave remaining ribbon through top, sides and bottom ch-1 sps around Bib *(do not weave ribbon through ch-3 sps of Border).* Fold ends to back of work and sew in place. ✿

Little Sweetie

continued from page 25

each st across neck edge, 3 sc in next corner, evenly space 44 sc across to next corner, turn.

Row 26: Ch 1, sc in each st across to next 3-sc corner, sc in next st, 3 sc in next st, (ch 1, skip next st, sc in next st) across to next 3-sc corner, 3 sc in next st; for **buttonholes,** ch 2, skip next st, (sc in next 6 sts, ch 2, skip next st) 5 times; sc in each st across, turn.

Row 27: Ch 1, sc in each sc and 2 sc in each ch-2 sp across to neck edge, sl st in next st leaving remaining sts unworked. Fasten off.

Sew buttons to edging opposite buttonholes.

BOOTIE (make 2)

Rnd 1: Starting at **toe,** ch 4, sc in second ch from hook, sc in next ch, 5 sc in last ch; working on opposite side of ch, sc in next ch, 4 sc in last ch, join with sl st in first sc. *(12 sc made)*

Rnd 2: Ch 2, hdc in same st, 2 hdc in each st around, join with sl st in top of ch-2. *(24 hdc)*

Rnd 3: Ch 3, (dc, ch 1, 2 dc) in same st, skip next 2 sts, *(2 dc, ch 2, 2 dc) in next st, skip next 2 sts; repeat from * around, join with sl st in top of ch-3. *(8 ch sps)*

Rnd 4: Sl st in next dc, sl st in next ch sp, ch 3, 2 dc in same sp, 3 dc in each ch sp around, join, **turn.** *(24 dc)*

Row 5: Working in rows, ch 3, (3 dc in center st of next 3-dc group) 6 times, dc in first dc of next 3-dc group leaving remaining sts unworked, turn. *(20 dc)*

Rows 6-9: Ch 3, 3 dc in center st of each 3-dc group across with dc in last dc, turn.

Rnd 10: Ch 2, (sc in first dc of next 3-dc group, ch 1, skip next dc, sc in last dc of same group, ch 1) around to last dc, ch 2, join with sl st in top of ch-3, **turn.**

For **center back seam,** flatten last row, working through both thicknesses, sl st in each sc and in each ch sp across. Fasten off.

Cut remaining ribbon in half, tie one piece in bow over top of each Bootie. ✿

Chapter
Two

31 Floral Doily
32 Scrubby Pad
35 Pixie Christmas Stocking
36 Sewing Helper
38 Lacy Bookmarks
40 Fans & Lace
42 Foot Warmers
44 Diagonal Dishcloth
47 Lace Tissue Holder
48 Ponytail Ruffles

2

The glowing ball of light in the night sky
was given the name of lunae dies or monan
daeg which later evolved into Monday.

Floral Doily

DESIGNED BY CAROL ALEXANDER

*This delightful design is for those of us who love to be surrounded
by flowers year-round but aren't fortunate enough to have a green thumb.
We can have colorful blooms every day — and we don't have to remember to water!*

FINISHED SIZE: 13" across.

MATERIALS: Size 10 crochet cotton thread — 60 yds. white, 50 yds. green variegated, 40 yds. green and 10 yds. peach; 6 mm pearl bead; white sewing thread; beading and tapestry needles; No. 7 steel hook or hook size needed to obtain gauge.

GAUGE: Rnds 1-3 = 2¾" across.

BASIC STITCHES: Ch, sl st, sc, dc, tr.

SPECIAL STITCHES: For **picot,** ch 4, sl st in top of last st made.

For **sc picot,** ch 4, sc in fourth ch from hook.

For **cluster,** yo 2 times, insert hook in next ch sp, yo, draw lp through, (yo, draw through 2 lps on hook) 2 times, *yo 2 times, insert hook in same ch sp, yo, draw lp through, (yo, draw through 2 lps on hook) 2 times; repeat from * 2 more times, yo, draw through all 5 lps on hook.

For **shell,** (2 dc, ch 2, 2 dc) in next ch sp.

For **beginning shell (beg shell),** ch 3, (dc, ch 2, 2 dc) in same sp.

DOILY

Rnd 1: With peach, ch 6, sl st in first ch to form ring, ch 3, 15 dc in ring, join with sl st in top of ch-3. *(16 dc made)*

Rnd 2: Ch 1, (sc, ch 4, 2 tr, ch 4, sc) in first st, sl st in next st, *(sc, ch 4, 2 tr, ch 4, sc) in next st, sl st in next st; repeat from * around, join with sl st in first sc.

Rnd 3: Ch 1, sc in first st, ch 4, 3 dc in sp between next 2 tr, **picot** *(see Special Stitches)*, 3 dc in same sp, ch 4, sc in next sc, *sc in next sc, ch 4, (3 dc, picot, 3 dc) in sp between next 2 tr, ch 4, sc in next sc; repeat from * around, join. Fasten off.

Rnd 4: Join white with sl st in any picot, **beg shell** *(see Special Stitches)*, ch 7, *shell *(see Special Stitches)* in next picot, ch 7; repeat from * around, join with sl st in top of ch-3.

Rnd 5: Sl st in next st, sl st in next ch sp, beg shell, ch 4, sc in center ch of next ch-7, ch 4, (shell in ch sp of next shell, ch 4, sc in center ch of next ch-7, ch 7) around, join.

Rnd 6: Sl st in next st, sl st in next ch sp, (ch 3, dc, ch 3, 2 dc) in same sp, ch 4, sc in next ch sp, sc in next sc, sc in next ch sp, ch 4, *(2 dc, ch 3, 2 dc) in next shell, ch 4, sc in next ch sp, sc in next sc, sc in next ch sp, ch 4; repeat from * around, join.

Rnd 7: Sl st in next st, sl st in next ch sp, (ch 3, dc, ch 4, 2 dc) in same sp, ch 4, sc in next ch sp, sc in next 3 sts, sc in next ch sp, ch 4, ,*(2 dc, ch 4, 2 dc) in next ch-3 sp, ch 4, sc in next ch sp, sc in next 3 sts, sc in next ch sp, ch 4; repeat from * around, join. Fasten off.

Rnd 8: Join green with sl st in first ch sp, ch 4, 11 tr in same sp, ch 4, skip next sc, sc in next 3 sc, ch 4, skip next ch sp, *12 tr in next ch sp, ch 4, skip next sc, sc in next 3 sc, ch 4, skip next ch sp; repeat from * around, join with sl st in top of ch-4.

Rnd 9: Ch 1, sc in first st, *[picot, sc in next 2 sts, (sc, picot, sc) in next st, sc in next st, (sc, picot, sc) in next st, sc in next 2 sts, picot, sc in next st, ch 4, skip next sc, sc in next st, ch 4], sc in next tr; repeat from * 6 more times; repeat between [ ], join with sl st in first sc. Fasten off.

Rnd 10: Join white with sl st in first st, ch 9 *(counts as tr and ch-5)*, skip next st, (dc in next st, ch 5, skip next 2 sts) 4 times, tr in next st,

continued on page 33

Scrubby Pad

DESIGNED BY JANIE HERRIN

No matter who is the designated dishwasher in your family,
this scrub pad made of sturdy nylon yarn will make quick work of the chore.
To keep it clean, toss it in the washer or run it through the dishwasher with the dishes!

FINISHED SIZE: 5¼" x 6¾".

MATERIALS: Nylon plastic canvas yarn — 2 oz. each green and white; K double-ended and H crochet hook or hook size needed to obtain gauge.

GAUGE: With **K double-end hook,** 6 sts = 2½"; 9 rows = 2".

BASIC STITCHES: Ch, sl st, sc.

GENERAL INSTRUCTIONS

To **draw up a lp**, insert hook in designated lp, bar or st, yo, draw lp through and leave on hook.

When **using a color already in use**, pick up color from row below, yo, draw through one lp on hook, (yo, draw through 2 lps on hook) across leaving last lp at end of row on hook (this is first vertical bar of next row).

To **work lps off with new color,** place slip knot on hook, draw slip knot through one lp on hook, (yo, draw through 2 lps) across leaving last lp at end of row on hook (this is first vertical bar of next row).

When **turning**, always slide lps to opposite end of hook. **Do not turn** unless otherwise stated.

To **turn,** rotate hook 180 degrees and slide stitches to opposite end.

If you have difficulty keeping all the stitches on the double-end hook, cap the unused end of hook with either a knitting needle protector or a clean wine cork.

SCRUBBY PAD

Note: Read General Instructions before beginning pattern.

Row 1: With white, ch 15, draw up lp in second ch from hook, draw up lp in each ch across, turn. *(15 lps on hook)*

Row 2: With green, work lps off hook, **do not turn.**

Row 3: Draw up lp in space between first 2 vertical bars, (draw up lp in space between next 2 vertical bars, yo, draw up lp in same space) across, draw up lp in last vertical bar, turn. *(42 lps on hook)*

Row 4: With white, yo, draw through one lp on hook, yo, draw through 3 lps on hook; (for **cluster, yo, draw through 4 lps on hook) across, do not turn.**

Row 5: Draw up lp in space between first 2 clusters, yo, draw up lp in same space, (draw up lp in space between next 2 clusters, yo, draw up lp in same space) across to last space, skip space between last cluster and last vertical bar, draw up lp in last vertical bar, turn. *(41 lps on hook)*

Row 6: With green, yo, draw through one lp on hook, cluster across to last 2 lps on hook, yo, draw through last 2 lps on hook, **do not turn.**

Row 7: Draw up lp in space between first vertical bar and first cluster, (draw up lp in space between next 2 clusters, yo, draw up lp in same space) across to last space between last cluster and last vertical bar, draw up lp in last space, yo, draw up lp in same space, draw up lp in vertical bar, **do not turn.** *(42 lps on hook)*

Rows 8-28: Repeat rows 4-7 consecutively, ending with row 4.

Row 29: Ch 1, sl st in each space across. Fasten off.

Rnd 30: Working around outer edge, with H hook and white, join with sc in first st at corner, 2 sc in same st, sc in each st and 2 sc in end of each row around with 3 sc in each corner, join with sl st in first sc. Fasten off. ✿

Floral Doily

continued from page 31

skip next sc, tr in next st, *[ch 5, skip next st, (dc in next st, ch 5, skip next 2 sts) 4 times, tr in next st, skip next sc], tr in next st; repeat from * 5 more times; repeat between [ ], join with sl st in fourth ch of ch-9.

Rnd 11: Ch 1, (5 sc in each of next 2 ch sps, 3 sc in next ch sp, 5 sc in each of next 2 ch sps) around, join with sl st in first sc. *(184 sc)*

Rnd 12: Ch 5, skip next st, dc in next st, (ch 2, skip next st, dc in next st) 10 times, *ch 2, dc in next st, (ch 2, skip next st, dc in next st) 11 times; repeat from * around, join with sl st in third ch of ch-5. *(96 ch sps)*

Rnd 13: Ch 1, 2 sc in each ch sp around, join with sl st in first sc. Fasten off. *(192 sc)*

Rnd 14: Join green variegated with sl st in first st, ch 5, dc in same st, ch 7, skip next 7 sts, *(dc, ch 2, dc) in next st, ch 7, skip next 7 sts; repeat from * around, join with sl st in third ch of ch-5.

Rnd 15: Sl st in next ch sp, beg shell, ch 3, sc in next ch-7 sp, ch 3, (shell in next ch sp, ch 3, sc in next ch-7 sp, ch 3) around, join with sl st in top of ch-3.

Rnd 16: Sl st in next st, sl st in next ch sp, (ch 3, dc, ch 3, 2 dc) in same sp, ch 3, sc in next ch sp, sc in next st, sc in next ch sp, ch 3, *(2 dc, ch 3, 2 dc) in next shell, ch 3, sc in next ch sp, sc in next sc, sc in next ch sp, ch 3; repeat from * around, join.

Rnd 17: Sl st in next st, sl st in next ch sp, (ch 3, dc, ch 4, 2 dc) in same sp, ch 4, sc in next ch sp, sc in next 3 sts, sc in next ch sp, ch 4, *(2 dc, ch 4, 2 dc) in next ch sp, ch 4, sc in next ch sp, sc in next 3 sts, sc in next ch sp, ch 4; repeat from * around, join.

Rnd 18: Sl st in next st, sl st in next ch sp, ch 1, sc in same sp, ch 12, skip next 2 ch sps, (sc in next ch sp, ch 12, skip next 2 ch sps) around, join with sl st in first sc. Fasten off.

Rnd 19: Join white with sl st in first sc, ch 2, **cluster** *(see Special Stitches on page __)* in next ch-12 lp, (ch 2, cluster in same lp) 4 times, ch 2, *sl st in next sc, ch 2, cluster in next ch lp, (ch 2, cluster in same lp) 4 times, ch 2; repeat from * around, join with sl st in first sl st. Fasten off.

Rnd 20: Join green with sl st in any sl st, ch 4, sl st in same st, ch 2, 3 sc in next ch sp, (**sc picot**—*see Special Stitches,* 3 sc in next ch sp) 3 times, ch 2, *(sl st, ch 4, sl st) in next sl st, ch 2, 3 sc in next ch sp, (sc picot, 3 sc in next ch sp) 3 times, ch 2; repeat from * around, join. Fasten off.

Sew bead to center of rnd 1 on Doily. ✿

Pixie Christmas Stocking

Designed by Sharon Hatfield

This adorable stocking is just the right personal touch for your favorite little elf. There's plenty of room inside for goodies and small toys — right down to the pointy toe! You can whip this stocking up in a day to make an extra Christmas visitor feel very welcome.

FINISHED SIZE: 19" long.

MATERIALS: Worsted yarn — 8 oz. each green, red and white; 2" square of cardboard; tapestry needle; N and G hooks or hook size needed to obtain gauge.

GAUGE: With **N hook,** 2 hdc = 1"; 1 hdc row = 1".

BASIC STITCHES: Ch, sl st, sc, hdc.

NOTES: Use two strands yarn held together unless otherwise stated.

Ch 1 at beginning of row is not used or counted as a stitch.

STOCKING

Foot Side (make 2)

Row 1: Starting at **toe,** with N hook and green, ch 4, 2 hdc in fourth ch from hook, turn. *(3 hdc made)*

Row 2: Ch 1, 2 hdc in first st, hdc in next st, 2 hdc in last st, turn. *(5)*

Rows 3-9: Ch 1, 2 hdc in first st, hdc in each st across with 2 hdc in last st, turn, ending with *(19 sts)* in last row.

Rows 10-18: Ch 1, hdc in each st across, turn. At end of last row, fasten off.

Sew row 18 on both Sides together for heel. Working at top of Foot, sew ends of rows 1-10 of Sides together for toe.

Leg

Rnd 1: Working around top opening of Foot with N hook and white, join with sl st in back seam, ch 1, evenly space 24 hdc around open-ing changing to red *(see illustration)* in last st made, join with sl st in top of first hdc, drop white. *(24 hdc made)*

Half Double Crochet Color Change

Rnd 2: Working this rnd in **back lps** only, ch 1, hdc in each st around changing to white in last st made, join, drop red.

Rnd 3: Ch 1, hdc in each st around changing to red in last st made, join, drop white.

Rnd 4: Ch 1, hdc in each st around changing to white in last st made, join, drop red.

Rnds 5-21: Repeat rnds 3 and 4 alternately, ending with rnd 3. Fasten off white.

Rnd 22: Ch 1, hdc in each st around, join. Fasten off.

Rnd 23: For **ruffle,** working in **front lps** of rnd 1, with top of Leg facing you, with N hook and green, join with sc in any st, skip next st, 5 hdc in next st, skip next st, (sc in next st, skip next st, 5 hdc in next st, skip next st) around, join with sl st in first sc. Fasten off.

Rnd 24: Join red with sc in any st, sc in each st around, join. Fasten off.

Rnd 25: Working this rnd in **back lps** only, join white with sc in any st, sc in each st around, join. Fasten off.

continued on page 37

Sewing Helper

DESIGNED BY DEBRA YORSTON

*It's great to keep a jar filled with tapestry needles, sewing needles
and other small necessities. This colorful jar topper also serves as a pincushion.
In addition to being so handy, it's also a charming decoration beside your sewing chair.*

FINISHED SIZE: Fits over small mouth canning jar.

MATERIALS: 1 oz. variegated worsted yarn; 16 x 16-hole piece clear 7-count plastic canvas; small mouth canning jar with lid; polyester fiberfill; *(optional craft glue);* I hook or hook size needed to obtain gauge.

GAUGE: 3 sc = 1"; 7 sc rows = 2".

BASIC STITCHES: Ch, sl st, sc, dc.

PIN CUSHION

Notes: Do not join or turn unless otherwise stated. Mark first st of each rnd.

Cut plastic canvas according to illustration.

Rnd 1: Starting at **bottom**, ch 2, 6 sc in second ch from hook. *(6 sc made)*

Rnd 2: 2 sc in each st around. *(12)*

Rnd 3: (2 sc in next st, sc in next st) around. *(18)*

Rnd 4: (2 sc in next st, sc in next 2 sts) around. *(24)*

Rnd 5: (2 sc in next st, sc in next 3 sts) around. *(30)*

Rnd 6: Working this rnd in **back lps** only, sc in each st around.

Rnds 7-8: Sc in each st around.

Rnd 9: (Sc next 2 sts tog, sc in next 3 sts) around. *(24)* Insert plastic canvas piece.

Rnd 10: (Sc next 2 sts tog, sc in next 2 sts) around. *(18)*

Rnd 11: (Sc next 2 sts tog, sc in next st) around. *(12)* Stuff over top of plastic canvas piece.

Rnd 12: (Sc next 2 sts tog) around, join with sl st in first sc. Leaving end for weaving, fasten off.

Weave end through sts of last rnd, pull to gather slightly, secure end.

RUFFLE

Rnd 1: Working in **front lps** of rnd 5 on Pin Cushion, join with sl st in any st, ch 3, dc in same st, dc in next st, (2 dc in next st, dc in next st) around, join with sl st in top of ch-3. *(45 dc made)*

Rnd 2: Ch 1, sc first 2 sts tog, ch 1, skip next st, (sc in next st, ch 1, skip next st) around, join with sl st in first sc. *(22 sc, 22 ch-1 sps)*

Rnd 3: Ch 1, sc in each st and in each ch sp around, join. Fasten off.

Weave 24" strand of yarn through ch sps of rnd 2. Place Pin Cushion on jar lid *(glue in place if desired)* pull yarn to gather around lid, tie ends into a bow. ❀

Cutting Illustration

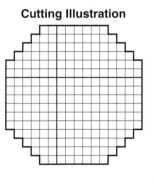

Pixie Christmas Stocking

continued from page 35

Hanger Ring

Row 1: Holding Stocking with Foot pointing left, with G hook and one strand green, join with sl st around post of top right-hand corner st, ch 8, sl st in same sp, turn.

Row 2: Ch 1, 10 sc in ch 8 ring, sl st in same sp as first sl st on row 1, turn. Fasten off. *(10 sc made)*

Row 3: Join red with sl st in same sp as first st on row 1, ch 1, sc in each st across last row, sl st in same sp as first st on row 1, turn. Fasten off.

Row 4: Join white with sl st in same sp as first st on row 1, ch 3, sc in first st on last row, (ch 2, sc in next sc) across, ch 3, sl st in same sp as first st on row 1. Fasten off.

Pom-pom

Wrap red around cardboard 100 times, slide loops off cardboard; tie separate strand red around middle of all loops. Cut loops. Trim ends. Sew to tip of toe. ❀

Lacy Bookmarks

Designed by Margret Willson

The avid reader on your gift list will love these pretty tasselled bookmarks.
The Blue Bookmark is wonderful for learning to make hairpin lace.
What an unexpected pleasure these will be when tucked into the gift of a new book or Bible.

FINISHED SIZES: Blue Bookmark is 8" long not including Fringe. Vanilla Bookmark is 7" long not including Fringe.

MATERIALS: Acrylic sport yarn — 30 yds. each blue and vanilla; adjustable hairpin loom; D hook or hook size needed to obtain gauge.

GAUGE: 7 sc = 1".

BASIC STITCHES: Ch, sl st, sc, hdc.

SPECIAL STITCH: For **picot,** ch 3, sl st in left 2 threads of sc just made.

BLUE BOOKMARK
Center Strip

Rnd 1: Adjust loom to 1" width; remove top bar. With blue, place slip knot on hook. Side loop off hook and onto left-hand prong of loom *(see illustration 1).* Replace top bar of loom. Draw yarn around right-hand side of loom to the back *(see illustration 2).* Insert hook into loop of slip knot and pull until knot is at center, yo, pull strand at back through lp on hook *(see illustration 3),* ch 1. *Drop lp from hook; insert hook in dropped lp from back to front, turn loom from right to left passing the yarn around to the back of the loom, yo, pull strand at back through lp on hook, ch 1, sc in top front strand of left-hand side of center sts *(see illustration 4);* repeat from * until you have 52 lps on each side *(see illustration 5).* **Do not fasten off.**

Border

Rnd 1: Slide lps off loom. Working around outer edge, ch 1, sc in spine at center, [*ch 4, insert hook from back to front through next 4 lps at same time, yo, draw lp through, complete as sc; repeat from * across, ch 4], sc in spine; repeat between [ ], join with sl st in first sc.

Rnd 2: Ch 1, (sc, ch 3, sc) in first st, *4 sc in next ch-4 sp, 3 sc in next sc, (sc in next ch-4 sp, 3 sc in next sc) across to last ch-4 sp on this side, 4 sc in next ch-4 sp*, (sc, ch 3, sc) in next sc; repeat between **, join. Fasten off.

Fringe

Cut seven strands blue each 8" long. Fold strands in half, insert hook in ch-3 sp at one end of Bookmark, draw fold through, draw all loose ends through fold, tighten. Trim ends.

VANILLA BOOKMARK
Center Strip

Rnd 1: Adjust loom to 1" width; remove top bar. With vanilla, place slip knot on hook. Side loop off hook and onto left-hand prong of loom *(see illustration 1)*. Replace top bar of loom. Draw yarn around right-hand side of loom to the back *(see illustration 2)*. Insert hook into loop of slip knot and pull until knot is at center, yo, pull strand at back through lp on hook *(see illustration 3)*, ch 1. *Drop lp from hook; insert hook in dropped lp from back to front, turn loom from right to left passing the yarn around to the back of the loom, yo, pull strand at back through lp on hook, ch 1, 2 hdc in top front strand of left-hand side of center sts; repeat from * until you have 24 lps on each side *(see illustration 5)*. **Do not fasten off.**

Border

Rnd 1: Slide lps off loom. Working around outer edge, ch 1, sc in spine at center, *ch 3, (insert hook from back to front through next lp, yo, draw lp through, complete as sc, sc in same lp) across to end, ch 3*, sc in spine at center;

repeat between **, Join with sl st in first sc.

Rnd 2: Ch 1, sc in first st, **picot** *(see Special Stitch)*, *(sc, picot) 2 times in next ch sp, (sc in next st, picot, skip next st) across to next ch-3 sp, (sc, picot) 2 times in next ch sp*, sc in next st at center, picot; repeat between **, join. Fasten off.

Fringe

Cut five strands vanilla each 6" long. Fold strands in half, insert hook in sc at one end of Bookmark, draw fold through; draw all loose ends through fold, tighten. Trim ends. ✿

Hairpin Lace Illustration

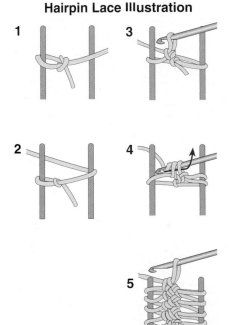

Fans & Lace

DESIGNED BY JOCELYN SASS

When you get the urge to do a little decorating, but your finances won't let you do a complete renovation, put your favorite pastime to work. You can satisfy your urge without the splurge with this charming, feminine pillow, bookend cover and trinket box cover.

FINISHED SIZES: Pillow is 9" x 13" with lace; Bookend Cover fits 4⅞" x 5½" bookend; Trinket Box Cover is 5½" across.

MATERIALS: 5 oz. pink worsted yarn; 400 yds. each white and variegated pink size 10 crochet cotton thread; 4 small and 4 large white porcelain roses; 2½ yds. white 1" gathered lace; 1⅔ yds. white ¼" ribbon; white sewing thread; polyester fiberfill; craft glue or hot glue gun; sewing and tapestry needles; D, F and H hooks or hook sizes needed to obtain gauges.

GAUGES: With **H hook**, 3 hdc= 1"; 2 hdc roses = 1". With **F hook,** 7 sc = 2"; 4 sc rows = 1".

BASIC STITCHES: Ch, sl st, sc, hdc, dc.

PILLOW

Cover Side (make 2)

Note: Use worsted yarn and H hook unless otherwise stated.

Row 1: With pink, ch 36, hdc in third ch from hook, hdc in each ch across, turn. *(35 hdc made)*

Rows 2-15: Ch 2, hdc in each st across, turn. At end of last row, **do not turn or fasten off.**

Row 16: Working around outer edge, ch 1, sc in end of each row and in each st around with 3 sc in each corner st, join with sl st in first sc. Fasten off.

Matching sts, working through both thicknesses in **back lps** only, join pink with sl st in any st, sl st in each st around, stuffing before closing, join with sl st in first sl st. Fasten off.

For **edging,** with D hook and one strand each white and variegated pink held together, join with sl st in any sl st of joining rnd, ch 3, 4 dc in same st, 5 dc in each st around, join with sl st in top of ch-3. Fasten off.

Fan (make 2)

Note: Use one strand each white and variegated pink held together and D hook unless otherwise stated.

Rnd 1: Ch 4, sl st in first ch to form ring, ch 1, 10 sc in ring, join with sl st in first sc. *(10 sc made)*

Row 2: Ch 1, sc in first st leaving remaining sts unworked, turn. *(1)*

Row 3: Ch 1, 3 sc in first st, turn. *(3)*

Rows 4-9: Ch 1, 2 sc in first st, sc in each st across with 2 sc in last st, turn, ending with *(15 sts)* in last row.

Row 10: Ch 1, sc in each st across, turn.

Rows 11-13: Repeat rows 4 and 10 alternately, ending with *(19 sts)* in last row.

Row 14: Skip first st, 5 dc in next st, (skip next st, sl st in next st, skip next st, 5 dc in next st) 4 times leaving last st unworked; working around outer edge, sc in end of each row and in each st around to opposite side of row 14, join with sl st in top of first dc made. Fasten off.

Finishing

1: Glue Fans to Pillow *(see photo).* Tie one 12" piece ribbon into a bow; glue bow over rows 2-3 of one Fan and one large rose to center of bow. Repeat on other Fan.

BOOKEND COVER

Cover Side (make 2)

Note: Use worsted yarn and F hook unless otherwise stated.

Row 1: With pink, ch 19, sc in second ch from hook, sc in each ch across, turn. *(18 sc made)*

Rows 2-19: Ch 1, sc in each st across, turn.

Rows 20-21: Ch 1, sc in first 2 sts tog, sc in each st across to last 2 sts, sc last 2 sts tog, turn. At end of last row, **do not turn or fasten off.** *(16, 14)*

Row 22: Repeat rnd 16 of Pillow Cover Side.

Matching sts, working through both thicknesses in **back lps** only, join pink and sl st in st at end of row 1 on bottom corner of cover, sl st in each st around to opposite bottom corner leaving remaining sts unworked for insert. Fasten off.

For **edging,** with D hook and one strand each white and variegated pink held together, join with sl st in first st of joining row, ch 3, 4 dc in same st, 5 dc in each st across. Fasten off.

Fan

Work same as Pillow Cover Fan.

continued on page 43

Foot Warmers

DESIGNED BY LENA CHAMBERLAIN

Keep your little one's feet warm and cozy this winter with these easy-to-make slippers. You may want to make several pairs in different colors to match favorite pj's and robes. Make them with easy-care acrylic worsted yarn, and you can machine wash and dry them time after time.

FINISHED SIZES: Instructions are for Child's small, 6" sole; changes for medium, 7" sole and large, 8" sole are in [ ].

MATERIALS: Worsted yarn — 4 oz. red, 3 oz. white; G hook or hook size needed to obtain gauge.

GAUGE: 4 sc = 1"; 3 sc rows = 1".

BASIC STITCHES: Ch, sl st, sc, hdc, dc.

SPECIAL STITCH: For **cross stitch (cr st),** skip next st, dc in next st; working in front of last st made, dc in skipped st.

SLIPPER (make 2)

Note: Do not join or turn unless otherwise stated. Mark first st of each rnd.

Rnd 1: With red, ch 20 [24, 26], sc in second ch from hook, sc in next 6 [10, 12] chs, hdc in next 3 chs, dc in next 8 [8, 10] chs, 6 dc in last ch; working on opposite side of ch, dc in next 8 [8, 10] chs, hdc in next 3 chs, sc in next 6 [10, 12] chs, 2 sc in same ch as first sc. *(43 sts made) [51 sts made, 59 sts made]*

Rnd 2: 2 sc in each of first 2 sts, hdc in each st around to next 6-dc group, 2 hdc in each of next 6 sts, hdc in each st around to last 3 sts, 2 sc in each of last 3 sts. *(54) [62, 70]*

Rnd 3: 2 sc in each of first 3 sts, sc in each st around to last 5 sts, 2 sc in each of last 5 sts. *(62 sc) [70 sc, 78 sc]*

Rnd 4: Sc in each st around, join wit sl st in first sc.

Rnd 5: Working this rnd in **back lps** only, ch 3, dc in each st around, join with sl st in top of ch-3. Fasten off.

Rnd 6: Join white with sc in second st of 2 center back sts, sc in next 20 [24, 28] sts, (sc next 2 sts tog) 10 times, sc in last 21 [25, 29] sts, join with sl st in first sc. *(52) [60, 68]*

Rnd 7: Ch 1, sc in each st around, join. Fasten off.

Rnd 8: Join red with sl st in first st, ch 3, **cr st** *(see Special Stitch)* around to last st, dc in last st, join with sl st in top of ch-3. Fasten off.

Rnd 9: Join white with sc in first st, sc in next 20 [24, 28] sts, (sc next 3 sts tog) 3 times, sc in last 23 [26, 30] sts, join with sl st in first sc. Fasten off. *(46) [54 62]*

Rnd 10: Join red with sl st in first st, ch 3, cr st 9 [11, 13] times, (dc next 2 sts tog) 3 times, cr st 10 [12, 14] times, dc in last st, join with sl st in top of ch-3. Fasten off. *(19 cr sts, 5 dc) [23 cr sts, 5 dc; 27 cr sts, 5 dc]*

Rnd 11: Join white with sc in first st, sc in next 11 [15, 19] sts, (ch 2, skip next st, sc in next 2 sts) 2 times, ch 2, skip next st, (sc next 2 sts tog) 3 times, ch 2, skip next st, (sc in next 2 sts, ch 2, skip next st) 2 times, sc in last 11 [15, 19] sts, join with sl st in first sc. Fasten off.

Row 12: Working in rows, join white with sl st in first st after last ch-2 sp on last rnd, ch 3, dc in each st across to first ch-2 sp leaving remaining sts unworked, **do not turn.**

Row 13: Ch 1; working from left to right, **reverse sc** *(see page 159)* in each st across. Fasten off.

For **trim,** working in **front lps** of rnd 4, join white with sl st in center st on heel, sl st in each st around, join with sl st in first sl st. Fasten off.

For **tie,** with red, ch 80. Fasten off.

Lace through ch-2 sps and end of row 12 *(see photo).* ✿

Fans & Lace

continued from page 41

Finishing

1: Glue Fan to Cover at slight angle *(see photo).* Tie 12" piece ribbon into a bow; glue to rows 2-3 of Fan. Glue one large and 2 small roses to center of bow *(see photo).*

2: Cut piece lace to fit around outer edge of Cover; glue in place.

TRINKET BOX COVER

Cover

Notes: Do not join or turn unless other wise stated. Mark first st of each rnd.

Use worsted yarn and F hook unless otherwise stated.

Rnd 1: With pink, ch 2, 6 sc in second ch from hook. *(6 sc made)*

Rnd 2: 2 sc in each st around. *(12)*

Rnd 3: (Sc in next st, 2 sc in next st) around. *(18)*

Rnd 4: (Sc in next 2 sts, 2 sc in next st) around. *(24)*

Rnd 5: (Sc in next 3 sts, 2 sc in next st) around. *(30)*

Rnd 6: (Sc in next 4 sts, 2 sc in next st) around. *(36)*

Rnd 7: (Sc in next 5 sts, 2 sc in next st) around. Fasten off. *(42)*

Rnd 8: With D hook and one strand each white and variegated pink held together, join with sl st in any st, ch 3, 4 dc in same st, (sl st in next st, 5 dc in next st) around, join. Fasten off.

Finishing

1: Scw remaining lace around outer edge of Cover. Glue Cover over top of trinket box.

2: Glue one large rose to center of Cover; glue one small rose to each side of large rose.

3: Tie remaining ribbon into a bow; glue below roses. ✿

Diagonal Dishcloth

DESIGNED BY DARLA FANTON

*Washing dishes can be a soothing experience after a long day at the office.
The hot soapy water and the simple act of cleaning a dish without having to think too deeply
is a calming experience, and this colorful handmade dishcloth adds to the contentment.*

FINISHED SIZE: 8½" square.

MATERIALS: Cotton worsted yarn — 1 oz. each burgundy and ecru; K double-ended and J crochet hook or hook size needed to obtain gauge.

GAUGE: With **K double-end hook,** 5 sts = 1"; 3 pattern rows = 1".

BASIC STITCHES: Ch, sl st, sc.

GENERAL INSTRUCTIONS

To **draw up a lp,** insert hook in designated lp, bar or st, yo, draw lp through and leave on hook.

When **using a color already in use,** pick up color from row below, yo, draw through one lp on hook, (yo, draw through 2 lps on hook) across leaving last lp at end of row on hook (this is first vertical bar of next row).

To **work lps off with new color,** place slip knot on hook, draw slip knot through one lp on hook, (yo, draw through 2 lps) across leaving last lp at end of row on hook (this is first vertical bar of next row).

When **turning,** always slide lps to opposite end of hook. **Do not** turn unless otherwise stated.

To **turn,** rotate hook 180 degrees and slide stitches to opposite end.

If you have difficulty keeping all the stitches on the double-end hook, cap the unused end of hook with either a knitting needle protector or a clean wine cork.

DISHCLOTH

Note: Read General Instructions before beginning pattern

Row 1: With K double-end hook and burgundy, ch 2, draw up lp in second ch from hook, turn. *(2 lps on hook)*

Row 2: With ecru, work lps off hook, **do not turn.**

Row 3: For **beginning increase (beg inc), ch 1, insert hook under first vertical bar, yo, draw through bar;** draw up lp in top strand of first **horizontal bar** *(see illustration);* for **end increase (end inc), insert hook under last vertical bar, yo, draw lp through;** turn. *(4 lps on hook)*

Row 4: With burgundy, work lps off hook, **do not turn.**

Row 5: Beg inc, draw up lp in top strand of each horizontal bar across, end inc, turn. *(6 lps on hook)*

Row 6: With ecru, work lps off hook, **do not turn.**

Row 7: Beg inc, draw up lp in top strand of each horizontal bar across, end inc, turn. *(8 lps on hook)*

Rows 8-50: Repeat rows 4-7 consecutively, ending with row 6. At end of last row, *(50 lps)* on hook.

Row 51: For **beginning decrease (beg dec), skip first horizontal bar;** draw up lp in top strand of each horizontal bar across to last horizontal bar; for **end decrease (end dec), insert hook under top strand of last horizontal bar, yo, draw through bar and one lp on hook;** turn. *(48 lps on hook.*

Row 52: With burgundy, work lps off hook, **do not turn.**

Row 53: Beg dec, draw up lp in top strand of each horizontal bar across to last horizontal bar, end dec, turn. *(46 lps on hook)*

Row 54: With ecru, work lps off hook, **do not turn.**

Rows 55-96: Repeat rows 51-54 consecutively, ending with row 52 and *(4 lps on hook).*

Row 97: Beg dec, draw up lp in top strand of next horizontal bar, end dec, turn. *(2 lps on hook)*

Row 98: With ecru, work lps off hook, turn. Draw up burgundy. Fasten off ecru.

Rnd 99: Working around outer edge in sts and in ends of rows, with J hook, ch 1, 3 sc in first st, ch 1, evenly spacing sts so piece lays flat, (sc, ch 1) around with (3 sc, ch 1) in each corner, join with sl st in first sc. Fasten off. ✿

Horizontal Bar

Lace Tissue Holder

DESIGNED BY MARGRET WILLSON

Broomstick lace is a popular stitch technique — it's fun to do and the results are beautiful.
This tissue holder is ideal as a companion gift with a set of matching towels
for a wedding or housewarming gift. Or simply treat yourself!

FINISHED SIZE: Covers standard-size tissue roll.

MATERIALS: Worsted yarn — 3 oz. blue; size 35 broomstick lace pin; G hook or hook size needed to obtain gauge.

GAUGE: 4 sc = 1".

BASIC STITCHES: Ch, sl st, sc.

HOLDER

Row 1: Starting at **bottom,** working from left to right, with G hook, ch 7, place last lp on pin. draw up lp in next ch, place on pin *(see illustration 1),* draw up lp in same ch, place on pin, *draw up lp in next ch and place on pin, (draw up lp in same ch, place on pin) 2 times; repeat from * across, **do not turn.** *(18 lps on pin)*

Row 2: Working from right to left, insert hook through 3 lps on pin, slide lps off pin and hold together as one *(see illustration 2),* yo, draw through lps, ch 1, 6 sc in same 3 lps *(see illustration 3),* (insert hook through next 3 lps on pin, slide lps off pin and hold together as one, yo, draw through lps and lp on hook, ch 1, 6 sc in same 3 lps) across, **do not turn.** Place last lp on pin. *(36 sc)*

Row 3: Working this row in **back lps** only, working from left to right, draw up lp in each sc across, **do not turn.** Place last lp on pin. *(36 lps on pin)*

Row 4: Repeat row 2, turn. *(72 sc)*

Row 5: Working this row in **front lps** only, ch 1, sc in each st across, turn.

Row 6: Working this row in **back lps** only, ch 1, sc in each st across, **do not turn.** Place last lp on pin.

Row 7: Repeat row 3. *(72 lps on hook)*

Row 8: Working right to left, insert hook through 6 lps on pin. slide lps off pin and hold together as one, yo, draw through lps, ch 1, 6 sc in same 6 lps, (insert hook through next 6 lps on pin, slide lps off pin and hold together as one, yo, draw through lps and lp on hook, ch 1, 6 sc in same 6 lps) across, **do not turn.**

Rows 9-20: Repeat rows 3 and 8 alternately.

Rows 21-22: Repeat rows 3 and 2. At end of last row, do not place last lp on pin. Fasten off.

Sew side seam looping yarn to match lps and sewing sc together snugly.

For **tie,** ch 100. Fasten off.

Weave through lps of row 19, place tissue in Cover; pull ends to gather and tie into a bow. ✿

Broomstick Lace

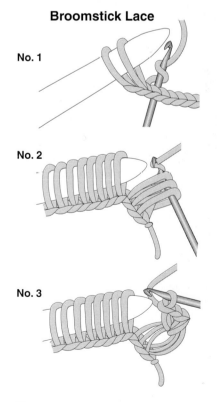

No. 1

No. 2

No. 3

Ponytail Ruffles

DESIGNED BY TERRI MCCAUGHIN

Tame your tresses with these soft and cushy ponytail ruffles.
You'll want to make several in your favorite jewel-toned colors of chenille yarn.
For a little girl who loves cheerleading or dance, make ruffles in team colors.

FINISHED SIZES: Blue Ponytail Ruffle is 1¾" wide. Purple Ponytail Ruffle is 2" wide.

MATERIALS FOR BOTH: Chenille yarn — ½ oz. each blue variegated, purple variegated and black; 2 large elastic hair bands; G hook.

BASIC STITCHES: Ch, sl st, sc, hdc, dc.

BLUE PONYTAIL RUFFLE

Rnd 1: With blue variegated, working around one hair band *(see page 159),* join with sc

around band, work 29 more sc around band, join with sl st in first sc. *(40 sc made)*

Rnd 2: Ch 6, skip next st, (dc in next st, ch 3, skip next st) around, join with sl st in third ch of ch-6. *(20 dc, 20 ch-3 sps)*

Rnd 3: Ch 1, sc in first st, (*ch 2, working in front of sts, sc in next skipped st on rnd 1, ch 2*, sc in next st on last rnd) 19 times; repeat between **, join with sl st in first sc. Fasten off. *(40 sc, 40 ch sps)*

Rnd 4: Working in ch-3 sps on rnd 2, join black with sc in any ch-3 sp, (hdc, dc, ch 2, dc, hdc, sc) in same sp, (sc, hdc, dc, ch 2, dc, hdc, sc) in each ch-3 sp around, join. Fasten off.

PURPLE PONYTAIL RUFFLE

Rnd 1: With purple variegated, repeat same rnd of Blue Ponytail Ruffle.

Rnd 2: Ch 8, dc in next st, ch 3, (dc in next st, ch 5, dc in next st, ch 3) around, join with sl st in third ch of ch-3. *(20 ch-3 sps, 20 ch-5 sps)*

Rnd 3: Sl st in first ch sp, ch 1, sc in same sp, ch 2, (sc in next ch sp, ch 2) around, join with sl st in first sc. Fasten off. *(40 sc, 40 ch-2 sps)*

*Note: For **sc front post (sc fp)**, insert hook from front to back around post of next st, yo, draw lp through, yo, draw through both lps on hook.*

Row 4: Join black with sc in any st, ch 5, dc in same st, *[sc in next ch sp, sc fp around next st, sc in next ch sp], (dc, ch 2, dc) in next st, repeat from * 18 more times; repeat between [ ], join with sl st in third ch of ch-5. Fasten off. ✿

Chapter Three

51 Christmas Shell Afghan
52 Teapot Tidee
53 Doily Sachet
54 Kitchen Extras
56 Photo Album
57 Puppy Poncho
58 Headband and Mittens
62 Cotton Candy
64 Cro-Tat™ Jar Topper
66 Cool Water Bottle Holder
68 Sweet Baby Hat

3

Tuesday was named tiwesdaeg to honor the European god of war, Tiwi, who would guide warriors who died in battle to paradise.

Christmas Shell Afghan

Designed by Katherine Eng

A season that's full of cheerful smiles and carol whistling deserves to have a tribute placed on display in your home. An afghan is a nice backdrop for a few sprigs of holly. You just need to be sure to leave enough space for sitting nearby as you open your gifts.

FINISHED SIZE: 44" x 66" not including Fringe.

MATERIALS: Worsted yarn — 29 oz. soft white, 10 oz. spruce and 9 oz. red; H hook or hook size needed to obtain gauge.

GAUGE: 2 shells and one sc = 3"; 3 pattern rows = 2".

BASIC STITCHES: Ch, sl st, sc, dc.

SPECIAL STITCH: For **shell,** (2 dc, ch 2, 2 dc) in next st or ch sp.

AFGHAN

Note: Leave 6" ends at beginning and end of rows to be worked into Fringe.

Row 1: With white, ch 224, sc in second ch from hook, (ch 2, skip next 2 chs, sc in next ch) across, turn. *(112 sc, 111 ch sps made)*

Row 2: Ch 1, sc in first st, *shell *(see Special Stitch)* in next sc, sc in next sc; repeat from * across, turn. Fasten off.

Row 3: Join spruce with sl st in first st, ch 3, 2 dc in same st, sc in ch sp of next shell, (shell in next sc, sc in ch sp of next shell) across to last sc, 3 dc in last sc, turn. Fasten off.

Row 4: Join red with sc in first dc, shell in next sc, (sc in next shell, shell in next sc) across to last 3 dc, sc in last dc, turn. Fasten off.

Row 5: Repeat row 3.

Row 6: Join white with sc in first dc, shell in next sc, (sc in next shell, shell in next sc) across to last 3 dc, sc in last dc, turn.

Row 7: (Ch 3, 2 dc) in first st, sc in next shell, (shell in next sc, sc in next shell) across to last sc, 3 dc in last sc, turn.

Row 8: Ch 1, sc in first dc, shell in next sc, (sc in next shell, shell in next sc) across to last 3 dc, sc in last dc, turn.

Rows 9-10: Repeat rows 7 and 8. At end of last row, fasten off.

Row 11: Join red with sl st in first st, ch 3, 2 dc in same st, sc in next shell, (shell in next sc, sc in next shell) across to last sc, 3 dc in last sc, turn. Fasten off.

Row 12: Join spruce with sc in first dc, shell in next sc, (sc in next shell, shell in next sc) across to last 3 dc, sc in last dc, turn. Fasten off.

Row 13: Repeat row 11.

Rows 14-18: Repeat rows 6-10.

Rows 19-24: Repeat rows 3-8. At end of last row, fasten off.

Rows 25-35: Repeat rows 3-13.

Rows 36-38: Repeat rows 6-8.

Row 39: Ch 1, sc in first st, *ch 2, (sc, ch 2, sc) in next shell, ch 2, sc in next sc; repeat from * across. Fasten off.

Row 40: Working in starting ch on opposite side of row 1, join white with sc in first ch, (ch 2, skip next 2 chs, sc in next ch) across, turn.

Rows 41-78: Repeat rows 2-39.

Fringe

For **each Fringe,** cut 2 strands yarn each 13" long. Holding both strands together, fold in half. Insert hook in end of row, pull fold through, pull all loose ends through fold including 6" ends at ends of rows, tighten. Trim ends.

Matching color of row, Fringe 2 times in each end of each dc row and one time in each end of each sc row on short ends of Afghan. ✿

Teapot Tidee

DESIGNED BY DEE MARRS

*The day is at an end, the children are in bed and now is the right time for some
peaceful reflection. Sit back and remember your favorite moments of the day
while sipping a delicious cup of tea and enjoying some precious quiet time for yourself.*

FINISHED SIZE: Flower is 1¾" across.

MATERIALS: Size 10 metallic crochet cotton thread — 20 yds. white/gold; 5 yds. beige size 10 crochet cotton thread; ½" flat button; gold wire hook with eye; 16" of gold elastic cord; 1 foam curler; tapestry needle; No. 7 steel hook or hook size needed to obtain gauge.

GAUGE: Rnds 1-3 of Flower = 1¼" across.

BASIC STITCHES: Ch, sl st, sc, hdc, dc.

FLOWER

Rnd 1: With white/gold, ch 6, sl st in first st

to form ring, ch 1, 12 sc in ring, join with sl st in first sc. *(12 sc made)*

Row 2: Ch 1, sc in first st, ch 3, skip next st, (sc in next st, ch 3, skip next st) around, join.

Rnd 3: For **petals,** sl st in first ch sp, ch 1, (sc, hdc, 2 dc, hdc, sc) in same ch sp and in each ch sp around, join with sl st in first sc.

Rnd 4: Working behind petals, ch 5, (sl st around post of first sc on next petal, ch 5) around, join with sl st in first ch of first ch-5.

Rnd 5: Ch 1, (sc, hdc, 5 dc, hdc, sc) in each ch sp around, join. Fasten off.

Rnd 6: With wrong side facing you, working in ch-5 sps on rnd 4 between sts of rnd 5, join white/gold with sl st between first 2 sts on one petal, ch 3, evenly space 5 more dc in ch sp between sts on this petal, evenly sp 6 dc in next ch sp between sts of petal around, join with sl st in top of ch-3.

Rnd 7: Ch 1, sc in each st around, join with sl st in first sc. Fasten off.

Rnd 8: Join beige with sl st in first st, sc in each st around, join. Fasten off.

Sew button to center of rnd 1 on right side of Flower.

Finishing

1: For **drip catcher,** cut 1" piece from foam roller.

2: Thread one end of cord through eye on hook; pull ends even.

3: Weave one end of cord through 2 sts on inside of Flower; repeat with other end of cord on opposite side of Flower.

4: Pull one end of cord through center of drip catcher. Tie ends of cord into a knot and pull knot into center of foam.

5: Place hook over handle of teapot; place Flower over center of lid and slip drip catcher under spout of teapot. ✿

Doily Sachet

DESIGNED BY JOSIE RABIER

A lacy crocheted sachet is always a welcome addition to a housewarming or wedding gift.
Make these small sachets in quiet moments so you'll have them on hand,
and add them to gifts of linens or other soft household or decorating items.

FINISHED SIZE: Doily measures 5" across.

MATERIALS: Size 10 crochet cotton thread — 40 yds. variegated green; 10" satin ¼" picot ribbon; one cotton ball; few drops perfume or potpourri scent; tapestry needle; No. 7 steel hook.

BASIC STITCHES: Ch, sl st, sc, dc, tr.

SPECIAL STITCH: For **cluster,** yo, insert hook in next ch sp, yo, draw lp through, yo, draw through 2 lps on hook, *yo, insert hook in same ch sp, yo, draw lp through, yo, draw through 2 lps on hook; repeat from *, yo, draw through all 4 lps on hook.

DOILY

Rnd 1: Ch 6, sl st in first ch to form ring, ch 7 *(counts as tr and ch-3),* (tr in ring, ch 3) 11 times, join with sl st in fourth ch of ch-7. *(12 ch-3 sps made)*

Rnd 2: (Sl st, ch 6, dc) in first ch sp, (dc, ch 3, dc) in each ch sp around, join with sl st in third ch of ch-6.

Rnd 3: (Sl st, ch 3, dc, ch 3, 2 dc) in first ch sp, (2 dc, ch 3, 2 dc) in each ch sp around, join with sl st in top of ch-3.

Rnd 4: Sl st in next dc, sl st in first ch sp, ch 6, (dc, ch 3, dc, ch 3, dc) in same sp, (dc, ch 3, dc, ch 3, dc, ch 3, dc) in each ch sp around, join with sl st in third ch of ch-6. *(36 ch-3 sps)*

Rnd 5: Sl st in first ch sp, ch 1, sc in same sp, ch 2, *(**cluster**—*see Special Stitch,* ch 2, cluster, ch 2, cluster, ch 2, cluster) in next ch sp, ch

2, sc in next 2 ch sps, ch 2; repeat from * 10 more times, (cluster, ch 2, cluster, ch 2, cluster, ch 2, cluster) in next ch sp, ch 2, sc in last ch sp, join with sl st in first sc. Fasten off.

For **sachet,** weave ribbon through ch sps of rnd 4, put a few drops of perfume or potpourri on cotton ball; place in middle of Doily, pull ends of ribbon tight. Tie into a bow. ✿

Kitchen Extras

DESIGNED BY SUE CHILDRESS

*Nothing in life has to be mundane — even washing dishes. Turn on the radio,
grab the dishcloth or towel, then sing, dance or just have fun as you clean.
This handy set helps you make quick work of everyday kitchen chores.*

FINISHED SIZES: Dish towel is 20" long when buttoned. Dishcloth is 8½" square.

MATERIALS: 100% cotton 3-ply yarn — 7 oz. pink; 1" tall novelty button; sewing thread; sewing and tapestry needles; G hook or hook size needed to obtain gauge.

GAUGE: 4 dc sts = 1"; 2 dc rows = 1".

BASIC STITCHES: Ch, sl st, sc, dc, tr.

SPECIAL STITCHES: For **cluster,** yo, insert hook in next ch sp, yo, draw lp through, yo, draw through 2 lps on hook, yo, insert hook in same sp, yo, draw lp through, yo, draw through 2 lps on hook, yo, draw through all 3 lps on hook.

For **V st,** (dc, ch 1, dc) in next ch sp.

For **shell,** 5 dc in next st.

TOWEL

Row 1: Ch 64, sc in second ch from hook, ch 2, skip next ch, sc in next ch, *skip next 3 chs, (3 tr, ch 4, sc) in next ch , ch 2, skip next ch, (sc, ch 4, 3 tr) in next ch, skip next 3 chs, sc in next ch, ch 2, skip next ch, sc in next ch; repeat from * across, turn. *(30 tr, 11 ch-2 sps made)*

Row 2: Ch 4, dc in first ch-2 sp, ch 1, skip next 3 tr, sc in top of next ch-4, ch 2, **cluster** *(see Special Stitches)* in next ch-2 sp, ch 2, sc in top of next ch-4, ch 1, skip next 3 tr, *V st *(see Special Stitches)* in next ch-2 sp, ch 1, skip next 3 tr, sc in top of next ch-4, ch 2, cluster in next ch-2 sp, ch 2, sc in top of next ch-4, ch 1, skip next 3 tr; repeat from * across to last ch-2 sp, dc in last ch-2 sp, ch 1, dc in last sc, turn.

Row 3: Ch 1, sc in same st, ch 2, skip next ch-1 sp, sc in next ch-1 sp, (3 tr, ch 4, sc) in next ch-2 sp, ch 2, skip next cluster, (sc, ch 4, 3 tr) in next ch-2 sp, sc in next ch-1 sp, *ch 2, skip next V st, sc in next ch-1 sp, (3 tr, ch 4, sc) in next ch-2 sp, ch 2, skip next cluster, (sc, ch 4, 3 tr) in next ch-2 sp, sc in next ch-1 sp; repeat from * across to last dc and ch-4, ch 2, skip next dc, sc in third ch of last ch-4, turn.

Rows 4-26: Repeat rows 2 and 3 alternately, ending with row 2. At end of last row, fasten off.

Top

Row 1: Working in starting ch on opposite side of row 1 on Towel, join with sl st in first ch, ch 3, dc in each ch across, turn. *(63 dc made)*

Row 2: Ch 3, dc in next st, (dc next 2 sts tog, dc in next st) across to last st, dc in last st, turn. *(43)*

Row 3: Ch 3, (dc next 2 sts tog) across, turn. *(22)*

Row 4: Ch 3, (dc next 2 sts tog) across to last st, dc in last st, turn. *(12)*

Row 5: Ch 3, dc in next 4 sts, dc next 2 sts tog, dc in last 5 sts, turn. *(11)*

Row 6: Ch 3, dc next 2 sts tog, dc in next 5 sts, dc next 2 sts tog, dc in last st, turn. *(9)*

Rows 7-11: Ch 3, dc in each st across, turn.

Row 12: Ch 3, dc next 2 sts tog, dc in next st; for **buttonhole,** ch 1, skip next st; dc next 2 sts tog, dc in last st, turn.

Row 13: Ch 3, dc next 2 sts tog, dc in next ch-1 sp, dc next 2 sts tog, dc in last st, turn. Fasten off.

Edging

Rnd 1: Working around outer edge in ends of rows and in sts, join with sc in row 1 of Towel, 2 sc in each dc row, sc in each sc row, sc in each ch and sc in each st around with 3 sc in each corner of row 26 and 2 sc in each corner of row 13 on Top, join with sl st in first sc.

Row 2: Working in rows, ch 1, sc in first st, skip next 2 sts, **shell** *(see Special Stitches)* in next st, skip next 2 sts, sc in next st, *skip next st, shell in next st, skip next st, sc in next st; repeat from * 33 more times leaving remaining sts unworked. Fasten off. *(35 shells)*

Center and sew button over row 6 of Top.

DISHCLOTH

Row 1: Ch 28, sc in second ch from hook, ch 2, skip next ch, sc in next ch, *skip next 3 chs, (3 tr, ch 4, sc) in next ch, ch 2, skip next ch, (sc, ch 4, 3 tr) in next ch, skip next 3 chs, sc in next ch, ch 2, skip next ch, sc in next ch; repeat from * across, turn. *(12 tr, 5 ch-2 sps made)*

Rows 2-12: Repeat rows 2 and 3 of Towel alternately, ending with row 2. At end of last row, **do not turn.**

Rnd 13: Working around outer edge in ends of rows and in sts, ch 1, 2 sc in each dc row, sc in each sc row, sc in each ch and sc in each st around with 3 sc in each corner, join with sl st in first sc. *(98)*

Rnd 14: Ch 1, sc in first st, skip next 2 sts, shell in next st, skip next 2 sts, *sc in next st, skip next st, shell in next st, skip next st; repeat from * around, join. Fasten off. ✿

Photo Album

DESIGNED BY MARIA NAGY

This pastel baby album is the perfect size to carry in your purse, where it will always be handy for sharing pictures of the little ones. It also makes a wonderful gift for a proud new grandmother or aunt, or anyone with a new baby in the family.

FINISHED SIZE: Fits 5" x 6½" photo album with 2" binding.

MATERIALS: Worsted yarn — 3 oz. blue/pink/white variegated, 1½ oz. pink and 1 oz. blue; 6" x 7⅛" piece of white fabric; 1 yd. white oval 5 mm x 7 mm strung pearl beads; white sewing thread; 4" ring; photo to fit in 4" ring; 5" x 6½" photo album with 2" binding; sewing needle; H crochet hook or size needed to obtain gauge.

GAUGE: 7 sc= 2"; 7 sc rows = 2".

BASIC STITCHES: Ch, sl st, sc, dc.

COVER

Row 1: With variegated, ch 21, sc in second ch from hook, sc in each ch across, turn. *(20 sc made)*

Note: *Front of row 1 is wrong side of work.*

Rows 2-45: Ch 1, sc in each st across, turn. At end of last row, do not turn. Fasten off.

For edging, working around outer edge, join pink with sc in first st on last row, skip next st, *(sc, ch 3, dc) in next st or end of next row; repeat from * around, join with sl st in first sc. Fasten off.

PHOTO FRAME

Rnd 1: Working around ring, *(see page 159),* join blue with sc around ring, work 63 more sc around ring, join with sl st in first sc. *(64 sc made)*

Rnd 2: Ch 1, sc in first st, ch 3, skip next st, (sc in next st, ch 3, skip next st) around, join. Fasten off.

FINISHING

1: For **flaps,** cut fabric in half lengthwise. Sew one long edge and short ends of one piece to each short end of Cover.

2: Weave strung beads through rnd 2 of Photo Frame. Tie ends into a 2-loop bow. With bow in corners *(see photo),* sew rnd 1 of Photo Frame to front of Cover inserting photo before closing. Tack bow to Cover to secure. ✿

Puppy Poncho
DESIGNED BY LIZ FIELD

Your little bundle of fur will love this new outfit. Designed for small, medium or large dogs, it's created in textured bouclé yarn. Make it in a color to match or contrast with a pretty collar, and your pet will be attired for a fashionable outing.

FINISHED SIZE: Fits small, medium or large dog.

MATERIALS: Worsted bouclé yarn — 5 oz. for small, 7 oz. for medium and 9 oz. for large; stitch markers; ⅞" flat button; sewing thread to match button; sewing needle; H hook or hook size needed to obtain gauge.

GAUGE: 3 sts = 1"; 3 dc rows = 2".

BASIC STITCHES: Ch, sl st, sc, hdc, dc.

NOTE: Push nubs on bouclé yarn to front of work as stitches are made.

PONCHO
Yoke

Rnd 1: Ch to fit around base of dog's neck in multiples of three, sl st in first ch to form ring, ch 1, sc in each ch around, join with sl st in first sc.

Rnd 2: Ch 1, sc in each st around, join.

Rnd 3: Ch 1, sc in first 2 sts, 2 sc in next st, (sc in next 2 sts, 2 sc in next st) around, join.

Rnd 4: Ch 1, sc in each st around

Rnd 5: Ch 2, hdc in each st around, join with sl st in top of ch-2.

Rnds 6-9 or to desired length to fit neck: Ch 3, dc in each st around, join with sl st in top of ch-3.

Body
Note: Place Yoke on dog, mark first st with marker, measure from marker across back, allowing 1½"

on each side for Edging, mark st on opposite side of Yoke.

Row 1: Ch 1, sl st in marked st, ch 3, dc in each st across to next marked st, dc in marked st leaving remaining sts unworked, turn.

Next Rows: Ch 3, dc in each dc across, turn, until piece measures 1½" from base of dog's tail. At end of last row, fasten off.

continued on page 61

Headband and Mittens

Designed by Shirley Patterson

If you dislike having your hair flattened by a hat, this thick and colorful headband is made just for you. With matching mittens, you'll be ready for cold weather. This set features an interesting stitch pattern that's easier than it looks.

HEADBAND

FINISHED SIZE: One size fits all.

MATERIALS: Worsted yarn — 2 oz. black, small amount each rose, green, lt. blue, dk. blue and variegated; tapestry needle; H hook or hook size needed to obtain gauge.

GAUGE: 7 sc = 2"; 4 **back lp** rows = 1".

BASIC STITCHES: Ch, sl st, sc.

HEADBAND

Row 1: With black, ch 16, sl st in second ch from hook, sl st in next 2 chs, sc in next 9 chs, sl st in last 3 chs, turn. *(15 sts made)*

*Notes: Work remaining rows in **back lps** only. Front of row 2 is right side of work.*

Rows 2-3: Ch 1, sl st in first 3 sl sts, sc in next 9 sts, sl st in last 3 sts, turn. Drop lp from hook.

Row 4: Join variegated with sc in ch at base of fourth st on row 1, ch 9, skip next 7 sts on row 1, sc in ch at base of next st on row 1. Fasten off.

Row 5: Pick up dropped lp, ch 1, sl st in first 3 sl sts changing to dk. blue in last st made *(see page 159),* sc in next 9 sts changing to black in last st made, sl st in last 3 sts, turn.

Row 6: Ch 1, sl st in first 3 sts changing to dk. blue in last st made, sc in next 4 sts, sc in next st and in ch lp below at same time, sc in next 4 sts changing to black in last st made, sl st in last 3 sts, turn.

Rows 7-10: Ch 1, sl st in first 3 sts changing to dk. blue in last st made, sc in next 9 sts changing to black in last st made, sl st in last 3 sts, turn. At end of last row, drop lp from hook.

Row 11: Join variegated with sc in **front lp** of fourth st on row 7, ch 9, skip next 7 sts, sc in **front lp** of next st on row 7 leaving remaining sts unworked. Fasten off.

Row 12: Repeat row 5.

Row 13: Ch 1, sl st in first 3 sts, sc in next 4 sts, sc in next st and in ch lp below at same time, sc in next 4 sts, sl st in last 3 sts, turn.

Rows 14-15: Repeat row 2. Drop lp from hook.

Row 16: Working in sts of row 13, repeat row 11.

Note: Substitute rose for dk. blue on rows 17-23.

Row 17: Pick up dropped lp, repeat row 7.

Rows 18-19: Repeat row 7.

Row 20: Repeat row 6.

Rows 21-23: Repeat row 7.

Row 24: Repeat row 2. Drop lp from hook.

Row 25: Working in sts of row 20, repeat row 11.

Row 26: Pick up dropped lp, repeat row 2.

Row 27: Repeat row 13.

Note: Substitute lt. blue for dk. blue on rows 28-31 and rows 33-35.

Rows 28-31: Repeat rows 7-10.

Row 32: Working in sts of row 27, repeat row 11.

Row 33: Pick up dropped lp, repeat row 7.

Row 34: Repeat row 6.

Row 35: Repeat row 7.

Rows 36-38: Repeat row 2. At end of last row, drop lp from hook.

Row 39: Working in sts of row 34, repeat row 11.

Note: Substitute green for dk. blue on rows 40-45.

Row 40: Pick up dropped lp, repeat row 7.

Row 41: Repeat row 6.

Rows 42-45: Repeat rows 7-10.

Row 46: Working in sts of row 41, repeat row 11.

Row 47: Pick up dropped lp, repeat row 2.

Row 48: Repeat row 13.

Rows 49-52: Repeat rows 7-10.

Row 53: Working in sts of row 48, repeat row 11.

Row 54: Pick up dropped lp, repeat row 7.

Row 55: Repeat row 6.

Rows 56-58: Repeat row 2.

Note: Substitute rose for dk. blue on row 59 and rows 61-66.

Row 59: Repeat row 7, drop lp from hook.

Row 60: Working in sts of row 55, repeat row 11.

Rows 61: Pick up dropped lp, repeat row 7.

Row 62: Repeat row 6.

Rows 63-66: Repeat rows 7-10.

Row 67: Working in sts of row 62, repeat row 11.

Row 68: Pick up dropped lp, repeat row 2.

Row 69: Repeat row 13.

Row 70: Repeat row 2.

Note: Substitute lt. blue for dk. blue on rows 71-74 and rows 76-78.

Rows 71-74: Repeat row 7.

Row 75: Working in row 69, repeat row 11.

Row 76: Repeat row 6.

Rows 77-78: Repeat row 7. At end of last row, drop lp from hook.

Row 79: Working in sts of row 75, repeat row 11.

Rows 80-82: Repeat row 2.

Note: Substitute green for dk. blue on rows 83-87 and rows 89-90.

Row 83: Repeat row 6.

Rows 84-87: Repeat rows 7-10.

Row 88: Working in sts of row 83, repeat row 11.

Row 89: Pick up dropped lp, repeat row 7.

Row 90: Repeat row 6

Row 91: Sl st row 90 and starting ch on opposite side of row 1 together.

MITTENS

FINISHED SIZE: Palm is 4½" wide x 7½" long.

MATERIALS: Worsted yarn — 7 oz. black, small amount each rose, green, lt. blue, dk. blue and variegated; tapestry needle; H hook or hook size needed to obtain gauge.

GAUGE: 7 sc = 2"; 4 sc rows = 1".

BASIC STITCHES: Ch, sl st, sc.

NOTE: Adjust Mittens to a larger or smaller size by using a larger or smaller hook.

PALM (make 2)

Row 1: With black, ch 42, sl st in second ch from hook, sl st in next 3 chs, sc in next 25 chs, sl st in last 12 chs, turn. *(41 sts made)*

*Note: Work all sl sts in **back lps** and all sc in **both lps** unless otherwise stated.*

Rows 2-17: Ch 1, sl st in each sl st and sc in each sc across, turn. At end of last row, fasten off.

TOP OF HAND (make 2)

Row 1: With black, ch 42, sl st in second ch from hook, sl st in next 3 chs, sc in next 25 chs, sl st in last 12 chs, turn. *(41 sts made)*

*Notes: Work all sl sts in **back lps** and all sc in **both lps** unless otherwise stated.*

Front of row 2 is right side of work.

Row 2: Ch 1, sl st in first 12 sl sts changing to dk. blue in last st made *(see page 159),* sc in next 25 sts changing to black in last st made, sl st in last 4 sts, turn.

Rows 3-4: With black sl st in each sl st and with dk. blue sc in each sc across, turn. At end of last row, drop lp from hook.

Row 5: With front facing you, join variegated with sc in ch at base of first sc on row 1, (ch 9, skip next 7 sts, sc in ch at base of next sc) 3 times

leaving remaining sts unworked. Fasten off.

Row 6: With wrong side facing you, pick up dropped lp, ch 1, sl st in first 4 sts, sc in next 4 sts, sc next sc and in ch lp below at same time, (sc in next 7 sts, sc next sc and in ch lp below at same time) 2 times, sc in next 4 sts, sl st in last 12 sts, turn.

Rows 7-9: With black sl st in each sl st and with rose sc in each sc across, turn.

Row 10: Ch 1, sl st in each sl st and sc in each sc across, turn.

Row 11: With black sl st in each sl st and with lt. blue sc in each sc across, turn. Drop lp from hook.

Row 12: With front facing you, join variegated with sc in **back bar** *(see illustration)* of first sc on row 6, (ch 9, skip next 7 sts, sc in back bar of next sc) 3 times leaving remaining sts unworked. Fasten off.

Back bar of sc:

Row 13: With wrong side facing you, pick up dropped lp, ch 1, sl st in first 4 sts changing to lt. blue in last st made, sc in next 4 sts, sc next sc and in ch lp below at same time, (sc in next 7 sts, sc next sc and in ch lp below at same time) 2 times, sc in next 4 sts changing to black in last st made, sl st in last 12 sts, turn.

Row 14: Repeat row 11.

Row 15: Ch 1, sl st in each sl st and sc in each sc across, turn.

Rows 16-18: With black sl st in each sl st and with green sc in each sc across, turn. At end of last row, drop lp from hook.

Row 19: With front facing you, join variegated with sc in back bar of first sc on row 13, (ch 9, skip next 7 sts, sc in back bar of next sc) 3 times leaving remaining sts unworked. Fasten off.

Row 20: With wrong side facing you, pick up dropped lp, ch 1, sl st in first 4 sts, sc in next 4 sts, sc next sc and in ch lp below at same time, (sc in next 7 sts, sc next sc and in ch lp below at same time) 2 times, sc in next 4 sts, sl st in last 12 sts. Fasten off.

LEFT MITTEN

Hold Palm piece and Back Of Hand piece wrong sides together with Back Of Hand facing you, matching sts, working through both thicknesses in both lps of sts, join black with sl st in first st at wrist edge, sl st in next 13 sts; for **thumb opening,** sl st in next 8 sts on Top Of Hand only skipping 8 sts on Palm; sl st through both thicknesses in each st across. Fasten off.

Working on opposite side, join black with sl st in first st of 4-sl st group, sl st in each st across to wrist edge. Fasten off.

Weave strand black through ends of rows at tips of fingers and pull to gather tightly; secure.

Thumb

Note: Do not join or turn unless otherwise stated. Mark first st of each rnd.

Rnd 1: Working around thumb opening over sl sts, join black with sc in first st 8-sl st group was worked in on Top Of Hand, sc in next 7 sts, sc in next 8 skipped sts on Palm. *(16 sc made)*

Rnds 2-3: Sc in each st around.

Rnd 4: (Sc in next 6 sts, sc next 2 sts tog) around. *(14)*

Rnd 5: (Sc in next 5 sts, sc next 2 sts tog) around. *(12)*

Rnd 6: (Sc in next 4 sts, sc next 2 sts tog) around. *(10)*

Rnds 7-10: Sc in each st around. At end of last rnd, join with sl st in first sc. Leaving long end for weaving, fasten off.

Weave end around opening at tip of Thumb and pull to gather tightly; secure.

RIGHT MITTEN

Hold Palm piece and Top Of Hand piece wrong sides together with Palm facing you, matching sts, working through both thicknesses in both lps of sts, join black with sl st in first st at wrist edge, sl st in next 13 sts; for **thumb opening,** sl st in next 8 sts on Palm only skipping 8 sts on Top Of Hand; sl st through both thicknesses in each st across. Fasten off.

Working on opposite side, join black with sl st in first st of 4-sl st group, sl st in each st across to wrist edge. Fasten off.

Weave strand black through ends of rows at tips of fingers and pull to gather tightly; secure.

Thumb

Note: Do not join or turn unless otherwise stated. Mark first st of each rnd.

Rnd 1: Working around thumb opening over sl sts, join black with sc in first st 8-sl st group was worked in on Palm, sc in next 7 sts, sc in next 8 skipped sts on Top Of Hand. *(16 sc made)*

Rows 2-10: Repeat same rnds of Left Mitten Thumb.

Weave end around opening at tip of Thumb and pull to gather tightly; secure. ✿

Puppy Poncho

continued from page 57

Edging

Row 1: Join with sl st in st on last rnd of Yoke before Body; working around Body, sc evenly across ends of rows, 3 sc in first st of last row on Body, sc in each st across with 3 sc in last st, sc evenly across ends of rows on Body, sl st in next 2 sts on last rnd of Yoke, turn.

Rows 2-3: Ch 3, skip first 2 sl sts, dc in each st across with 3 dc in center st of each 3-dc group, sl st in next 2 sts on last rnd of Yoke, turn. At end of last row, fasten off.

Strap

Row 1: Join with sc in center st on one side of Body, sc in next 3 sts, turn. *(4 sc made)*

Next rows: Ch 3, dc in each st across, turn, until Strap fits around dog's tummy. At end of last row, fasten off.

Sew button to end of Strap using space between sts on opposite side of Body as buttonhole. ✿

Cotton Candy

DESIGNED BY KATHY WIGINGTON

Whether you've got the sniffles from a cold or a sad movie, you'll want to keep this lovely tissue cover handy. It's fresh and feminine in pink and white, but it will be equally beautiful in colors to match your bedroom or bath.

FINISHED SIZE: Fits boutique tissue box.

MATERIALS: 100 yds. white and 75 yds. pink 1" wide tulle or 2 oz. white and 1½ oz. pink worsted yarn; tapestry needle; F hook or hook size needed to obtain gauge.

GAUGE: 9 sc sts = 2"; 9 sc rows = 2".

BASIC STITCHES: Ch, sl st, sc, dc.

SIDES

Rnd 1: With white, ch 80, sl st in first ch to form ring, ch 1, sc in each ch around, join with sl st in first sc. *(80 sc made)*

Rnds 2-3: Ch 1, sc in each st around, join. At end of last rnd, fasten off.

Rnd 4: Working this rnd in **back lps** only, join pink with sl st in first st, ch 3, dc in each st around, join with sl st in top of ch-3. Fasten off.

Rnd 5: Working this rnd in **back lps** only, join white with sc in first st, sc in each st around, join.

Rnds 6-11: Ch 1, sc in each st around, join. At end of last rnd, fasten off.

Rnds 12-21: Repeat rnds 4-11 consecutively, ending with rnd 5.

Rnds 22-23: Repeat rnd 2. At end of last rnd, fasten off.

TOP

Row 1: With white, ch 21, sc in second ch from hook, sc in each ch across, turn. *(20 sc made)*

Rows 2-9: Ch 1, sc in each st across, turn.

Row 10: Ch 1, sc in first 5 sts; for **opening,** ch 10, skip next 10 sts; sc in last 5 sts, turn. *(10 sc, 1 ch-10 sp)*

Row 11: Ch 1, sc in each st and in each ch across, turn. *(20)*

Rows 12-20: Ch 1, sc in each st, across, turn. At end of last row, fasten off.

For **trim around Top opening,** join pink with sl st in first skipped st of row 9, ch 3, skip next st, (sl st in next st, ch 3, skip next st) 4 times, sl st in end of next row, ch 3; working on opposite side of ch-10 on row 10, (sl st in next ch, ch 3, skip next ch) 5 times, sl st in end of next row, ch 3, join with sl st in first sl st. Fasten off.

For **trim that joins Top to Sides,** holding wrong sides of Top and Sides together, matching corners and working through both thicknesses, with Sides towards you, join pink with sc in first st, sc in each st and in end of each row around, join with sl st in first sc. Fasten off.

For **trim around rnd 3 of Sides,** working in **front lps** of rnd 3 on Sides, join pink with sl st in any st, ch 3, skip next st, (sl st in next st, ch 3, skip next st) around, join with sl st in first sl st. Fasten off.

Repeat on rnd 20.

ZIG ZAG TRIM

Working in **front lps** of rnds 4 and 11 on Sides, join pink with sl st in second st on rnd 4, ch 4, skip first 4 sts on rnd 11, sl st in next st, ch 4, skip next 4 sts on rnd 4, (sl st in next st, ch 4, skip next 4 sts on rnd 11, sl st in next st, ch 4, skip next 4 sts on rnd 4) around, join with sl st in first st, fasten off.

Repeat rnds 12 and 19.

BEADING TRIM

Rnd 1: Working in starting ch on opposite side of rnd 1 on Sides, join pink with sc in any ch, sc in each ch around, join with sl st in first sc.

Rnd 2: Ch 4, skip next st, (dc in next st, ch 1, skip next st) around, join with sl st in third ch of ch-4. Fasten off.

For **tie,** with pink, ch 100. Fasten off.

Pull Cover over tissue box. Weave tie through rnd 2 of Beading Trim. Pull tightly to fit snugly around bottom; tie into a bow. ✿

Cro-Tat™ Jar Topper

DESIGNED BY ERMA FIELDER

It's great fun to put together a gift basket filled with treats and handmade items that include all the recipient's favorites. Add a jar of homemade goodies to the basket, topped with a frilly bit of lace and ribbon. Long after the treats are gone, the pretty jar will be lovingly used.

Crochet Tatting™ used with permission of trademark owner, Annie's Attic.

Cro-Tat™
The Ease of Crochet, The Elegance of Tatting

FINISHED SIZE: Fits small mouth canning jar.

MATERIALS: Size 10 crochet cotton thread — 100 yds. pink and 25 yds white; 22" of narrow ribbon; crochet tatting hook.

GAUGE: Rnds 1-3 of Bottom = 2" across.

BASIC STITCHES: Ch, sl st, sc, hdc, dc.

SPECIAL STITCHES: For **double stitch (ds),** to make **first half,** hold the thread with the left hand and wrap clockwise around left index finger; scoop the hook under the thread from front to back toward the fingertip *(see photo a)* and lift the thread off your finger to form a loop on the hook, pull the thread snug. Move the right index finger over the last loop made to hold it in place. To make **second half** of stitch, wrap the thread counter-clockwise around left index finger; scoop the hook under the thread from the back toward the fingertip *(see photo b),* lifting the thread off your finger to form a loop on the hook. Pull the thread snug against the last lp and hold in place with the right index finger.

For **picot (p),** with right index finger, hold the thread against the hook and make the next ds, approximately ¼" from the last ds *(see photo c),* slide the last ds made over to the previous ds forming a loop; the loop is the picot. Pull the picot to tighten the thread around the hook.

To **close ring,** make a loop a little longer than the stitches on hook, *(see photo d),* yo, above loop and pull through all lps on hook making sure not to lose first loop *(see photo e),* keeping loop made after pulling through sts on hook, insert hook into first loop, *(see photo f),* pull second loop to tighten first loop around hook, pull end of thread to tighten second loop around hook, continue pulling until both lps are snug on hook, yo, pull through both lps on hook forming a ring.

For **joined picot (joined p),** insert hook in corresponding picot from front to back, yo, pull lp through picot and place on hook.

For **bullion stitch**, yo 10 times on hook, insert hook in ch or st, yo, pull lp through, yo, pull through all lps on hook at same time, ch 1. *If making this stitch for the first time, practice before starting instructions. A dtr can be substituted for the bullion stitch if desired.*

For **reverse sl st,** working from left to right, insert hook in next st to the right, yo, pull lp through st and lp on hook.

BOTTOM

Rnd 1: With white, ch 2, 12 dc in second ch from hook, join with sl st in top of first dc. *(12 dc made)*

continued on page 67

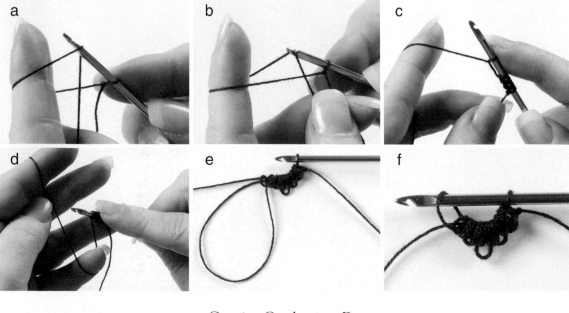

Cool Water Bottle Holder

DESIGNED BY ELIZABETH ANN WHITE

This stylish water bottle holder made with sport yarn is the perfect accessory for walking or exercising. Make the strap as long as you like for a perfect fit. This clever carrier makes a wonderful gift for fitness buffs.

FINISHED SIZE: Fits 20 fl. oz. water bottle.

MATERIALS: 230 yds. sport yarn; tapestry needle; No. 0 steel hook or hook size needed to obtain gauge.

GAUGE: 8 V sts = 3"; 3 V st rows = 1".

BASIC STITCHES: Ch, sl st, dc.

SPECIAL STITCH: For **V st,** (dc, ch 1, dc) in next st or ch sp.

BOTTOM

Rnd 1: Ch 4, sl st in first ch to form ring, ch 3, 11 dc in ring, join with sl st in top of ch-3. *(12 dc made)*

Rnd 2: (Ch 3, dc) in first st, 2 dc in each st around, join. *(24)*

Rnd 3: (Ch 3, dc) in first st, dc in next st, (2 dc n next st, dc in next st) around, join. *(36)*

Rnd 4: (Ch 3, dc) in first st, dc in next 2 sts, (2 dc in next st, dc in next 2 sts) around, join. *(48)*

Rnd 5: (Ch 3, dc) in first st, dc in next 3 sts, (2 dc in next st, dc in next 3 sts) around, join. *(60)*

Rnd 6: Working this rnd in **back lps** only, ch 3, dc in each st around, join.

Rnd 7: (Ch 4, dc) in first ch sp *(counts as first V st),* skip next 2 sts, (**V st** in next st—*see Special Stitch,* skip next 2 sts) around, join with sl st in third ch of ch-4. *(20 V sts)*

Rnds 8-22 (Sl st, ch 4, dc) in first ch sp, V st in each ch sp around, join.

Rnd 23: Ch 3, dc in each st and in each ch sp around, join. *(60 dc)*

Row 24: Working in rows; for **first half of strap,** ch 2, *(is not used or counted as a st),* dc in next 22 sts, dc next 2 sts tog leaving remaining sts unworked, turn. *(23 dc)*

Rows 25-30: Ch 2, dc in each st across to last 2 sts, dc last 2 sts tog, turn, ending with 11 sts in last row.

Row 31: Ch 2, dc in each st across, turn. *(10)*

Rows 32-106: Ch 3 *(counts as first st),* dc in each st across, turn. At end of last row, fasten off.

Row 24: For **second half of strap,** skip next 5 unworked sts on rnd 23, join with sl st in next st, ch 2 *(is not used or counted as a st),* dc in next 22 sts, dc next 2 sts tog leaving remaining sts unworked, turn. *(23 dc)*

Rows 25-30: Ch 2, dc in each st across to last 2 sts, dc last 2 sts tog, turn, ending with 11 sts in last row.

Row 32: Ch 2, dc in each st across, turn. *(10)*

Rows 33-106: Ch 3, *(counts as first st),* dc in each st across, turn. At end of last row, fasten off.

Sew last rows of strap halves together. ✿

Cro-Tat™ Jar Topper

continued from page 65

Rnd 2: (Ch 3, dc) in first st, 2 dc in each st around, join. *(24)*

Rnd 3: Ch 3, 2 dc in next st, (dc in next st, 2 dc in next st) around, join. *(36)*

Rnd 4: Ch 3, dc in next st, 2 dc in next st, (dc in next 2 sts, 2 dc in next st) around, join. *(48)*

Rnd 5: Ch 3, dc in next 2 sts, 2 dc in next st, (dc in next 3 sts, 2 dc in next st) around, join. Fasten off. *(60)*

TOP

Rnd 1: With pink, ch 2, 6 sc in second ch from hook, join with sl st in first sc. *(6 sc made)*

Rnd 2: Ch 2 *(not counted as a st),* **bullion st** *(see Special Stitches)* in first st, ch 1, bullion st in same st, ch 1, (bullion st, ch 1) 2 times in each st around, join with sl st in top of first bullion st. *(12 bullion sts, 12 ch sps)*

Rnd 3: Sl st in next ch sp, ch 1, sc in same sp, ch 3, (sc in next ch sp, ch 3) around, join with sl st in first sc. *(12 ch sps)*

Rnd 4: Sl st in next ch sp, working this rnd from left to right, make ring of **4 ds** *(see Special Stitches),* **p** *(see Special Stitches),* (4 ds, p) 2 times, 4 ds, **close ring** *(see Special Stitches),* **reverse sl st** *(see Special Stitches)* in same ch sp, *reverse sl st in next 2 chs of next ch sp, make ring of 4 ds, **joined p** *(see Special Stitches)* in last picot of last ring, (4 ds, p) 2 times, 4 ds, close ring, reverse sl st in same ch sp; repeat from * 9 more times, reverse sl st in next 2 chs of next ch sp, make ring of 4 ds, joined p in last picot of last ring, 4 ds, p, 4 ds, joined p in first picot of first ring, 4 ds, close ring, reverse sl st in same ch sp. Fasten off.

Rnd 5: Join pink with sc in center picot of any ring, ch 5, (sc in center picot of next ring, ch 5) around, join with sl st in first sc.

Rnd 6: Ch 2, working around first ch sp on last rnd of Top into sts on last rnd of Bottom, bullion st in next 5 sts; (working around next ch sp on Top, bullion st in next 5 sts on Bottom) around, join with sl st in top of first bullion st.

Rnd 7: Ch 1, sc in each st around, join with sl st in first sc.

Rnd 8: Ch 4, skip next st, (dc in next st, ch 1, skip next st) around, join with sl st in third ch of ch-4.

Rnd 9: Ch 1, sc in each st and in each ch sp around, join with sl st in first sc.

Rnd 10: Ch 1, sc in first st, ch 4, (sc in next st, ch 4) around, join. *(60 ch sps)*

Rnd 11: Sl st in next ch sp, ch 2, work 4 bullion sts in same ch sp, work 4 bullion sts in each ch sp around, join with sl st in top of first bullion st. Fasten off.

Rnd 12: Working in spaces between bullion sts, join white with sc in any sp, (ch 3, sc, ch 3) in same sp, (sc, ch 3) 2 times in each sp around, join with sl st in first sc. Fasten off.

Weave ribbon through ch sps of rnd 8, place Topper on jar, pull ribbon ends to gather around jar lid, tie ends into a bow. ✿

Sweet Baby Hat

Designed by Michele Wilcox

Bursting with energy, a toddler is always adorable. Add this fun and bouncy hat, and she's simply irresistible! Imagine how this perky headwarmer will bring a smile to the face and a bounce to the step of your little one.

FINISHED SIZE: Fits 6 to 18 mos.

MATERIALS: Cotton sport yarn — small amount each rose, white, purple, green, yellow, blue, pink and aqua; tapestry needle; E hook or hook size needed to obtain gauge.

GAUGE: 9 sts = 2"; 4 pattern rows = 1".

BASIC STITCHES: Ch, sl st, sc, dc.

HAT

Ribbing

Row 1: With rose, ch 9, sc in second ch from hook, sc in each ch across, turn. *(8 sc made)*

Rows 2-60 or to desired measurement around head ending in even rows: Working these rows in **back lps** only, ch 1, sc in each st across, turn. At end of last row, **do not turn.**

Top

Row 1: Working in ends of rows, ch 1, sc in each row across, turn. Fasten off.

Row 2: Join white with sc in first st, dc in next st, (sc in next st, dc in next st) across, turn. Fasten off.

Row 3: Join purple with sc in first st, dc in next st, (sc in next st, dc in next st) across, turn.

Row 4: Ch 1, sc in first st, dc in next st, (sc in next st, dc in next st) across, turn. Fasten off.

Rows 5-20: Working in color sequence of white/green, white/yellow, white/blue, white/pink/ white/aqua, repeat rows 2-4 consecutively, ending with row 2.

Sew Ribbing and ends of rows on Top together.

With seam at center back, flatten and sew Top opening closed.

Curls (make one each green, purple, yellow, blue)

(Ch 15, 3 sc in second ch from hook, 3 sc in each ch across) 3 times. Fasten off.

Sew two Curls to top of Hat on each side *(see photo).* ✿

Wednesday

Chapter
Four

70 Doily & Bowl Cover
73 Present Pillow
75 Hooded Scarf
76 Bright Basics
79 Elegant Pastels
81 Pillow Toppers
84 Helpful Holders
86 Simply Beautiful Bibs
88 Floor Doily
90 Autumn Doily

4

The Viking god, Woden, traveled all
over the world looking for wisdom.
His day was called Wodnesdaeg.

Doily & Bowl Cover

DESIGNED BY NORMA J. GALE

Create a tranquil moment of peace with a touch of candlelight to accompany the evening meal or simply to add a little atmosphere to the middle of the work week. A pleasant way to enhance some quality time for yourself.

FINISHED SIZES: Doily is 7½" across. Cover fits 5" tall x 15½" circumference bowl.

MATERIALS FOR BOTH: Size 10 crochet cotton thread — 225 yds. silver and 150 yds. lilac; 8 purple 7 mm faceted acrylic gemstones; craft glue or hot glue gun; blocking board or Styrofoam®; plastic wrap; rustproof pins; No. 10 steel hook or hook size needed to obtain gauge.

GAUGE: Rnds 1-5 of Doily = 2" across; 5 dc and 4 ch sps on Cover = 1".

BASIC STITCHES: Ch, sl st, sc, dc, tr.

SPECIAL STITCHES: For **V st,** (tr, ch 1, tr) in next ch sp.

For **mesh,** dc in next dc, ch 2, skip next ch sp or 2 dc.

For **block,** dc in next dc, 2 dc in next ch sp, **or,** dc in next 3 dc.

DOILY

Rnd 1: With silver, ch 6, sl st in first ch to form ring, ch 3, 11 dc in ring, join with sl st in top of ch-3. *(12 dc made)*

Rnd 2: Ch 5 *(counts as first dc and ch-2),* (dc in next st, ch 2) around, join with sl st in third ch of ch-5.

Rnd 3: Ch 3, (dc, ch 1, dc) in next ch sp, *dc in next st, (dc, ch 1, dc) in next ch sp; repeat from * around, join with sl st in top of ch-3.

Rnd 4: Ch 3, dc in each st around with (dc, ch 1, dc) in each ch sp, join.

Rnd 5: Ch 5, skip next 2 sts, (dc, ch 2, dc) in next ch sp, ch 2, skip next 2 sts, *dc in next st, ch 2, skip next 2 sts, (dc, ch 2, dc) in next ch sp, ch 2, skip next 2 sts; repeat from * around, ch 2, join with sl st in third ch of ch-5.

Rnd 6: Ch 5, dc in next st, (dc, ch 2, dc) in next ch sp, dc in next st, ch 2, *dc in next st, ch 2, dc in next st, (dc, ch 2, dc) in next ch sp, dc in next st, ch 2; repeat from * around, join as before.

Rnd 7: Ch 4 *(counts as first dc and ch-1),* dc in next ch sp, dc in next 2 sts, ch 2, skip next ch sp, dc in next 2 sts, dc in next ch sp, ch 1, (dc in next st, ch 1, dc in next ch sp, dc in next 2 sts, ch 2, skip next ch sp, dc in next 2 sts, dc in next ch sp, ch 1) around, join with sl st in third ch of ch-4.

Rnd 8: Sl st in next ch, sl st in next st, ch 3, dc in next 2 sts, ch 2, skip next ch sp, dc in next 3 sts, ch 3, skip next st, (*dc in next 3 sts, ch 2, skip next ch sp, dc in next 3 sts, ch 3*, skip next st) 10 times; repeat between **, join with sl st in top of ch-3.

Rnd 9: Ch 3, dc in next 2 sts, ch 4, skip next ch sp, (dc in next 3 sts, ch 4, skip next ch sp) around, join.

Rnd 10: Ch 5, skip next st, dc in next st, (dc, ch 2, dc) in next ch sp, *dc in next st, ch 2, skip next st, dc in next st, (dc, ch 2, dc) in next ch sp; repeat from * around, join with sl st in third ch of ch-5.

Rnd 11: Ch 5, skip next ch sp, (dc in next 2 sts, ch 2, skip next ch sp) around to last st, dc in last st, join.

Rnd 12: Ch 1, sc in each st and 2 sc in each ch sp around, join with sl st in first sc. *(192 sc)*

Rnd 13: Working this rnd in **back lps** only, ch 6, skip next 2 sts, dc in next 2 sts, ch 2, skip next 2 sts, (dc in next 2 sts, ch 3, skip next 2 sts, dc in next 2 sts, ch 2, skip next 2 sts) around to last st, dc in last st, join with sl st in third ch of ch-6.

Rnd 14: Ch 7, skip next ch sp, dc in next 2 sts, ch 2, skip next ch sp, (dc in next 2 sts, ch 4, skip next ch sp, dc in next 2 sts, ch 2, skip next ch sp) around to last st, dc in last st, join with sl st in third ch of ch-7.

Rnd 15: Ch 7, skip next ch sp, dc in next 2 sts, ch 3, skip next ch sp, (dc in next 2 sts, ch 4, skip next ch sp, dc in next 2 sts, ch 3, skip next ch sp) around to last st, dc in last st, join.

Rnd 16: Ch 1, sc in each st around with 4 sc in each ch-4 sp and 3 sc in each ch-3 sp, join with sl st in first sc. Fasten off. *(264 sc)*

Rnd 17: Join lilac with sc in any st, ch 3, sc in next st, ch 3, skip next st, (sc in next st, ch 3, sc in next st, ch 3, skip next st) around, join.

Rnd 18: Sl st in next ch sp, ch 4, dc in same sp, (dc, ch 1, dc) in each ch sp around, join with sl st in third ch of ch-4.

Rnd 19: Sl st in next ch sp, ch 5, tr in same sp, **V st** *(see Special Stitches)* in each ch sp around, join with sl st in fourth ch of ch-5. Fasten off.

Rnd 20: Working in sps between V sts, join silver with sc in any sp, ch 3, dc in last sc made, (sc in next sp, ch 3, dc in last sc made) around, join with sl st in first sc. Fasten off.

Rnd 21: Working in **front lps** of rnd 12, join lilac with sc in any st, ch 3, sc in next st, ch 3, skip next st, (sc in next st, ch 3, sc in next st, ch 3, skip next st) around, join.

Rnds 22-24: Repeat rnds 18-20.

Finishing

Apply fabric stiffener according to manufacturer's instructions. Pin to plastic covered blocking board, shape. Let dry.

COVER

Rnd 1: With silver, ch 180, sl st in first ch to form ring, ch 5, *(counts as first dc and ch-2 sp)*, skip next 2 chs, (dc in next ch, ch 2, skip next 2 chs) around, join with sl st in third ch of ch-5. *(60 ch sps made)*

Rnds 2-4: Ch 5, skip next ch sp, **mesh** *(see Special Stitches on page 71)* around, join.

Rnd 5: Ch 5, skip next ch sp, mesh 6 times, **block** *(see Special Stitches),* (mesh 14 times, block) 3 times, mesh 7 times, join with sl st in third ch of ch-5.

Rnd 6: Ch 5, skip next ch sp, mesh 5 times, block, dc in next dc, ch 5, skip next ch sp, block, (mesh 12 times, block, dc in next dc, ch 5, skip next ch sp, block) 3 times, mesh 6 times, join as before.

Rnd 7: Ch 5, skip next ch sp, mesh 4 times, block, dc in next dc, ch 3, sc in next ch sp, ch 3, skip next 3 dc, block, (mesh 10 times, block, dc in next dc, ch 3, sc in next ch sp, ch 3, skip next 3 dc, block) 3 times, mesh 5 times, join.

Rnd 8: Ch 5, skip next ch sp, mesh 3 times, block, dc in next dc, ch 5, sc in next ch sp, sc in next sc, sc in next ch sp, ch 5, skip next 3 dc, block, (mesh 8 times, block, dc in next dc, ch 5, sc in next ch sp, sc in next sc, sc in next ch sp, ch 5, skip next 3 dc, block) 3 times, mesh 4 times, join.

Rnd 9: Ch 5, skip next ch sp, mesh 4 times, dc in dc before next ch sp, 3 dc in next ch sp, ch 5, skip next sc, sc in next sc, ch 5, skip next sc, 3 dc in next ch sp, (mesh 10 times, dc in dc before next ch sp, 3 dc in next ch sp, ch 5, skip next sc, sc in next sc, ch 5, skip next sc, 3 dc in next ch sp) 3 times, mesh 5 times, join.

Rnd 10: Ch 5, skip next ch sp, mesh 5 times, dc in next dc before next ch sp, 3 dc in next ch sp, ch 2, 3 dc in next ch sp, (mesh 12 times, dc in next dc before next ch sp, 3 dc in next ch sp, ch 2, 3 dc in next ch sp) 3 times, mesh 6 times, join.

Rnds 11-12: Ch 5, skip next ch sp, mesh 6 times, block, (mesh 14 times, block) 3 times, mesh 7 times, join.

Rnds 13-18: Repeat rnds 6-11.

Rnds 19-22: Repeat rnd 2.

Rnd 23: Ch 1, sc in each st and 2 sc in each ch sp around, join with sl st in first sc.

Rnd 24: Ch 4, skip next st, (dc in next st, ch 1, skip next st) around, join with sl st in third ch of ch-4. Fasten off.

Rnd 25: Join lilac with sc in any st, ch 3, (sc in next st, ch 3) around, join with sl st in first sc.

Rnd 26: Sl st in next ch sp, ch 4, dc in same sp, (dc, ch 1, dc) in each ch sp around, join with sl st in third ch of ch-4.

Rnd 27: Sl st in next ch sp, ch 5, tr in same sp, V st in each ch sp around, join with sl st in fourth ch of ch-5. Fasten off.

Rnd 28: Working in sps between V sts, join silver with sc in any sp, ch 3, dc in last sc made, (sc in next sp, ch 3, dc in last sc made) around, join with sl st in first sc. Fasten off.

Rnd 29: Working in starting ch on opposite side of rnd 1, join silver with sl st in ch at base of any dc, ch 4, dc in ch at base of next dc, ch 1, dc in next ch, ch 1, (dc in ch at base of next dc, ch 1, dc in ch at base of next dc, ch 1, dc in next ch, ch 1) around, join with sl st in third ch of ch-4. Fasten off.

Rnd 30: Join lilac with sc in any st, ch 3, (sc in next st, ch 3) around, join with sl st in first sc.

Rnd 31: Sl st in next ch sp, ch 4, dc in same sp, (dc, ch 1, dc) in each ch sp around, join with sl st in third ch of ch-4.

Rnd 32: Sl st in next ch sp, ch 5, tr in same sp, V st in each ch sp around, join with sl st in fourth ch of ch-5. Fasten off.

Rnd 33: Working in sps between V sts, join

continued on page 75

Present Pillow

DESIGNED BY ELIZABETH ANN WHITE

A special gift pillow makes a wonderful decorative heirloom.
All you will need to do is place a treasured photo in the frame and
present it as a momento to friends or family and it will last a lifetime.

FINISHED SIZE: 7½" x 11½".

MATERIALS: 352 yds. green rayon chenille; frame appliqué; 3 yds. gold 3" wired ribbon; polyester fiberfill; sewing thread; tapestry and sewing needles, H hook or hook size needed to obtain gauge.

GAUGE: 3 sc = 1"; 7 sc rows = 2".

BASIC STITCHES: Ch, sc.

SIDE (make 4)

Row 1: Ch 36, sc in second ch from hook, sc in each ch across, turn. *(35 sc made)*

Rows 2-25: Ch 1, sc in each st across, turn. At end of last row, fasten off.

END (make 2)

Row 1: Ch 26, sc in second ch from hook, sc in each ch across, turn. *(25 sc made)*

Rows 2-25: Ch 1, sc in each st across, turn. At end of last row, fasten off.

FINISHING

1: Sew long edges of Sides together.

2: Sew Ends to short edges of Sides forming a box, stuffing before closing.

3: With sewing thread and needle, stitch around seams on sides forming a corded edge.

4: Wrap and tie ribbon in bow around box *(see photo)*. Tack appliqué to bow. ✿

Hooded Scarf

DESIGNED BY ELIZABETH ANN WHITE

When the weather turns cooler, you'll love this lacy hooded scarf. Its generous size and built-in hood keep the chilliest of winds at bay. It's perfect for wearing to fall football games and other events, and it's also dressy enough for more formal gatherings.

FINISHED SIZE: 37" long not including Fringe.

MATERIALS: Worsted yarn — 9 oz.; H hook or hook size needed to obtain gauge.

GAUGE: 7 dc = 2"; 3 dc rows = 2".

BASIC STITCHES: Ch, sc, dc.

SPECIAL STITCH: For **shell,** (2 dc, ch 2, 2 dc) in next ch or ch sp.

SCARF

Row 1: Ch 34, (dc, ch 2, 2 dc) in fourth ch from hook, *skip next 2 chs, dc in next 5 chs, skip next 2 chs, **shell** *(see Special Stitch)* in next ch; repeat from * 2 more times, turn. *(15 dc, 4 shells made)*

Rows 2-54: Ch 3, shell in ch sp of first shell, (dc in next 5 sts, shell in ch sp of next shell) across, turn.

Row 55: For **hood portion,** ch 3, shell in first shell, (dc in next 5 sts, shell in next shell) 3 times, ch 1, sc in turning ch-3 on row below, turn.

Row 56: Ch 1, shell in first shell, (dc in next 5 sts, shell in next shell) 3 times, turn.

Row 57: Ch 3, shell in first shell, (dc in next 5 sts, shell in next shell) 3 times, **do not turn;** to **join at center back of head,** fold Scarf crosswise between rows 54 and 55 matching ends of rows *(fold is at center top of Scarf);* to **join,** ch 1, sc in ch-3 sp at end of corresponding row on other side of Scarf, turn.

Row 58: Repeat row 56.

Row 59: Ch 3, shell in first shell, (dc in next 5 sts, shell in next shell) 3 times, ch 1, sc in ch-3 sp at end of corresponding row on other side of Scarf, turn.

Rows 60-70: Repeat rows 56 and 59 alternately, ending with row 56.

Rows 71-107: Repeat row 2. At end of last row, fasten off.

FRINGE

For **each Fringe,** cut six strands each 16" long. With all six strands held together, fold in half, insert hook in sp, draw fold through, draw all loose ends through fold, tighten. Trim ends.

Working on one short end of Scarf, Fringe in sp on each side of each 5-dc group, and in ch sp of each end shell.

Repeat on opposite short end. ✿

Doily & Bowl Cover

continued from page 72

continued from page 72

silver with sc in any sp, ch 3, dc in last sc made, (sc in next sp, ch 3, dc in last sc made) around, join with sl st in first sc. Fasten off.

Finishing

1: Glue one gemstone to center of each spider web design *(see photo).*

2: For **tie** (make 2), with lilac, ch 190. Fasten off. Weave one tie through sts of rnds 24 and 29. Place Cover on bowl, pull ends of ties to make Cover snug around bowl; ties ends of each tie into a bow. ✿

Bright Basics

DESIGNED BY ELLEN ANDERSON EAVES

*Brighten your mornings with a pair of colorful kitchen helpers.
These are as much fun to make as they are to use and can be made in any color
combination for your own use, for gifts or for selling in bazaars and fund-raisers.*

DIAMONDS POT HOLDER

FINISHED SIZE: 10" x 11" not including hanging loop.

MATERIALS: Size 3 crochet cotton — 190 yds. blue, 100 yds. white and 10 yds. pink; F hook or hook size needed to obtain gauge.

GAUGE: 9 sc = 2"; 11 sc rows = 2"; 2 sc rows and one front post row = 1".

BASIC STITCHES: Ch, sl st, sc.

SPECIAL STITCHES: For **dc front post (dc fp,** *see page 159),* yo, insert hook from front to back around post of next st on row before last, yo, draw lp through, (yo, draw through 2 lps on hook) 2 times. Skip next st on last row behind post st.

For tr front post (tr fp), yo 2 times, insert hook from front to back around post of next st 3 rows below, yo, draw lp through, (yo, draw through 2 lps on hook) 3 times. Skip next st on last row behind post st.

FRONT

Row 1: With white, ch 44, sc in second ch from hook, sc in each ch across, turn. *(43 sc made)*

Rows 2-3: Ch 1, sc in each st across, turn. At end of last row, **do not turn.** Fasten off.

Row 4: With right side facing you, join blue with sc in first st, *sc in next st, **dc fp** (*see Special Stitches*) around next st on row

before last, **tr fp** *(see Special Stitches)* around next st 3 rows below, dc fp around next st on row before last; repeat from * across to last 2 sts, sc in last 2 sts, turn. *Front of row 4 is right side of work.*

Row 5-6: Ch 1, sc in each st across, turn. At end of last row, **do not turn.** Fasten off.

Rows 7: With right side facing you, join

white with sc in first st, tr fp, (dc fp, sc in next st, dc fp, tr fp) across to last st, sc in last st, turn.

Rows 8-49: Repeat rows 2-7 consecutively. At end of last row, **do not turn.**

Rnd 50: Working around outer edge in ends of rows, ch 1, (skip first row, sc in each row across to last row, skip last row); working in starting ch on opposite side of row 1, 3 sc in first ch, sc in each ch across with 3 sc in last ch; working in ends of rows; repeat between ( ); working in sts across last row, 3 sc in first st, sc in each st across with 3 sc in last st, join with sl st in first sc. Fasten off. *(188 sc)*

BACK

Row 1: With blue, ch 44, sc in second ch from hook, sc in each ch across, turn. *(43 sc made)*

Rows 2-49: Ch 1, sc in each st across, turn. At end of last row, **do not turn.**

Rnd 50: Repeat same rnd of Front.

BORDER

Rnd 1: Hold Front and Back wrong sides together with Front facing you, matching sts, working through both thicknesses, join pink with sc in any center corner st, 2 sc in same st, sc in each st around with 3 sc in each center corner st, join with sl st in first sc. Fasten off.

Rnd 2: Join white with sc in center corner st at top left-hand corner, sc in same st, **turn;** for **hanging loop,** (sl st, ch 10, sl st) in next st, **turn,** ch 1, 20 sc in ch lp just made; sl st in next st, sc in each st around with 3 sc in each center corner st, sc in same st as first sc, join. Fasten off.

HEXAGON POT HOLDER

FINISHED SIZE: 8" across not including hanging loop.

MATERIALS: Size 3 crochet cotton — 70 yds. each yellow and blue and 25 yds. white; F hook or hook size needed to obtain gauge.

GAUGE: 9 dc = 2"; 5 dc rows = 2".

BASIC STITCHES: Ch, sl st, sc, dc.

SPECIAL STITCHES: For **beginning popcorn (beg pc),** ch 3, 4 dc in same st, drop lp from hook, insert hook in top of ch-3, draw dropped lp through.

For **popcorn (pc),** 5 dc in next st, drop lp from hook, insert hook in first st of 5-dc group, draw dropped lp through.

FRONT

Row 1: With yellow, ch 4, 11 dc in fourth ch from hook, join with sl st in top of ch-3. *(12 dc made)*

Rnd 2: Beg pc *(see Special Stitches),* 3 dc in next st, ***pc** *(see Special Stitches)* in next st, 3 dc in next st; repeat from * around, join with sl st in top of beg pc. *(18 dc, 6 pc)*

Rnd 3: Ch 3, pc in next st, 3 dc in next st, pc in next st, (dc in next st, pc in next st, 3 dc in next st, pc in next st) around, join with sl st in top of ch-3. *(24 dc, 12 pc)*

Rnd 4: Ch 3, dc in next st, pc in next st, 3 dc in next st, pc in next st, (dc in next 3 sts, pc in next st, 3 dc in next st, pc in next st) around to last st, dc in last st, join. *(36 dc, 12 pc)*

Rnd 5: Ch 3, *[pc in next st, dc in next 2 sts, 3 dc in next st, dc in next 2 sts, pc in next st], dc in next st; repeat from * 4 more times; repeat between [ ], join. *(48 dc, 12 pc)*

Rnd 6: Beg pc, dc in next 4 sts, 3 dc in next st, dc in next 4 sts, (pc in next st, dc in next 4 sts, 3 dc in next st, dc in next 4 sts) around, join with sl st in top of beg pc. *(66 dc, 6 pc)*

Rnd 7: Ch 3, dc in next 5 sts, 3 dc in next st, (dc in next 11 sts, 3 dc in next st) 5 times, dc in last 5 sts, join with sl st in top of ch-3. Fasten off. *(84 dc)*

Rnd 8: Join white with sl st in first st, ch 3, dc in next 6 sts, 3 dc in next st, (dc in next 13 sts, 3 dc in next st) 5 times, dc in last 6 sts, join. Fasten off. *(96)*

Rnd 9: Join blue with sl st in first st, ch 3, dc in next 7 sts, 3 dc in next st, (dc in next 15 sts, 3 dc in next st) 5 times, dc in last 7 sts, join. Fasten off. *(108)*

BACK

Rnd 1: With blue, ch 4, 11 dc in fourth ch from hook, join with sl st in top of ch-3. *(12 dc)*

Rnd 2: Ch 3, 3 dc in next st, (dc in next st, 3 dc in next st) around, join. *(24)*

Rnds 3-9: Ch 3, 3 dc in each st around with
continued on page 79

Elegant Pastels

DESIGNED BY TAMMY HILDEBRAND

Soft, fuzzy colors of pastel pink, mint and yellow make this sherbet-inspired throw.
It's pure delight and makes up quickly with chunky yarns.
Whether your baby is brand new or all grown up, she'll love this cozy afghan.

FINISHED SIZE: 45" x 57½" not including Fringe.

MATERIALS: Fuzzy chunky yarn — 24 oz. white; 7 oz. each lt. pink, mint and lt. yellow; J hook or hook size needed to obtain gauge.

GAUGE: 8 dc = 3"; 7 dc rows = 5".

BASIC STITCHES: Ch, dc.

SPECIAL STITCH: For **V st,** (dc, ch 1, dc) in next st.

NOTE: Leave 6" end at beginning and end of each row to be worked into Fringe later.

AFGHAN

Row 1: With white, ch 155, dc in fourth ch from hook, dc in each ch across, **do not turn.** Fasten off. _(153 dc made)_

Note: Work the following rows in **back lps** only.

Row 2: Join lt. pink with sl st in first st, ch 3, *skip next st, **V st** (see Special Stitch) in next st, skip next st, dc in next st; repeat from * across, **do not turn.** Fasten off. _(39 dc, 38 V sts)_

Row 3: Join white with sl st in first st, ch 3, dc in each st and in each ch across, **do not turn.** Fasten off. _(153)_

Row 4: With mint, repeat row 2.

Row 5: Repeat row 3.

Row 6: With lt. yellow, repeat row 2.

Row 7: Repeat row 3.

Rows 8-63: Repeat rows 2-7 consecutively, ending with row 3.

FRINGE

For **each Fringe,** cut 6 strands yarn each 12" long. With all 6 strands held together, fold in half, insert hook in end of row, draw fold through, draw all loose ends through fold including 6" end at beginning or end of rows, tighten. Trim ends.

Matching row colors, Fringe in end of each row across each short end of Afghan. ✿

Bright Basics

continued from page 77

3 dc in center st of each 3-dc group, join, ending with 108 dc in last rnd. At end of last rnd, fasten off.

BORDER

Rnd 1: Hold Front and Back wrong sides together with front facing you, matching sts, working through both thicknesses, join white with sc in center st of any 3-dc group, sc in same st, sc in each st around with 3 sc in center st of each 3-dc group, sc in same st as first st, join with sl st in first sc. _(120 sc made)_

Rnd 2: Ch 1, sc in first 2 sts, **turn;** for **hanging loop,** (sl st, ch 10, sl st) in next st, **turn,** ch 1, 20 sc in ch lp just made; sl st in next st, (sc in next st, ch 3, skip next st) 9 times, (sc, ch 3, sc) in next st, *ch 3, skip next st, (sc in next st, ch 3, skip next st) 9 times, (sc, ch 3, sc) in next st; repeat from * 3 more times, (ch 3, skip next st, sc in next st) 9 times, sc in last st, join. Fasten off. ✿

Pillow Toppers

DESIGNED BY KATHERINE ENG

A window seat with a garden view is the right place for keeping these cheerful throw pillows handy for leisurely comfort. Tuck a journal under one of the pillows so it's easily accessible for jotting down your thoughts for the day.

CAROLINA

FINISHED SIZE: 13" square not including Ruffle.

MATERIALS: Worsted yarn — 2½ oz. green, 2 oz. each lavender and variegated; 13" square lavender pillow with 3" ruffle; lavender sewing thread; sewing needle; G hook or hook size needed to obtain gauge.

GAUGE: 4 sc = 1"; 4 sc rows =1".

BASIC STITCHES: Ch, sl st, sc, hdc, dc, tr.

TOPPER

Rnd 1: With lavender, ch 4, sl st in first ch to form ring, ch 1, 8 sc in ring, join with sl st in first sc. *(8 sc made)*

Rnd 2: (Ch 3, sl st in next st) around, join with sl st in joining sl st of last rnd. *(8 ch sps)*

Rnd 3: (Sl st, ch 3, sl st) in next ch sp, ch 3, *(sl st, ch 3, sl st) in next ch sp, ch 3; repeat from * around, join with sl st in first sl st. *(16 ch sps)*

Rnd 4: Sl st in next ch sp, ch 1, sc in same sp, 5 dc in next ch sp, (sc in next ch sp, 5 dc in next ch sp) around, join with sl st in first sc.

Rnd 5: Ch 1, sc in first st, ch 2, skip next 2 dc, (sc, ch 2, sc) in next dc, ch 2, skip next 2 dc, *sc in next sc, ch 2, skip next 2 dc, (sc, ch 2, sc) in next dc, ch 2, skip next 2 dc; repeat from * around, join. Fasten off.

Rnd 6: Skip next ch-2 sp, join variegated with sc in next ch-2 sp, ch 1, 5 dc in next sc, ch 1, skip next ch-2 sp, (sc in next ch-2 sp, ch 1, 5 dc in next sc, ch 1, skip next ch-2 sp) around, join.

Rnd 7: Ch 1, sc in first st, *[sc in next ch-1 sp, sc in next 3 dc, hdc in next 2 dc, dc in next ch-1 sp, (2 tr, ch 2, 2 tr) in next sc, dc in next ch-

1 sp, hdc in next 2 dc, sc in next 3 dc, sc in next ch-1 sp], sc in next sc; repeat from * 2 more times; repeat between [ ], join.

Rnd 8: Ch 1, sc in each st around with (sc, ch 3, sc) in each corner ch-2 sp, join, **turn.** *(21 sc between each corner ch-3 sp)*

Rnd 9: (Sl st, ch 1, sc) in next st, *ch 1, skip next st, (sc in next st, ch 1, skip next st) across to next corner ch sp, (sc, ch 3, sc) in next corner ch sp; repeat from * 3 more times, ch 1, skip next st, (sc in next st, ch 1, skip next st) across, join, **turn.**

Rnd 10: Ch 1, sc in each st and in each ch-1 sp around with (sc, ch 3, sc) in each corner ch-3 sp, join, **turn.** Fasten off.

Rnd 11: Join lavender with sc in sixth sc after any corner ch sp, *ch 1, skip next st, (sc in next st, ch 1, skip next st) across to next corner ch sp, (sc, ch 3, sc) in next corner ch sp; repeat from * 3 more times, ch 1, skip next st, (sc in next st, ch 1, skip next st) across, join, **turn.**

Rnd 12: Repeat rnd 10, **do not fasten off.**

Rnd 13: Ch 1, sc in first st, *ch 1, skip next st, (sc in next st, ch 1, skip next st) across to next corner ch sp, (sc, ch 3, sc) in next corner ch sp; repeat from * 3 more times, ch 1, skip next st, (sc in next st, ch 1, skip next st) across, join, **turn.** Fasten off.

Row 14: Working in rows, for **first corner,** join green with sc in first st after any corner ch sp, sc in each ch-1 sp and in each st across to next corner ch-3 sp, turn. *(31 sc)*

Rows 15-28: Ch 1, sc first 2 sts tog, sc in each st across to last 2 sts, sc last 2 sts tog, turn, ending with *(3 sts)* in last row.

Row 29: Ch 1, sc first 2 sts tog, ch 2, sc last worked st and last st tog, turn. Fasten off.

Repeat on sts between corner ch sps on rnd 13 for remaining three corners.

BORDER

Rnd 1: Join lavender with sc in ch-2 sp at tip of any corner, ch 2, sc in same sp, *evenly space 47 sc across to ch-2 sp at tip of next corner, (sc, ch 2, sc) in next ch sp; repeat from * 2 more times, evenly space 47 more sc across, join with sl st in first sc, **turn.**

Rnd 2: (Sl st, ch 1, sc) in next st, *ch 1, skip next st, (sc in next st, ch 1, skip next st) across to next corner ch sp, (sc, ch 3, sc) in next ch sp; repeat from * 3 more times, ch 1, join with sl st in first sc, **turn.** Fasten off.

Rnd 3: Join variegated with sc in any ch-1 sp, ch 3, sc in same sp, (sc, ch 3, sc) in each ch-1 sp around with (sc, ch 2, sc, ch 3, sc, ch 2, sc) in each corner ch-3 sp, join. Fasten off.

Sew rnd 1 of Border to outer edge of pillow, leaving ruffle free.

BLUES

FINISHED SIZE: 13" square not including ruffle.

MATERIALS: Worsted yarn — 2½ oz. variegated, and 1 oz. blue; 13" square lavender pillow with 3" ruffle; lavender sewing thread; sewing needle; G hook or hook size needed to obtain gauge.

GAUGE: 4 sc = 1"; 4 sc rows =1".

BASIC STITCHES: Ch, sl st, sc, dc.

SQUARE (make 4)

Rnd 1: With variegated, ch 4, sl st in first ch to form ring, ch 1, 8 sc in ring, join with sl st in first sc. *(8 sc made)*

Rnd 2: Ch 1, sc in first st, (2 dc, ch 2, 2 dc) in next st, *sc in next st, (2 dc, ch 2, 2 dc) in next st; repeat from * around, join. Fasten off.

Rnd 3: Join blue with sc in any sc, ch 3, sc in same st, *[ch 2, skip next 2 dc, (sc, ch 2, sc) in next ch-2 sp, ch 2, skip next 2 dc], (sc, ch 3, sc) in next sc; repeat from * 2 more times; repeat between [ ], join. Fasten off.

Rnd 4: Join variegated with sl st in any ch-3 sp, (ch 3, 2 dc, ch 3, 3 dc) in same sp, *[ch 2, skip next ch-2 sp, sc in next ch-2 sp, ch 2, skip next ch-2 sp], (3 dc, ch 2, 3 dc) in next ch-3 sp; repeat from * 2 more times; repeat between [ ], join with sl st in top of ch-3. Fasten off.

Rnd 5: Join blue with sc in any sc, sc in each st and 2 sc in each ch-2 sp around with (sc, ch 3, sc) in each corner ch-3 sp, join with sl st in first sc. Fasten off. *(13 sc between each corner ch-3 sp)*

Rnd 6: Join variegated with sc in any corner ch-3 sp, ch 3, sc in same sp, *[ch 1, skip next st, (sc in next st, ch 1, skip next st) across to next corner], (sc, ch 3, sc) in next corner ch sp; repeat from * 2 more times; repeat between [ ], join.

Rnd 7: Ch 1, sc in each sc and in each ch-1 sp around with (sc, ch 3, sc) in each corner ch-3 sp, join. Fasten off.

Holding Squares wrong sides together, matching sts, sew together through **back lps** in two rows of two Squares each.

BORDER

Rnd 1: Join variegated with sc in any corner ch-3 sp, ch 3, sc in same sp, *[ch 1, skip next st, (sc in next st, ch 1, skip next st) 8 times, sc in ch sp before next seam, ch 1, sc in ch sp after seam, ch 1, skip next st, (sc in next st, ch 1, skip next st) across to next corner], (sc, ch 3, sc) in next corner ch sp; repeat from * 2 more times; repeat between [ ], join with sl st in first sc.

Rnd 2: Repeat rnd 7 of Square. *(41 sc between corner ch-3 sps)*

Rnds 3-4: With blue, repeat rnds 6 and 7 of Square.

Rnds 5-6: With variegated, repeat rnds 6 and 7 of Square.

Sew rnd 4 of Border to outer edge of pillow, leaving ruffle free.

CONFETTI

SIZE: 13" square not including ruffle.

MATERIALS: Worsted yarn — 3½ oz. variegated and 2½ oz. lavender; 13" square lavender pillow with 3" ruffle; lavender sewing thread; sewing needle; G hook or hook size needed to obtain gauge.

GAUGE: 4 sc = 1"; 4 sc rows =1".

BASIC STITCHES: Ch, sl st, sc, hdc, dc.
SPECIAL STITCH: For **shell,** 5 dc in next st.

TOPPER

Rnd 1: With lavender, ch 8, sl st in first ch to form ring, ch 1, 8 sc in ring, join with sl st in first sc. Fasten off. *(8 sc made)*

Rnd 2: Join variegated with sc in any st, (ch 3, sc) in same st, ch 2, *(sc, ch 3, sc) in next st, ch 2; repeat from * around, join. Fasten off.

Rnd 3: Join lavender with sc in any ch-2 sp, ch 2, skip next ch-3 sp, (sc in next ch-2 sp, ch 2, skip next ch-3 sp) around, join. *(8 sc, 8 ch-2 sps)*

Rnd 4: Ch 1, sc in first sc, *[(sc, hdc) in next ch-2 sp, (2 dc, ch 2, 2 dc) in next sc, (hdc, sc) in next ch-2 sp], sc in next sc; repeat from * 2 more times; repeat between [ ], join.

Rnd 5: Ch 1, sc in each st around with (sc, ch 2, sc) in each corner ch-2 sp, join. Fasten off.

Row 6: Working in rows, for **corner,** join variegated with sc in first st after any corner ch sp, sc in next 10 sts leaving remaining sts unworked, turn. *(11 sc)*

Rows 7-10: Ch 1, sc first 2 sts tog, sc in each st across to last 2 sts, sc last 2 sts tog, turn, ending with *(3 sts)* in last row.

Row 11: Ch 1, sc first 2 sts tog, ch 2, sc last worked st and last st tog. Fasten off.

Repeat rows 6-11 in sts between corner ch sps on rnd 5 for remaining three corners.

Rnd 12: Join lavender with sc in any corner ch sp, ch 2, sc in same sp, *[evenly space 8 sc across ends of rows to center of block, sc in next ch sp on rnd 5, evenly space 8 sc across to next corner], (sc, ch 2, sc) in next corner ch sp; repeat from * 2 more times; repeat between [ ], join.

Rnd 13: Ch 1, sc in each st around with (sc, ch 2, sc) in each corner ch sp, join. Fasten off.

Row 14: For **corner,** join variegated with sc in first st after any corner ch sp, sc in next 20 sts, turn. *(21 sc)*

Rows 15-23: Ch 1, sc first 2 sts tog, sc in each st across to last 2 sts, sc last 2 sts tog, turn, ending with *(3 sts)* in last row.

Row 24: Repeat row 11.

Repeat rows 14-24 on sts between corner ch sps on rnd 13 for remaining three corners.

BORDER

Rnd 1: Join lavender with sc in any corner ch sp, ch 2, sc in same sp, *[evenly space 15 sc across ends of rows to center of block, sc in next ch sp on rnd 13, evenly space 16 sc across to next corner], (sc, ch 2, sc) in next corner ch sp; repeat from * 2 more times; repeat between [ ], join. *(34 sc between corner ch sps)*

Rnds 2-3: Ch 1, sc in each st around with (sc, ch 2, sc) in each corner ch sp, join, ending with *(38 sc)* between corner ch sps. At end of last rnd, fasten off.

Rnd 4: Join variegated with sc in any corner ch sp, ch 2, sc in same sp, sc in each st around with (sc, ch 2, sc) in each corner ch sp, join.

Rnd 5: Sl st in next ch sp, ch 3, 6 dc in same sp, *[(skip next 2 sts, sc in next st, skip next 2 sts, **shell** in next st—*see Special Stitch*) 6 times, skip next 2 sts, sc in next st, skip next st], 7 dc in next corner ch sp; repeat from * 2 more times; repeat between [ ], join with sl st in top of ch-3.

Rnd 6: (Sl st, ch 1, sc) in next st, *[skip next st, 7 dc in next st, skip next st, sc in next st, (shell in next sc, sc in center st of next shell) 6 times, shell in next sc, skip next st], sc in next st; repeat from * 2 more times; repeat between [ ], join with sl st in first sc.

Rnd 7: Ch 3, *[(hdc in next 3 sts, (2 dc, ch 2, 2 dc) in next st, hdc in next 3 sts, (dc in next sc, hdc in next dc, sc in next 3 dc, hdc in next dc) 7 times], dc in next sc; repeat from * 2 more times; repeat between [ ], join with sl st in top of ch-3. Fasten off.

Rnd 8: Join lavender with sc in any st, sc in each st around with (sc, ch 2, sc) in each corner ch sp, join. *(55 sc between corner ch sps)*

Rnd 9: Ch 1, sc in each st around with (sc, ch 2, sc) in each corner ch sp, join. Fasten off.

Rnd 10: Join variegated with sl st in any corner ch sp, ch 3, sl st in same sp, *[ch 2, skip next st, (sl st in next st, ch 2, skip next st) across to next corner], (sl st, ch 3, sl st) in next corner ch sp; repeat from * 2 more times; repeat between [ ], join with sl st in first sl st. Fasten off.

Sew rnd 8 of Border to outer edge of pillow, leaving ruffle free. ✿

Helpful Holders

DESIGNED BY SUE CHILDRESS

For someone who travels a great deal, it's comforting to bring along a little bit of home sweet home in the form of a lovingly stitched set of accessory holders. These beautifully appliquéd pink and white bags keep jewelry, hosiery and other items contained regardless of the destination.

FINISHED SIZES: Hosiery Bag is 5½" x 6¼"; Jewelry Bag is 2½" tall.

MATERIALS: Size 5 crochet cotton — 200 yds pink; 1 yd. pink rattail cord; ½ yd. pink ⅛" ribbon; 2 appliqués; pearl 8 mm shank button; pink sewing thread; sewing needle; B hook or hook size needed to obtain gauge.

GAUGE: 6 hdc =1"; 4 hdc rows/rnds = 1".

BASIC STITCHES: Ch, sl st, sc, hdc, dc.

SPECIAL STITCH: For **picot,** ch 3, sl st in top of last st made.

HOSIERY BAG

Front Side

Row 1: Ch 39, hdc in third ch from hook, hdc in each ch across, turn. *(38 hdc made)*

Rows 2-22: Ch 2, hdc in each st across, turn. At end of last row, fasten off.

Back Side

Rows 1-22: Repeat same rows of Front Side. At end of last row, **do not fasten off.**

Rows 23-28: For **flap,** ch 3, skip next 2 hdc, hdc in each st across to last 4 sts, skip next 2 sts, dc in next st leaving last st unworked, turn, ending with *(8 sts)* in last row.

Row 29: Ch 3, skip next 2 sts, hdc in next st, skip next 2 sts, dc in next st leaving last st unworked. Fasten off.

Rnd 30: Hold Front and Back wrong sides together with Front facing you, matching rows 1-22; working in rnds through both thicknesses, join with sl st in end of row 22, ch 2, sc in same row, (ch 2, sc in end of next row) across, ch 2, sc in end of same row; working in starting ch on opposite side of row 1, (ch 2, skip next ch, sc in next ch) across, (ch 2, sc in end of next row) across; working in ends of rows on flap only, (sc in end of next row, 7 dc in end of next row) 3 times, sc in end of last row; for **buttonhole,** (sc, ch 6, sc) in next hdc; sc in end of same row, (7 dc in end of next row, sc in end of next row) 3 times, join with sl st in first sl st, **turn.**

Row 31: Ch 1, *sc in next sc, (dc in next dc, **picot**—*see Special Stitch)* 7 times*; repeat between ** 2 more times, sc in next 2 sc, 6 sc

in next ch-6 sp, sc in next sc; repeat between ** 3 times, sl st in next st leaving remaining sts unworked. Fasten off.

Sew button centered on row 13.

Sew one appliqué 1" from right-hand edge over rows 4-6. Tie 9" of ⅛" ribbon into a bow around st above appliqué.

JEWELRY BAG

Rnd 1: Ch 3, 6 hdc in third ch from hook, join with sl st in top of ch-2. *(7 hdc made)*

Rnd 2: Ch 2, hdc in same st, 2 hdc in each st around, join. *(14)*

Rnd 3: Ch 2, 2 hdc in next st, (hdc in next st, 2 hdc in next st) around, join. *(21)*

Rnds 4-5: Ch 2, (hdc in next st, 2 hdc in next st) around, join. *(31, 46)*

Rnd 6: Working this rnd in **back lps** only, ch 2, hdc in each st around, join.

Rnd 7: Ch 2, hdc in same st, hdc in next 3 sts, (2 hdc in next st, hdc in next 5 sts) around, join. *(54)*

Rnds 8-15: Ch 2, hdc in each st around, join.

Rnd 16: Ch 4, skip next st, (dc in next st, ch 1, skip next st) around, join with sl st in third ch of ch-4. *(27 ch sps)*

Rnd 17: Sl st in first ch sp, ch 3, 6 dc in same sp, sc in next 2 ch sps, (7 dc in next ch sp, sc in next 2 ch sps) around, join with sl st in top of ch-3.

Rnd 18: Ch 6, sl st in third ch from hook, (dc in next st, picot) 6 times, skip next st, sc in next st, *(dc in next st, picot) 7 times, skip next st, sc in next st; repeat from * around, join. Fasten off.

Rnd 19: Working in **front lps** of rnd 5, join with sc in any st, ch 3, skip next st, (sc in next st, ch 3, skip next st) around, join with sl st in first sc. Fasten off.

For **front,** sew appliqué over rnds 9-12. Tie 9" of ⅛" ribbon into a bow around st above appliqué.

Cut rattail cord in half. Starting at one side, weave one length through ch sps on rnd 16; tie ends into a bow. Starting at opposite side, repeat with remaining length. ✿

Simply Beautiful Bibs

DESIGNED BY KYLEIGH C. HAWKE

If your busy lifestyle doesn't allow a lot of time to shop for baby shower gifts, make these adorable bibs during moments of relaxation. Then you'll never have to rush around for a baby gift. Made with absorbent washcloths, these bibs are always very much appreciated.

FINISHED SIZES: Girl's Bib is 13½" x 14". Boy's Bib is 14" square.

MATERIALS FOR ONE: Size 10 crochet cotton —150 yds. each Main Color (MC) and Contrasting Color (CC); 48" MC ⅜" satin ribbon and matching sewing thread; 11½" wide x 12" long washcloth for girls and 12" square washcloth for boys; Fray Check®; 4" plastic lid; sewing needle; No. 6 steel hook or hook size needed to obtain gauge.

GAUGE: 8 sc = 1".

BASIC STITCHES: Ch, sl st, sc.

SPECIAL STITCHES: For **scallop,** ch 2, (2 dc in next ch sp, ch 2) 4 times, skip next st, sc in next 3 sts.

For **corner scallop,** ch 2, (2 dc in next ch sp, ch 2) 5 times, skip next st, sc in next 3 sts.

PREPARATION

For **neck opening,** fold washcloth in half, measure 2" from each side of fold and mark. Measure 2½" down from center and mark. Place bottom half of lid along marks and trace around lid with pencil. Apply fray check along outline and allow to dry. Cut out semi-circle for neck.

TRIM FOR GIRL'S BIB

Rnd 1: Starting at right shoulder corner at neck edge, with CC, place slip knot on hook, working ³⁄₁₆" from edge of Bib, push hook through Bib, complete as sc, working approximately 8 sts per inch,

work 28 more sc evenly spaced across shoulder, work 90 sc evenly spaced across next side, work 90 sc evenly spaced across bottom, work 90 sc evenly spaced across next side, work 29 sc evenly spaced across next shoulder, 3 sc in next corner, work 55 sc evenly spaced across neck opening, 3 sc in last corner, join with sl st in first sc. Fasten off. *(389 sc made)*

Rnd 2: Join MC with sc in first st, sc in next 9 sts, ch 3, skip next 2 sts, (sc in next st, ch 3, skip next 2 sts) 2 times, *sc in next 7 sts, ch 3, skip next 2 sts, (sc in next st, ch 3, skip next 2 sts) 2 times; repeat from * 19 more times, sc in next 11 sts, 3 sc in next st, sc in next 57 sts, 3 sc in next st, sc in last st, join.

Rnd 3: Ch 1, sc in first 9 sts, ch 3, skip next ch sp, 2 dc in next ch sp, (ch 2, 2 dc) 2 times in same sp, ch 3, skip next ch sp, skip next st, sc in next 5 sts, ch 3, skip next ch sp, [◊2 dc in next ch sp, (ch 2, 2 dc) 3 times in same sp, ch 3, skip next ch sp and next st, sc in next 5 sts, ch 3, skip next ch sp, *2 dc in next ch sp, (ch 2, 2 dc) 2 times in same sp, ch 3, skip next ch sp and next st◊, sc in next 5 sts, ch 3, skip next ch sp; repeat from * across to next corner ch sp]; repeat between [ ] 2 more times; repeat between ◊◊, sc in each st across with 3 sc in each corner st, join.

Row 4: Working in rows, ch 1, skip first st, sc in next 7 sts, **scallop** *(see Special Stitches),* **corner scallop** *(see Special Stitches),* (scallop 5 times, corner scallop) 3 times, ch 2, (2 dc in next ch sp, ch 2) 4 times, skip next st, sc in next 7 sts, sl st in next st leaving remaining sts unworked, turn. Fasten off.

Row 5: Skip first 5 sc, join white with sc in next st, sc in next ch sp, (ch 6, sc in next ch sp) 4 times, [◊skip next st, sc in next st, skip next st, sc in next ch sp, (ch 6, sc in next ch sp) 5 times, *skip next st, sc in next st, skip next st, sc in next ch sp, (ch 6, sc in next ch sp) 4 times◊; repeat from * 4 more times]; repeat between [ ] 2 times; repeat between ◊◊, skip next st, sc in next st leaving remaining sts unworked, turn.

Row 6: Ch 1, sc in first st, skip next st, 6 sc in each of next 4 ch sps, skip next st, sc in next st, skip next st, *[6 sc in each of next 5 ch sps, skip next st, sc in next st, skip next st], (6 sc in each of next 4 ch sps, skip next st, sc in next st, skip next st) 5 times; repeat from * 2 more times; repeat between [ ], 6 sc in each of next 4 ch sps, skip next st, sc in last st. Fasten off.

Finishing
Cut two pieces ribbon each 17" long. Sew one end of one piece to each corner at neck edge.

Tie remaining ribbon into a bow and sew below neck edge on center front.

TRIM FOR BOY'S BIB
Rnd 1: Repeat same rnd of Trim For Girl's Bib.

Rnd 2: Join MC with sc in first st, sc in each st around with 3 sc in each corner st, join with sl st in first sc.

Rnd 3: Ch 1, sc in first 3 sts, ch 4, skip next 3 sts, (dc in next st, ch 2, dc in next st, ch 2, skip next 3 sts) 4 times, *[dc in next st, ch 2, dc in next st, ch 2, skip next st, dc in next st, ch 2, dc in same st, ch 2, skip next st, dc in next st, ch 2, dc in next st, ch 2, skip next 3 sts]; repeat between ( ) 16 times; repeat from * 2 more times; repeat between [ ]; repeat between ( ) 3 times, dc in next st, ch 2, dc in next st, ch 4, skip next 3 sts, sc in each st across with 3 sc in each corner st, join.

Row 4: Working in rows, ch 1, sc in first 3 sts, ch 2, (dc in next dc, ch 5, dc in next dc) across to last ch sp, ch 2, skip last ch sp, sc in next 3 sts leaving remaining sts unworked, turn.

Row 5: Ch 1, skip first st, sc in next 2 sts, (4 sc, ch 2, 4 sc) in each ch-5 sp across to last ch sp, ch 2, skip last ch sp, sc in each of next 2 sts leaving last st unworked, turn. Fasten off.

Row 6: Join white with sc in first st, sc in next st, ch 2, skip next ch sp, sc next 2 sts tog, sc in next 2 sts, (sc, ch 2, sc) in next ch sp, *sc in next 3 sts, sc next 2 sts tog, sc in next 3 sts, (sc, ch 2, sc) in next ch sp; repeat from * around to last 6 sts, sc in next 2 sts, sc next 2 sts tog, ch 2, skip next ch sp, sc in last 2 sts. Fasten off.

Finishing
Work same as Trim for Girl's Bib's Finishing. ✿

Floor Doily

AN ANNIE ORIGINAL DESIGN

*The pineapple is a long-recognized symbol of welcome and hospitality.
This floor doily is a lacy, yet sturdy way to welcome guests and highlight your
home's décor. It's an unusual accent that's sure to inspire lots of compliments.*

FINISHED SIZE: 54" across.

MATERIALS: 35 oz. aran worsted yarn; Q crochet hook or hook size needed to obtain gauge.

GAUGE: With **3 strands held tog,** rnds 1-2 = 6" across.

BASIC STITCHES: Ch, sl st, sc, dc, tr.

SPECIAL STITCHES: For **beginning shell (beg shell),** (sl st, ch 3, dc, ch 2, 2 dc) in first st.

For **shell,** (2 dc, ch 2, 2 dc) in next st.

NOTE: Rug is worked with three strands of yarn held together as one throughout.

RUG

Rnd 1: Ch 4, sl st in first ch to form ring, ch 3, 11 dc in ring, join with sl st in top of ch-3. *(12 dc made)*

Rnd 2: (Ch 3, dc) in first st, 2 dc in each st around, join. *(24)*

Rnd 3: (Ch 3, dc) in first st, dc in next st, (2 dc in next st, dc in next st) around, join. *(36)*

Rnd 4: (Ch 3, dc) in first st, dc in next 2 sts, (2 dc in next st, dc in next 2 sts) around, join. *(48)*

Rnd 5: (Ch 3, dc) in first st, dc in next 3 sts, (2 dc in next st, dc in next 3 sts) around, join. *(60)*

Rnd 6: Beg shell *(see Special Stitches),* ch 3, skip next 4 sts, *****shell** *(see Special Stitches)* in next st, ch 3, skip next 4 sts; repeat from * around, join.

Rnd 7: Sl st in next st, beg shell in ch sp of beg shell, ch 3, 12 tr in ch sp of next shell, ch 3, (shell in ch sp of next shell, ch 3, 12 tr in ch sp of next shell, ch 3) around, join.

Rnd 8: Sl st in next st, beg shell in ch sp of beg shell, ch 3, (dc in next tr, ch 1) 11 times, dc in next tr, ch 3, *shell in next shell, ch 3, (dc in next tr, ch 1) 11 times, dc in next tr, ch 3; repeat from * around, join.

Rnd 9: Sl st in next st, beg shell in first shell, ch 3, skip next ch sp, (sc in next ch sp, ch 3) 11 times, *shell in next shell, ch 3, skip next ch sp, (sc in next ch sp, ch 3) 11 times; repeat from * around, join.

Rnd 10: Sl st in next st, beg shell in first shell, ch 3, skip next ch sp, (sc in next ch sp, ch

3) 10 times, *shell in next shell, ch 3, skip next ch sp, (sc in next ch sp, ch 3) 10 times; repeat from * around, join.

Rnd 11: Sl st in next st, beg shell in first shell, ch 3, skip next ch sp, (sc in next ch sp, ch 3) 9 times, *shell in next shell, ch 3, skip next ch sp, (sc in next ch sp, ch 3) 9 times; repeat from * around, join.

Rnd 12: Sl st in next st, beg shell in first shell, ch 3, skip next ch sp, (sc in next ch sp, ch 3) 8 times, *shell in next shell, ch 3, skip next ch sp, (sc in next ch sp, ch 3) 8 times; repeat from * around, join.

Rnd 13: Sl st in next st, (beg shell, ch 2, 2 dc) in first shell, ch 3, skip next ch sp, (sc in next ch sp, ch 3) 7 times, skip next ch sp, *(shell, ch 2, 2 dc) in next shell, ch 3, skip next ch sp, (sc in next ch sp, ch 3) 7 times, skip next ch sp; repeat from * around, join.

Row 14: Working in rows, for **first pineapple,** sl st across to second ch sp, beg shell in second ch sp, ch 3, skip next ch sp, (sc in next ch sp, ch 3) 6 times, skip next ch sp, shell in next shell leaving remaining sts unworked, turn.

Row 15: Ch 3, shell in first shell, ch 3, skip next ch sp, (sc in next ch sp, ch 3) 5 times, skip next ch sp, shell in next shell, turn.

Row 16: Ch 3, shell in first shell, ch 3, skip next ch sp, (sc in next ch sp, ch 3) 4 times, skip next ch sp, shell in next shell, turn.

Row 17: Ch 3, shell in first shell, ch 3, skip next ch sp, (sc in next ch sp, ch 3) 3 times, skip next ch sp, shell in next shell, turn.

Row 18: Ch 3, shell in first shell, ch 3, skip next ch sp, (sc in next ch sp, ch 3) 2 times, skip next ch sp, shell in next shell, turn.

Row 19: Ch 3, shell in first shell, ch 3, skip next ch sp, sc in next ch sp, ch 3, skip next ch sp, shell in next shell, turn.

Row 20: Ch 3, shell in first shell, shell in last shell. Fasten off.

Row 14: For **second pineapple,** join with sl st in ch sp of next unworked shell on rnd 13, (ch 3, dc, ch 2, 2 dc) in same ch sp, ch 3, skip next ch sp, (sc in next ch sp, ch 3) 6 times, shell in next shell leaving remaining sts unworked, turn.

Row 15: Ch 3, shell in first shell, ch 3, skip

continued on page 92

Autumn Doily

DESIGNED BY DENISE AUGOSTINE

*This autumn-inspired doily is reminiscent of the bounty and beauty of the season.
Its delightful leaf shapes bring to mind images like the chill in the air, the smell
of wood smoke, and the satisfying crunch of brilliantly colored leaves underfoot.*

FINISHED SIZE: 10½" across.

MATERIALS: Size 10 crochet cotton thread — 175 yds. ecru; No. 7 steel hook or hook size needed to obtain gauge.

GAUGE: 5 sts = ½"; 5 dc rows = 1".

BASIC STITCHES: Ch, sl st, hdc, dc.

SPECIAL STITCH: For **picot,** ch 5, dc in fifth ch from hook.

Doily

Rnd 1: Ch 8, sl st in first ch to form ring, ch 3, 23 dc in ring, join with sl st in top of ch-3. *(24 dc made)*

Rnd 2: Ch 5 *(counts as first dc and ch-2),* skip next st, (dc in next st, ch 2, skip next st) around, join with sl st in third ch of ch-5. *(12 dc, 12 ch sps)*

Rnd 3: Sl st in first ch sp, ch 3, 2 dc in same sp, **front post (fp,** *see page 159)* around next st, 3 dc in next ch sp, ch 2, (3 dc in next ch sp, fp around next st, 3 dc in next ch sp, ch 2) around, join with sl st in top of ch-3.

Rnd 4: (Ch 3, dc) in first st, dc in next 2 sts, fp around next fp, dc in next 2 sts, 2 dc in next st, ch 2, (2 dc in next st, dc in next 2 sts, fp around next fp, dc in next 2 sts, 2 dc in next st, ch 2) around, join.

Rnd 5: (Ch 3, dc) in first st, (*dc in next 2 sts, 2 dc in next st, fp around next fp, 2 dc in next st, dc in next 2 sts, 2 dc in next st, ch 2*, 2 dc in next st) 5 times; repeat between **, join.

Rnd 6: Ch 3, dc in next 5 sts, fp around next fp, dc in next 6 sts, ch 2, dc in next ch sp, ch 2, (dc in next 6 sts, fp around next fp, dc in next 6 sts, ch 2, dc in next ch sp, ch 2) around, join.

Rnd 7: Ch 3, dc in next 5 sts, fp around next fp, dc in next 6 sts, (ch 2, dc in next ch sp) 2 times, ch 2, *dc in next 6 sts, fp around next fp, dc in next 6 sts, (ch 2, dc in next ch sp) 2 times, ch 2; repeat from * around, join.

Rnd 8: Ch 2 *(not used or counted as a st),* dc in next 5 sts, fp around next fp, dc in next 4 sts, dc next 2 sts tog, ch 2, skip next ch sp, 5 dc in next ch sp, ch 2, skip next ch sp, (dc next 2 sts tog, dc in next 4 sts, fp around next fp, dc in next 4 sts, dc next 2 sts tog, ch 2, skip next ch sp, 5 dc in next ch sp, ch 2, skip next ch sp) around, join with sl st in top of first dc.

Rnd 9: Ch 2, dc in next 4 sts, fp around next fp, dc in next 3 sts, dc next 2 sts tog, ch 2, 2 dc in each of next 2 sts, fp around next st, 2 dc in each of next 2 sts, ch 2, (dc next 2 sts tog, dc in next 3 sts, fp around next fp, dc in next 3 sts, dc next 2 sts tog, ch 2, 2 dc in each of next 2 sts, fp around next st, 2 dc in each of next 2 sts, ch 2) around, join as before.

Rnd 10: Ch 2, dc in next 3 sts, fp around next fp, dc in next 2 sts, dc next 2 sts tog, ch 3, 2 dc in next st, dc in next 3 sts, fp around next fp, dc in next 3 sts, 2 dc in next st, ch 3, (dc next 2 sts tog, dc in next 2 sts, fp around next fp, dc in next 2 sts, dc next 2 sts tog, ch 3, 2 dc in next st, dc in next 3 sts, fp around next fp, dc in next 3 sts, 2 dc in next st, ch 3) around, join.

Rnd 11: Ch 2, dc in next 2 sts, fp around next fp, dc in next st, dc next 2 sts tog, ch 3, dc in next ch sp, ch 3, 2 dc in next st, dc in next 4 sts, fp around next fp, dc in next 4 sts, 2 dc in next st, ch 3, dc in next ch sp, ch 3, (dc next 2 sts tog, dc in next st, fp around next fp, dc in next st, dc next 2 sts tog, ch 3, dc in next ch sp, ch 3, 2 dc in next st, dc in next 4 sts, fp around next fp, dc in next 4 sts, 2 dc in next st, ch 3, dc in next ch sp, ch 3) around, join.

Rnd 12: Ch 2, dc in next st, fp around next fp, dc next 2 sts tog, (ch 3, dc in next ch sp) 2 times, ch 3, dc in next 6 sts, fp around next fp, dc in next 6 sts, (ch 3, dc in next ch sp) 2 times, ch 3, *dc next 2 sts tog, fp around next fp, dc next 2 sts tog, (ch 3, dc in next ch sp) 2 times, ch 3, dc in next 6 sts, fp around next fp, dc in next 6 sts, (ch 3, dc in next ch sp) 2 times, ch 3; repeat from * around, join.

Rnd 13: Ch 2, dc next 2 sts tog, ch 3, skip next ch sp, 5 dc in next ch sp, ch 3, skip next ch sp, dc in next 6 sts, fp around next fp, dc in next 6 sts, ch 3, skip next ch sp, 5 dc in next ch sp, ch 3, skip next ch sp, (dc next 3 sts tog, ch 3, skip next ch sp, 5 dc in next ch sp, ch 3, skip next ch sp, dc in next 6 sts, fp around next fp, dc in next 6 sts, ch 3, skip next ch sp, 5 dc in next ch sp, ch 3, skip next ch sp) around, join.

Rnd 14: Sl st in next 3 chs, (sl st, ch 3, dc) in next st, *[dc in next st, fp around next st, dc in next st, 2 dc in next st, ch 3, dc next 2 sts tog, dc in next 4 sts, fp around next fp, dc in next 4 sts, dc next 2 sts tog, ch 3, 2 dc in next st, dc in next st, fp around next st, dc in next st, 2 dc in next st, ch 2, (dc in next ch sp ch 2) 2 times], 2 dc in next st; repeat from * 4 more times; repeat between [ ], join with sl st in top of ch-3.

Rnd 15: (Ch 3, dc) in first st, *[dc in next 2 sts, fp around next fp, dc in next 2 sts, 2 dc in next st, ch 3, dc next 2 sts tog, dc in next 3 sts, fp around next fp, dc in next 3 sts, dc next 2 sts tog, ch 3, 2 dc in next st, dc in next 2 sts, fp around next fp, dc in next 2 sts, 2 dc in next st, ch 2, skip next ch sp, dc in next ch sp, ch 2, skip next ch sp], 2 dc in next st; repeat from * 4 more times; repeat between [ ], join.

Rnd 16: Ch 3, dc in next 3 sts, *[fp around next fp, dc in next 4 sts, ch 2, dc in next ch sp, ch 2, dc next 2 sts tog, dc in next 2 sts, fp around next fp, dc in next 2 sts, dc next 2 sts tog, ch 2, dc in next ch sp, ch 2, dc in next 4 sts, fp around next fp, dc in next 4 sts, ch 2, (dc in next ch sp, ch 2) 2 times], dc in next 4 sts; repeat from * 4 more times; repeat between [ ], join.

Rnd 17: Ch 2, dc in next 3 sts, *[fp around next fp, dc in next 2 sts, dc next 2 sts tog, (ch 2, dc in next ch sp) 2 times, ch 2, dc next 2 sts tog, dc in next st, fp around next fp, dc in next st, dc next 2 sts tog, (ch 2, dc in next st) 2 times, ch 2, dc next 2 sts tog, dc in next 2 sts, fp around next fp, dc in next 2 sts, dc next 2 sts tog, (ch 2, dc in next ch sp) 3 times, ch 2], dc next 2 sts tog, dc in next 2 sts; repeat from * 4 more times; repeat between [ ], join with sl st in top of first dc.

Rnd 18: Ch 2, dc in next 2 sts, *[fp around next fp, dc in next st, dc next 2 sts tog, (ch 2, dc in next ch sp) 3 times, ch 2, dc next 2 sts tog, fp around next fp, dc next 2 sts tog, (ch 2, dc in next ch sp) 3 times, ch 2, dc next 2 sts tog, dc in next st, fp around next fp, dc in next st, dc next 2 sts tog, (ch 2, dc in next ch sp) 4 times, ch 2], dc next 2 sts tog, dc in next st; repeat from * 4 more times; repeat between [ ], join as before.

Rnd 19: Ch 2, dc in next st, fp around next fp, dc next 2 sts tog, (ch 2, dc in next ch sp) 4 times, ch 2, dc next 3 sts tog, (ch 2, dc in next ch sp) 4 times, ch 2, dc next 2 sts tog, fp around next fp, dc next 2 sts tog, (ch 2, dc in next ch sp) 5 times, ch 2, *dc next 2 sts tog, fp around next fp, dc next 2 sts tog, (ch 2, dc in next ch sp) 4 times, ch 2, dc next 3 sts tog, (ch 2, dc in next ch sp) 4 times, ch 2, dc next 2 sts tog, fp around next fp, dc next 2 sts tog, (ch 2, dc in next ch sp) 5 times, ch 2; repeat from * around, join.

Rnd 20: Ch 2, dc next 2 sts tog, (ch 3, dc in next ch sp) 10 times, ch 3, dc next 3 sts tog, (ch 3, dc in next ch sp) 6 times, ch 3, *dc next 3 sts tog, (ch 3, dc in next ch sp) 10 times, ch 3, dc next 3 sts tog, (ch 3, dc in next ch sp) 6 times, ch 3; repeat from * around, join.

Rnd 21: Sl st in next ch sp, ch 6 *(counts as first dc and ch-3)*, dc in next ch sp, (ch 3, dc in next ch sp) around, ch 1; to **join,** hdc in third ch of ch-6.

Rnd 22: Ch 2, dc in next ch sp, **picot** *(see Special Stitch),* (dc same ch sp and next ch sp tog, picot) around, dc same ch sp and first ch sp tog, picot, join with sl st in top of first dc. Fasten off. ✿

Floor Doily
continued from page 89

continued from page 89

next ch sp, (sc in next ch sp, ch 3) 5 times, skip next ch sp, shell in next shell, turn.

Row 16: Ch 3, shell in first shell, ch 3, skip next ch sp, (sc in next ch sp, ch 3) 4 times, skip next ch sp, shell in next shell, turn.

Row 17: Ch 3, shell in first shell, ch 3, skip next ch sp, (sc in next ch sp, ch 3) 3 times, skip next ch sp, shell in next shell, turn.

Row 18: Ch 3, shell in first shell, ch 3, skip next ch sp, (sc in next ch sp, ch 3) 2 times, skip next ch sp, shell in next shell, turn.

Row 19: Ch 3, shell in first shell, ch 3, skip next ch sp, sc in next ch sp, ch 3, skip next ch sp, shell in next shell, turn.

Row 20: Ch 3, shell in first shell, shell in last shell. Fasten off.

For **next pineapple,** repeat rows 14-20 of second pineapple 4 more times. ✿

Chapter
Five

95   Black & White Afghan
96   Striped Chair Pad
98   Bath Duo
101   Peach Parfait
103   Pastel Bookmarks
105   Cro-Tat™ Snowflakes
110   Lacy Towel Edgings
112   Wild Rose Doily
114   Colorful Carryall
116   Baby Night Cap

5

Believing that thunder and lightning was
caused by the hammer of an angry god,
Thor, Europeans named his day Thuresdaeg.

Black & White Afghan

DESIGNED BY DARLA SIMS

*Clearly defined lines of elegance in a simple black and white design.
Vibrant colors have their place, but sometimes just two
basic colors are all that is needed to create one dynamic statement.*

FINISHED SIZE: 45" x 52".

MATERIALS: Worsted yarn — 20 oz. black and 14 oz. white with iridescent thread; I and J hooks or hook size needed to obtain gauge.

GAUGE: With **J hook,** two 5-dc groups and one sc = 3½"; 2 dc rows and one sc row worked in pattern = 3".

BASIC STITCHES: Ch, sl st, sc, hdc, dc.

AFGHAN

Row 1: With J hook and white, ch 64, 2 dc in fourth ch from hook, (skip next 2 chs, sc in next ch, skip next 2 chs, 5 dc in next ch) 9 times, skip next 2 chs, sc in next ch, skip next 2 chs, 3 dc in last ch, turn. Fasten off. *(10 sc, 9 5-dc groups, 6 dc made)*

Row 2: Join black with sc in first dc; *working into spaces on each side of sc, ch 1, skip next sp, dc in next sp, ch 1, dc in skipped space, ch 1, skip next 2 dc, sc in next dc; repeat from * across, turn.

Row 3: Ch 1, sc in first st, (5 dc in ch sp between next 2 dc, ch 1) across to last st, sc in last st, turn. Fasten off.

Row 4: Join white with sl st in first st, (ch 3, dc) in same st, (ch 1, skip next 2 dc, sc in next dc, ch 1; working over ch sp of last row into sps on each side of sc on row before last, skip next sp, dc in next sp, ch 1, dc in skipped sp) 9 times, ch 1, skip next 2 dc on last row, sc in next dc, ch 1, 2 dc in last st, turn.

Row 5: (Ch 3, 2 dc) in first st, ch 1, (5 dc in ch sp between next 2 dc, ch 1) 9 times, 3 dc in last st, turn. Fasten off.

Row 6: Join black with sc in first st, ch 1; (working over ch sp of last row into sps on each side of sc on row before last, skip next sp, dc in next sp, ch 1, dc in skipped sp, ch 1, skip next 2 dc, sc in next dc) 10 times, turn.

Row 7: Ch 1, sc in first st, (5 dc in ch sp between next 2 dc, ch 1) across to last st, sc in last st, turn. Fasten off.

Rows 8-44: Repeat rows 4-7 consecutively, ending with row 4. At end of last row, fasten off.

BORDER

Rnd 1: Join black with sl st in first st, (ch 3, 2 dc) in same st, (3 dc in next sc, 3 dc in ch sp between next 2 dc) 9 times, 3 dc in next sc, 3 dc in last st, ch 1; working in ends of rows *3 dc in end of same row, (3 dc in end of next black section, 3 dc in end of next white section) across, ch 1*; working in starting ch on opposite side of row 1, 3 dc in first ch, (3 dc in base of next sc, 3 dc in base of next dc group) across; ch 1, repeat between **; to **join,** hdc in top of ch-3.

Rnds 2-5: (Ch 3, 2 dc) around joining hdc; working in spaces between 3-dc groups, 3 dc in each sp around with (3 dc, ch 1, 3 dc) in each corner ch sp, 3 dc in same sp as first 3 dc, join as before. At end of last rnd, fasten off.

Rnd 6: Join white with sl st around joining hdc, (ch 3, 2 dc) in same sp; working in spaces between 3-dc groups, 3 dc in each sp around with (3 dc, ch 1, 3 dc) in each corner ch sp, 3 dc in same sp as first 3 dc, join.

Rnd 7: Repeat rnd 2. Fasten off.

Rnd 8: With black, repeat rnd 6. Fasten off.

Rnds 9-10: Repeat rnds 6 and 7.

Rnd 11: With black, repeat rnd 6.

Rnds 12-20: Repeat rnd 2. At end of last rnd, fasten off.

continued on page 97

Striped Chair Pad

DESIGNED BY KATHY WIGINGTON

Make your home more inviting with the addition of cushiony chair pads in traditional stripes. Whether you make an entire set for the chairs in your dining room or just one for a treasured antique rocker, you can be sure your guests will be more comfortable.

FINISHED SIZE: 14½" square.

MATERIALS: Worsted yarn — 6 oz. each green and off-white; 14" square piece of batting; Four bobby pins for markers; tapestry needle; H hook or hook size needed to obtain gauge.

GAUGE: 7dc sts = 2"; 4 dc rows and 1 sc row = 2"

BASIC STITCHES: Ch, sl st, sc, dc.

SPECIAL STITCHES: For **small corner (sm corner),** fp around next st, dc in same st, fp around same st.

For **large corner (lg corner),** fp around next st, 3 dc in same st, fp around same st.

NOTE: Pillow may cup slightly until pieces are sewn together.

FIRST SIDE

Rnd 1: With off-white, ch 5, sl st in first ch to form ring, ch 3, 19 dc in ring, join with sl st in top of ch-3. Fasten off. *(20 dc made)*

Rnd 2: Join green with sl st in first st, ch 3, **front post (fp,** *see page 159)* around same st, dc in next st, place marker, fp around each of next 2 sts, dc in next st, ***sm corner** (see Special Stitches),* dc in next st, place marker, fp around each of next 2 sts, dc in next st; repeat from * around, fp around same st as first st, join with sl st in top of ch-3. *(8 fp, 8 dc, 4 sm corners)*

Rnds 3-4: Ch 3, fp around same st, dc in each st around to marker, slip marker, fp around each of next 2 sts, dc in each around to center st of next sm corner, (sm corner, dc in each st around to marker, slip marker, fp around each of next 2 sts, dc in each st around to center st of next sm corner) around, fp around same st as first st, join. At end of last rnd, join. Fasten off. *(24 dc, 8 fp, 4 sm corners)*

Rnd 5:. Join off-white with sl st in first st, ch 3, fp around same st, dc in each st around to marker, slip marker, fp around each of next 2 sts, dc in each st around to center st of next sm corner, (sm corner, dc in each st around to marker, slip marker, fp around each of next 2 sts, dc in each st around to center st of next sm corner) around, fp around same st as first st, join. Fasten off. *(32 dc, 8 fp, 4 sm corners)*

Rnd 6: Join green with sl st in first st, ch 3, fp around same st, sc in each st around to marker, slip marker, fp around each of next 2 sts, sc in each st around to center st of next sm corner, (sm corner, sc in each st around to marker, slip marker, fp around each of next 2 sts, sc in each st around to center st of next sm corner) around, fp around same st as first st, join. Fasten off. *(40 sc, 8 fp, 4 sm corners)*

Rnd 7: Repeat rnd 5. *(48 dc, 8 fp, 4 sm corners)*

Rnd 8: With green, repeat rnd 5. *(56 dc, 8 fp, 4 sm corners)*

Rnds 9-10: Repeat rnds 3 and 4, ending with *(72 dc, 8 fp and 4 sm corners)* in last rnd.

Rnds 11-15: Repeat rnds 5-9, ending with *(112 dc, 8 fp and 4 sm corners)* in last rnd.

Rnd 16: Ch 3, dc in same st, fp around same st, dc in each st around to marker, slip marker, fp around each of next 2 sts, dc in each st around to center st of next sm corner, ***lg corner** *(see Special Stitches)*, dc in each st around to marker, slip marker, fp around each of next 2 sts, dc in each st around to center st of next sm corner; repeat from * around, fp around same st as first st, dc in same st as first st, join. Fasten off. *(120 dc, 8 fp, 4 lg corners)*

Rnd 17: Join off-white with sl st in first st, ch 3, dc in same st, fp around same st, dc in each st around to marker, slip marker, fp around each of next 2 sts, dc in each st around to center st of next lg corner, (lg corner, dc in each st around to marker, slip marker, fp around each of next 2 sts, dc in each st around to center st of next lg corner) around, fp around same st as first st, dc in same st as first st, join. Fasten off. *(136 dc, 8 fp, 4 lg corners)*

Rnd 18: Join green with sl st in first st, ch 3, dc in same st, fp around same st, sc in each st around to marker, slip marker, fp around each of next 2 sts, sc in each st around to center st of next lg corner, (lg corner, sc in each st around to marker, slip marker, fp around each of next 2 sts, sc in each st around to center st of next lg corner) around, join. Fasten off. *(152 sc, 8 fp, 4 lg corners)*

Rnd 19: Repeat rnd 17. *(168 dc, 8 fp, 4 lg corners)*

SECOND SIDE

Reversing color sequence, work same as First Side.

EDGING

Holding Sides wrong sides together with batting between, matching sts, working through both thicknesses, join green with sc in any st, sc in each st around with 3 sc in each corner st, join with sl st in first sc. Fasten off.

TIES

For **first pair of ties,** with green, ch 30, sl st in any corner st, ch 30. Fasten off.

For **second pair of ties,** repeat in next corner st.

FINISHING

For **quilting,** working through both thicknesses, with green, sew rnd 7 together and rnd 16 together. ❀

Black & White Afghan

continued from page 95

Rnd 21: With I hook and white, join with sc around joining hdc, 2 sc in same sp, sc in each st around with 3 sc in each corner ch sp, join with sl st in first sc.

Rnd 22: Sl st in next st, ch 7, dc in fourth ch from hook, dc in same sc, (skip next 3 sts, dc in next st, ch 4, dc in fourth ch from hook, dc in same st; repeat from * around to last 2 or 3 sts, join with sl st in third ch of ch-7. Fasten off. ❀

Bath Duo

Designed by Sandra Fentress

Looking for a way to recycle old skirts, dresses or shirts? By tearing these into strips and using a large crochet hook, you can get something that is both functional and attractive all in one. For material, you only have to look in that bag of cast-off clothing that's in the bottom of the closet.

FINISHED SIZES: Basket is 3¾" tall not including Handle. Toilet Tissue Holder holds one roll of tissue.

MATERIALS FOR BASKET: 100% cotton 45" wide fabric — 1 yd. print and ¼ yd. solid; scissors; Q hook or hook size needed to obtain gauge.

MATERIALS FOR TOILET TISSUE HOLDER: 100% cotton 45" wide fabric — 1½ yds. print and ½ yd. solid; pinking shears; P and Q hooks or hook size needed to obtain gauge.

GAUGE: With **Q hook,** 3 sc = 2"; 3 sc rnds = 2"; 2 dc rows = 3".

PREPARATION: To make one long 2" wide strip *(see illustration),* cut print-fabric through selvage in 4½" sections and tear up to ¼" from opposite selvage. Continue to cut and tear remaining fabric, rolling into a ball.

With iron, press ¼" of raw edges inward on each side; then fold in half lengthwise; press again.

Repeat with solid fabric.

Fabric Cutting Illustration

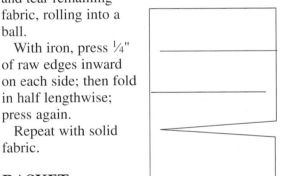

BASKET

Notes: Do not join or turn unless otherwise stated. Mark first st of each rnd.

To add a new piece, unfold 3" of new strip, overlap and refold fabric pieces together.

Wrong side of sc stitches will be on outside of both items.

*Work in **back lps** unless otherwise stated.*

Weave in ends with fingers.

Rnd 1: Starting at **bottom,** with Q hook and print fabric, ch 5, sl st in first ch to form ring, ch 1, (sc in ring, ch 1) 6 times changing to solid fabric *(see page 159)* in last st made. *(6 sc, 6 ch sps made)*

Rnd 2: (Sc in next st, ch 1, sc in next ch, ch 1) around changing to print fabric in last st made. *(12 sc, 12 ch sps)*

Rnd 3: Sc in each st and in each ch around. *(24)*

Rnds 4-5: Sc in each st around. At end of last rnd, change to solid fabric in last st made.

Rnd 6: Sc in each st around changing to print fabric in last st made.

Rnd 7: For **ruffles,** ch 1, (insert hook in next st, holding 1½" lp to wrong side of piece, yo, draw lp through st and through lp on hook at same time) around, join with sl st in first ch-1. Fasten off. *(24 ruffles)*

HANDLE

With Q hook and print fabric, join with sl st in first sl st on rnd 7, ch 14, sl st in st on opposite side of Basket, sl st in next st, sl st in each ch of Handle, sl st in st beside first sl st; working on opposite side of ch, ch 1, sl st in each ch across, join with sl st in second sl st. Fasten off.

For **bows,** cut two strips each print and solid 2½" x 15". Tie print strips into bows. Slide end of one solid strip through one stitch at base of Handle pulling ends even. Holding one print bow against Handle, tie solid strip into a bow around print bow. Trim ends if necessary. Cut V-shaped notches in ends. Repeat on opposite side of Handle.

TOILET TISSUE HOLDER

Row 1: With Q hook and print fabric, ch 10, dc in fourth ch from hook, dc in each ch across, turn. *(8 dc made)*

Rows 2-17: Ch 3, dc in each st across, turn. At end of last row, fasten off.

For **edging,** with P hook and solid fabric, join with sl st in end of row 1, sl st in end of each row across; for **top,** fold Tissue Holder in half crosswise, holding row 1 against row 17 and working through both thicknesses, sl st in each st across; working through one thickness, sl st in end of each row across, sl st in next st on corner. Fasten off.

For **trim,** with P hook, working over top of sts and through both thicknesses, holding row 16 against row 2, join solid fabric with sl st in first st, sl st in each st across. Fasten off.

For **hanger,** working in sts across top, with P hook, join solid fabric with sl st in third st from

continued on page 102

Peach Parfait

Designed by Lucille LaFlamme

*This lovely little decorative accent looks good enough to eat,
just like a perfect peach should! The lacy and openwork look of the shells,
clusters and picots all flow together fluidly in a feast for the eyes.*

FINISHED SIZE: 12" x 16" after blocking.

MATERIALS: Size 20 crochet cotton — 250 yds. peach; No. 11 steel hook or hook size needed to obtain gauge.

GAUGE: 10 shell rows = 3".

BASIC STITCHES: Ch, sl st, sc, tr.

SPECIAL STITCHES: For **beginning shell (beg shell),** sl st to first ch sp, (ch 4, 2 tr, ch 2, 3 tr) in same sp.

For **shell,** (3 tr, ch 2, 3 tr) in next ch sp.

For **picot,** ch 3, sl st in top of sc just made.

For **cluster (cl),** yo 2 times, insert hook in next st or ch sp, yo, draw lp through, (yo, draw through 2 lps on hook) 2 times, *yo 2 times, insert hook in same st or ch sp, yo, draw lp through, (yo, draw through 2 lps on hook) 2 times; repeat from *, yo, draw through all 4 lps on hook.

For **diamond,** sc in next 7 chs, **turn,** (ch 3, dc in next 6 sts, turn) 2 times, ch 1, sc in next 7 sts, **do not turn.**

For **V st,** (tr, ch 3, tr) in next st.

NOTE: Doily may ruffle slightly until blocked.

DOILY

Row 1: Ch 16, **shell** *(see Special Stitches)* in fourth ch from hook, ch 9, skip next 11 chs, shell in last ch, turn. *(2 shells made)*

Row 2: Ch 3, shell in ch sp of next shell, ch 11, shell in ch sp of last shell, turn.

Row 3: Ch 3, shell in next shell, ch 7, sc over next ch sps of last 2 rows and starting ch at same time, ch 1, **turn, diamond** *(see Special Stitches),* shell in next shell, turn. *(2 shells, 1 diamond)*

Row 4: Repeat row 2.

Row 5:. Ch 3, shell in next shell, ch 9, shell in last shell, turn.

Row 6: Repeat row 2.

Row 7: *Ch 3, shell in next shell, ch 7; working over ch sps of last 3 rows at same time, sc in point of last diamond worked*, ch 1, **turn,** diamond, shell in last shell, turn.

Rows 8-18: Repeat rows 4-7 consecutively, ending with row 6.

Row 19: Repeat between ** on row 7, ch 7, shell in last shell, **do not turn.**

Rnd 20: Working around outer edge, ch 1, sc in last tr made, (ch 7, skip next row, sc in next turning ch) 9 times, ch 7, sc in base of next shell on row 1, ch 9, sc in base of next shell, ch 7, sc in turning ch of row 1, (ch 7, skip next row, sc in next turning ch) 9 times, ch 7, sc in next shell, ch 9, skip next 2 ch-7 sps, sc in next shell, ch 7, join with sl st in first sc. *(24 sc, 24 ch sps)*

Rnd 21: (Ch 4, 2 tr, ch 2, 3 tr) in same st, *ch 7, 3 tr in next sc, (ch 5, 3 tr in next sc) 7 times, ch 7, shell in next sc, ch 5, sc in next ch sp, ch 5, (tr, ch 1) 7 times in next ch sp, tr in same sp, ch 5, sc in next ch sp, ch 5*, shell in next sc; repeat between **, join with sl st in top of ch-3.

Rnd 22: Beg shell *(see Special Stitches),* *ch 7, 7 tr in second tr of next 3-tr group, (ch 2, 7 tr in second tr of next 3-tr group) 7 times, ch 7, shell in next shell, ch 3, (tr in next ch sp, ch 3) 2 times, tr in next tr, (2 tr in next ch sp, tr in next tr) 7 times, ch 3, (tr in next ch sp, ch 3) 2 times*, shell in next shell; repeat between **, join.

Rnd 23: Beg shell, *ch 5, tr in fourth ch of next ch-7, ch 5, tr in fourth tr of next 7-tr group, (ch 5, sc in next ch sp, **picot**—*see Special Stitches,* ch 5, tr in fourth tr of next 7-tr group) 7 times, ch 5, tr in fourth ch of next ch-7, ch 5, shell in next shell, ch 3, (tr in next ch sp, ch 3) 2 times, skip next tr, tr in next tr, (ch 1, tr in next tr) 21 times, ch 3, skip next ch sp, (tr in next ch sp, ch 3) 2 times*, shell in next shell; repeat between **, join.

Rnd 24: Beg shell, *ch 7, 3 tr in next tr, (ch 5, 3 tr in next tr) 9 times, ch 7, shell in next shell, ch 5, skip next ch-3 sp, tr in next ch-3 sp, ch 3, skip next ch-3 sp, **cl** *(see Special Stitches)* in next ch-2 sp, (ch 2, cl in next ch-2 sp) 20 times, ch 3, skip next ch-3 sp, tr in next ch-3 sp, ch 5*, shell in next shell; repeat between **, join.

Rnd 25: Beg shell, *ch 7, 7 tr in second tr of next 3-tr group, (ch 2, 7 tr in second tr of next 3-tr group) 9 times, ch 7, shell in next shell, ch 5, **V st** *(see Special Stitches)* in next tr, skip next ch-3 sp, (V st in next ch-2 sp, skip next ch-2 sp) 4 times, V st in each of next 4 ch-2 sps, (skip next ch-2 sp, V st in next ch-2 sp) 4 times, V st in next tr, ch 5*, shell in next shell; repeat between **, join.

Rnd 26: Beg shell, *ch 5, tr in fourth ch of next ch-7, ch 5, tr in fourth tr of next 7-tr group, (ch 5, sc in next ch sp, picot, ch 5, tr in fourth tr of next 7-tr group) 9 times, ch 5, tr in fourth ch of next ch-7 , ch 5, shell in next shell, ch 5, skip next ch-5 sp, (cl in next V st, ch 3) 5 times, (cl, ch 3, cl) in each of next 4 V sts, (ch 3, cl in next V st) 5 times, ch 5*, shell in next shell; repeat between **, join.

Rnd 27: Beg shell, *ch 5, shell in next tr, ch 5, 3 tr in next tr, (ch 7, 3 tr in next tr) 9 times, ch 5, shell in next tr, ch 5, shell in next shell, ch 5, skip next ch-5 sp, sc in next ch-3 sp, (ch 7, sc in next ch-3 sp) 13 times, ch 5*, shell in next shell; repeat between **, join.

Rnd 28: Beg shell, *ch 5, shell in next shell, ch 3, (7 tr in second tr of next 3-tr group, ch 3) 10 times, shell in next shell, ch 5, shell in next shell, ch 7, skip next ch-5 sp, (sc in next ch-7 lp, ch 7) 13 times*, shell in next shell; repeat between **, join.

Rnd 29: Beg shell, *ch 5, tr in third ch of next ch-5, ch 5, shell in next shell, ch 5, V st in fourth tr of next 7-tr group, ch 5, (sc in next ch sp, picot, ch 5, V st in fourth tr of next 7-tr group, ch 5) 9 times, shell in next shell, ch 5, tr in third ch of next ch-5, ch 5, shell in next shell, ch 5, skip next ch-7 sp, cl in next ch-7 sp, (ch 7, cl in next ch-7 sp) 11 times, ch 5*, shell in next shell; repeat between **, join.

Rnd 30: Beg shell, *ch 5, (tr in third ch of next ch-5, ch 5) 2 times, shell in next shell, ch 5, skip next ch-5 sp, shell in next V st, (ch 5, skip next 2 ch sps, shell in next V st) 9 times, ch 5, shell in next shell, ch 5, (tr in third ch of next ch-5, ch 5) 2 times, shell in next shell, ch 5, skip next ch-5 sp, V st in third ch of next ch-5, (ch 3, V st in third ch of next ch-5) 10 times, ch 5*, shell in next shell; repeat between **, join.

Rnd 31: Beg shell, *ch 4, sc in next ch-5 sp, picot, ch 4, shell in third ch of next ch-5, (ch 4, sc in next ch-5 sp, picot, ch 4, shell in next shell) 12 times, ch 4, sc in next ch-5 sp, picot, ch 4, shell in third ch of next ch-5, ch 4, sc in next ch-5 sp, picot, ch 4, shell in next shell, (ch 4, skip next ch sp, sc in next V st, picot, ch 4, skip next ch sp, shell in next V st) 5 times, ch 4, skip next ch sp, sc in next V st, picot, ch 4*, shell in next shell; repeat between **, join.

Rnd 32: Beg shell, ch 7, (shell in next shell, ch 7) around, join.

Rnd 33: Sl st to first ch sp, (ch 4, 4 tr, ch 5, sl st in fourth ch from hook, ch 1, 5 tr) in same sp, ch 3, sc in next ch sp, ch 3, *(5 tr, ch 5, sl st in fourth ch from hook, ch 1, 5 tr) in next shell, ch 3, sc in next ch sp, ch 3; repeat from * around, join. Fasten off. ✿

Bath Duo

continued from page 99

continued from page 99

corner, ch 10, skip next 2 sts, sl st in next st. Fasten off.

For bows, cut one strip each print and solid 1" x 15". Trim outer edges with pinking shears. Tie print strip into a bow. Slide end of solid strip through one stitch under hanger pulling ends even. Holding print bow against Tissue Holder, tie solid strip into a bow around print bow. Trim ends. Cut V-shaped notches in ends. ✿

Pastel Bookmarks

DESIGNED BY KYLEIGH C. HAWKE

After answering the phone or a question from a family member, do you return to your book only to discover you've lost your place? These bookmarks are not only good for solving that problem, they're beautiful as well. And they're so much fun to make, you may not want to stop at one.

FINISHED SIZE: 9½" long not including tassel.

MATERIALS FOR ONE: Size 10 crochet cotton thread — small amount each main color (MC) and contrasting color (CC); tapestry needle; No. 6 steel hook or hook size needed to obtain gauge.

GAUGE: Rows 1-4 = 1¼" tall.

BASIC STITCHES: Ch, sl st, sc, dc, tr.

SPECIAL STITCH: For **shell,** (3 dc, ch 2, 3 dc) in next ch-2 sp.

NOTE: Bookmark may ruffle until blocked.

CENTER

Row 1: With MC, ch 6, sl st in first ch to form ring, ch 3, (2 dc, ch 2, 3 dc) in ring, turn.

Rows 2-24: Ch 3, **shell** *(see Special Stitch)* in next ch sp, dc in top of last ch-3, turn. At end of last row, **do not turn.** Fasten off.

EDGING

Rnd 1: Working around outer edge, join CC with sl st in ch sp of last shell made on Center, ch 4, 14 tr in same sp, 3 sc in end of each row around to row 1, 15 tr in beginning ring on row 1, 3 sc in end of each row around, join with sl st in top of ch-4, **do not turn.** *(168 sts)*

Rnd 2: Ch 1, sc in first st, ch 3, skip next st, (sc in next st, ch 3, skip next st) around, join with sl st in first sc. Fasten off.

For **tassel,** cut twelve strands CC each 10" long. Holding all strands tog, fold in half, insert hook in center ch lp on either end, draw fold through, draw all loose ends through fold, tighten. Trim ends. ✿

Cro-Tat™ Snowflakes

DESIGNED BY ERMA FIELDER

Is it tatting or is it crochet? It's cro-tatting, a technique that combines crochet with the elegance of tatting. It's done with a special straight-shanked crochet-tatting hook. These beautiful snowflakes make wonderful tree decorations, package trims and gifts.

FINISHED SIZES: 3¼" to 6" across.

MATERIALS FOR ONE: 25 yds. white size 10 crochet cotton thread; fabric stiffener; plastic wrap; blocking board or Styrofoam®; rustproof pins; crochet tatting hook.

BASIC STITCHES: Ch, sl st, sc.

SPECIAL STITCHES: For **double stitch (ds),** to make **first half,** hold the thread with the left hand and wrap clockwise around left index finger; scoop the hook under the thread from front to back toward the fingertip *(see photo A on page 106)* and lift the thread off your finger to form a loop on the hook, pull the thread snug. Move the right index finger over the last loop made to hold it in place. To make **second half** of stitch, wrap the thread counter-clockwise around left index finger; scoop the hook under the thread from the back toward the fingertip *(see photo B),* lifting the thread off your finger to form a loop on the hook. Pull the thread snug against the last lp and hold in place with the right index finger.

For **picot (p),** with right index finger, hold the thread against the hook and make the next ds, approximately ¼" from the last ds *(see photo C),* slide the last ds made over to the previous ds forming a loop; the loop is the picot. Pull the picot to tighten the thread around the hook.

To **close ring,** make a loop a little longer than the stitches on hook *(see photo D),* yo, above loop and pull through all lps on hook making sure not to loose first loop *(see photo E),* keeping loop made after pulling through sts on hook, insert hook into first loop *(see photo F),* pull second loop to tighten first loop around hook, pull end of thread to tighten second loop around hook, yo, pull through both lps on hook forming a ring.

For **joined picot (joined p),** insert hook in corresponding picot from front to back, yo, pull lp through picot and place on hook.

SNOWFLAKE NO. 1

Rnd 1: Make ring of **3 ds** *(see Special Stitches on page 105.),* **p** *(see Special Stitches),* (4 ds, p) 7 times, ds, **close ring** *(see Special Stitches).* Fasten off.

Rnd 2: Work rnd 2 in the following steps:

Step 1: Make large ring of 5 ds, p, 5 ds, **joined p** *(see Special Stitches)* in any picot on last rnd, 5 ds, p, 5 ds, close ring, (make ring of 3 ds, p, 3 ds, close ring) 3 times, sl st in base of first large ring. Fasten off.

Step 2: Make large ring of 5 dc, joined p in last picot of last large ring, 5 dc, joined p in next picot on last rnd, 5 ds, p, 5 ds, close ring, (make ring of 3 ds, p, 3 ds, close ring) 3 times, sl st in base of last large ring. Fasten off. Repeat step 2

for five more times.

Step 3: Make large ring of 5 ds, joined p in last picot of last large ring, 5 ds, joined p in next picot of last rnd, 5 ds, joined p in first picot of first large ring, 5 ds, close ring, (make ring of 3 ds, p, 3 ds, close ring) 3 times, sl st in base of last large ring. Fasten off.

Apply fabric stiffener according to manufacturers instructions. Pin to plastic covered blocking board, shape. Let dry.

SNOWFLAKE NO. 2

Make large ring of **3 ds** *(see Special Stitches on page 105.),* **p** *(see Special Stitches)* (3 ds, p) 2 times, 3 ds, **close ring** *(see Special Stitches),* ch 5, make small ring of ds, (p, ds), 3 times, close ring, ch 5, make small ring of 3 ds, p, 3 ds, close ring, ch 5, make small ring of ds (p, dc) 3 times, close ring, ch 5, *make large ring of 3 ds, **joined p** *(see Special Stitches)* in last picot of last large ring, (3 ds, p) 2 times, 3 ds, close ring, ch 5, make small ring of ds, (p, ds), 3 times, close ring, ch 5,

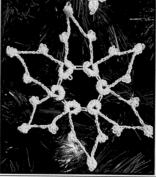

make small ring of 3 ds, p, 3 ds, close ring, ch 5, make small ring of ds (p, dc) 3 times, close ring, ch 5; repeat from * 3 more times, make large

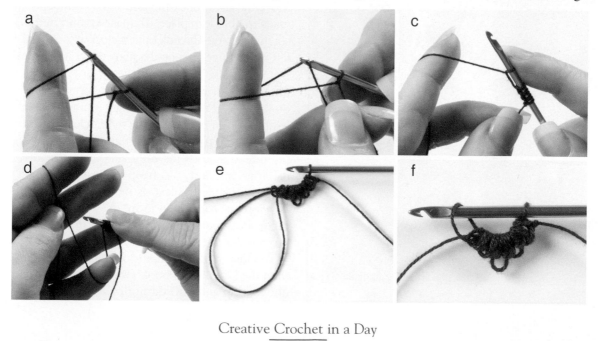

ring of 3 ds, joined p in last picot of last large ring, 3 ds, p, 3 ds, joined p in first picot of first large ring, 3 ds, close ring, ch 5, make small ring of ds, (p, ds) 3 times, close ring, ch 5, make small ring of 3 ds, p, 3 ds, close ring, ch 5, make ring of ds, (p, dc) 3 times, close ring, ch 5, join with sl st in base of first large ring. Fasten off.

Apply fabric stiffener according to manufacturers instructions. Pin to plastic covered blocking board, shape. Let dry.

SNOWFLAKE NO. 3

Rnd 1: Make large ring of **2 ds** *(see Special Stitches on page 105.)*, **p** *(see Special Stitches)*, (3 ds, p) 7 times, ds, **close ring** *(see Special Stitches)*. Fasten off.

Rnd 2: Join with sl st in any picot of last rnd, make ring of 5 ds, p, 5 ds, close ring, sl st in same picot, ch 2, (sl st in next picot on last rnd, make ring of 5 ds, p, 5 ds, close ring, sl st in same picot, ch 2) around, join with sl st in base of first ring.

Rnd 3: [Ch 5, sl st in picot of same ring, ch 10, *make ring of (3 ds, p) 3 times, 3 ds, close ring; repeat from * 2 more times, sl st in base of first ring of 3-ring group, ch 10, sl st in same picot as first ch-10 on last rnd, ch 5, sl st in base of same ring, sl st in next ch-2 sp, ch 5, (make ring of 2 ds, p, 2 ds, close ring) 3 times, sl st in base of first ring of 3-ring group, ch 5, sl st in same ch-2 sp, sl st in base of next ring]; repeat between [ ] around. Fasten off.

Apply fabric stiffener according to manufacturers instructions. Pin to plastic covered blocking board, shape. Let dry.

SNOWFLAKE NO. 4

Rnd 1: *Make ring of **ds** *(see Special Stitches on page 105.)*, **p** *(see Special Stitches)*, ds, **close ring** *(see Special Stitches)*; repeat from * 7 more times, join with sl st in first ds.

Rnd 2: *Ch 5, (make ring of ds, p, ds, close ring, ch 1) 2 times, (make ring of 2 ds, p, 2 ds, close ring) 3 times, sl st in base of first ring of 3-ring group, (ch 1, make ring of ds, p, ds, close ring) 2 times, sl st in fifth ch of ch-5, ch 5, sl st in sp between next 2 picot on rnd 1; repeat from *around. Fasten off.

Apply fabric stiffener according to manufacturers instructions. Pin to plastic covered blocking board, shape. Let dry.

SNOWFLAKE NO. 5

Rnd 1: Make ring of **ds** *(see Special Stitches on page 105.)*, **p** *(see Special Stitches)*, (2 ds, p) 7 times, ds, **close ring** *(see Special Stitches)*. Fasten off.

Rnd 2: Make ring of 6 ds, **joined p** *(see Special Stitches)* in any picot of rnd 1, 6 ds, close ring, ch 7, *make ring of 6 ds, joined p in next picot of rnd 1, 6 ds, close ring, ch 7; repeat from * around, join with sl st in base of first ring.

Rnd 3: Sl st in next 3 chs, sl st in same ch sp, ch 7, (sl st in next ch sp, ch 7) around, join with sl st in first sl st. Fasten off.

Rnd 4: [Make ring of 6 ds, joined p in any ch sp on last rnd, 6 ds, close ring, ch 7, make ring of (3 ds, p) 3 times, 3 ds, close ring, *make ring of 3 ds, joined p in last picot of last ring, (3 ds, p) 2 times, 3 ds, close ring; repeat from *, join with sl st in base of first ring of 3-ring group, ch 7]; repeat between [ ] around, join with sl st in base of first ring. Fasten off.

Apply fabric stiffener according to manufacturers instructions. Pin to plastic covered blocking board, shape. Let dry.

SNOWFLAKE NO. 6

Rnd 1: *Make ring of **6 ds** (see Special Stitches on page 105.), **p** (see Special Stitches), (6 ds, p) 2 times, 6 ds, **close ring** (see Special Stitches); repeat from *, sl st in base of first ring. Fasten off.

Rnd 2: Join with sc in first picot of second ring, *ch 10, sc in next picot on next ring, ch 5,

sl st in next picot, make ring of 5 ds, (p, 5 ds) 3 times, close ring, sl st in same picot, ch 5*, sc in next picot; repeat between **, join with sl st in first sc.

Rnd 3: Sl st in next ch sp, (ch 3, dc, ch 2, 4 ds, ch 2, 4 ds, ch 2, 2 dc) in same sp, ch 3, (2 dc, ch 2, 2 dc) in next ch sp, ch 5, skip next picot on next ring, sl st in next picot, make ring of 3 ds, (p, 3 ds) 3 times, close ring, sl st in same picot, ch 5, (2 dc, ch 2, 2 dc) in next ch-5 sp, ch 3, (2 dc, ch 2, 4 ds, ch 2, 4 ds, ch 2, 2 dc) in next ch sp, ch 3, (2 dc, ch 2, 2 dc) in next ch sp, make ring of 3 ds, (p, 3 ds) 3 times, close ring, sl st in same picot, ch 5, (2 dc, ch 2, 2 dc) in next ch-5 sp, ch 3, join with sl st in top of ch-3.

Rnd 4: Sl st in next st, sl st in next ch sp, [*ch 3, make ring of 3 ds, p, 3 ds, close ring, ch 3, sl st in same ch sp*, sl st in next 4 sts, sl st in next ch sp, make ring of 3 ds, (p, ds) 2 times, p, 3 ds, close ring, sl st in same ch sp, sl st in next 4 sts, sl st in next ch sp; repeat between **, sl st in next 2 sts, sl st in next ch sp, ch 3, sl st in same ch sp, sl st in next 2 sts; repeat between **, sl st in next 2 sts, sl st in next ch sp, ch 3, sl st in same ch sp, ch 5, sl st in center picot of next ring, make ring of 3 ds, (p, ds) 2 times, p, 3 ds, close ring, sl st in same picot, ch 5, sl st in next ch sp, ch 3, sl st in same ch sp, sl st in next 2 sts; repeat between **, sl st in next 2 sts, sl st in next ch sp, ch 3, sl st in same sp], sl st in next 2 sts; repeat between [ ], join with sl st in first sl st. Fasten off.

Apply fabric stiffener according to manufac-

turers instructions. Pin to plastic covered blocking board, shape. Let dry.

SNOWFLAKE NO. 7

Rnd 1: Working this rnd from left to right, make ring of **5 ds** (see Special Stitches on page 105.), **p** (see Special Stitches), (5 ds, p) 2 times, 5 ds, **close ring** (see Special Stitches), *make ring of 5 ds, **joined p** (see Special Stitches) in last picot of last ring, (5 ds, p) 2 times, 5 ds, close ring; repeat from * 3 more times, make ring of 5 ds, joined p in last picot of last ring, 5 ds, p, 5 ds, joined p in first picot of first ring, 5 ds, close ring, join with sl st in base of first ring. Fasten off.

Rnd 2: Make ring of 5 ds, p, 5 ds, joined p in center picot of any ring on last rnd, 5 ds, p, 5 ds, close ring, ch 1, (make ring of ds, close ring) 3 times, ch 1, make ring of 5 ds, (p, ds) 4 times, p, 5 ds, close ring, ch 1, (make ring of ds, close ring) 3 times, ch 1, *make ring of 5 ds, p, 5 ds, joined p in center picot of next ring on last rnd, 5 ds, p, 5 ds, close ring, ch 1, (make ring of ds, close ring) 3 times, ch 1, make ring of 5 ds, (p, ds) 4 times, p, 5 ds, close ring, ch 1, (make ring of ds,

close ring) 3 times, ch 1; repeat from * around, join with sl st in base of first ring. Fasten off.

Apply fabric stiffener according to manufacturers instructions. Pin to plastic covered blocking board, shape. Let dry.

SNOWFLAKE NO. 8

*Note: For **double stitch chain (ds ch)**, (make ring of ds, close ring) 4 times.*

Rnd 1: Working this rnd from left to right, make ring of **2 ds** (see Special Stitches on page 105.), **p** (see Special Stitches), (2 ds, p) 5 times, 2 ds, **close ring** (see Special Stitches); **ds ch** (see Note); p, ds ch, *[make ring of (2 ds, p) 2 times, 2 ds, **joined p** (see Special Stitches) in fourth picot of last ring, (2 ds, pc) 3 times, 2 ds, close ring, make ring of 2 ds, joined p in last picot of last ring, 4 ds, (p, 2 ds) 6 times, p, 4 ds], p, 2 ds, close ring, make ring of 2 ds, joined p in last picot of last ring, (2 ds, p) 5 times, ds ch, joined p in picot between first 2 ds chs, ds ch; repeat from * 2 times; repeat between [ ], joined p in first picot of first ring, 2 ds, close ring, join with sl st in base of first ring. Fasten off.

Rnd 2: Working right to left, join with sl st in first right-hand unjoined picot of any large ring, *[make ring of 3 ds, p, 3 ds, close ring, sl st in same picot, ch 1, (sl st in next picot, make ring of 3 ds, p, 3 ds, close ring, ch 1) 2 times, sl st in next picot, ch 4, (make ring of 3 ds, p, 3 ds, close ring) 3 times, sl st in base of first ring of 3-ring group, ch 4, sl st in same picot, (ch 1, sl st in next picot, make ring of 3 ds, p, 3 ds, close ring) 3 times, ch 3, (sl st, ch 3, sl st) in next picot on next ring, ch 3, sl st in next picot, ch 2, make ring of 3 ds, p, 3 ds, close ring, ch 2, sl st in next unjoined picot of next ring, ch 3, (sl st, ch 3, sl st) in next picot, ch 3], sl st in next unjoined p on next large ring; repeat from * 2 more times; repeat between [ ], join with sl st in base of first ring. Fasten off.

Apply fabric stiffener according to manufacturers instructions. Pin to plastic covered blocking board, shape. Let dry.

SNOWFLAKE NO. 9

Rnd 1: Make ring of **ds** *(see Special Stitches on page 105.)*, **p** *(see Special Stitches)*, (2 ds, p) 5 times, ds, **close ring.** Fasten off.

*Note: For **double stitch chain (ds ch)**, (make ring of ds, close ring) 3 times.*

Rnd 2: Join with sl st in any picot, make ring of 6 ds, p, 6 ds, close ring, sl st in same picot, ch 2, (sl st in next picot, make ring of 6 ds, p, 6 ds, close ring, sl st in same picot, ch 2) around, join with sl st in base of first ring. Fasten off.

Rnd 3: Join with sl st in any ch-2 sp, **ds ch** *(see Note)*, (make ring of 2 ds, p, 2 ds, close ring) 3 times, sl st in base of first ring of 3-ring group, ds ch, make ring of 6 ds, (p, 6 ds) 3 times, close ring, ds ch, (make ring of 2 ds, p, 2 ds, close ring) 3 times, sl st in base of first ring of 3-ring group, ds ch, *sl st in next ch-2 sp, ds ch, (make ring of 2 ds, p, 2 ds, close ring) 3 times, sl st in base of first ring of 3-ring group, ds ch, make ring of 6 ds, (p, 6 ds) 3 times, close ring, ds ch, (make ring of 2 ds, p, 2 ds, close ring) 3 times,

sl st in base of first ring of 3-ring group, ds ch; repeat from * around, join with sl st in first sl st. Fasten off.

Apply fabric stiffener according to manufacturers instructions. Pin to plastic covered blocking board, shape. Let dry.

SNOWFLAKE NO. 10

Rnd 1: Make ring of **ds** *(see Special Stitches on page 105.)*, **p** *(see Special Stitches)*, (ds, p) 5 times, ds, **close ring.** Fasten off.

*Note: For **double stitch chain (ds ch)**, (make ring of ds, close ring) 5 times.*

Rnd 2: Make ring of 6 ds, **joined p** *(see Special Stitches)* in any picot on last rnd, 6 ds, close ring, **ds ch** *(see Note)*, (make ring of 6 ds, p, 6 ds, close ring) 3 times, sl st in base of first ring of 3-ring group, ds ch, *make ring of 6 ds, joined p in next picot on last rnd, 6 ds, close ring, ds ch, (make ring of 6 ds, p, 6 ds, close ring) 3

times, sl st in base of first ring of 3-ring group, ds ch; repeat from * around, join with sl st in base of first ring, fasten off. ✿

Lacy Towel Edgings

DESIGNED BY JENNIFER MCCLAIN

*These special towels really add decorating charm to a guest bathroom, and they're
ever so easy to make. It's a fast and economical way to dress up plain towels
for a designer look. Choose yarn and ribbon colors to match or contrast with towel color.*

FINISHED SIZES: Pink Edging is 2½" wide. Off-white Edging is 2" wide.

MATERIALS FOR ONE: Acrylic sport yarn — 2 oz. main color *(MC)*; enough ¼" satin ribbon in color matching towel to fit across towel plus 1"; matching sewing thread; sewing needle; C hook or hook size needed to obtain gauge.

GAUGE: 3 tr rows = 2".

BASIC STITCHES: Ch, sl st, sc, dc, tr.

SPECIAL STITCHES: For **shell,** (2 dc, ch 1, 2 dc) in next ch sp.

For **2-dc cluster (2-dc cl),** yo, insert hook in next st, yo, draw lp through, yo, draw through 2 lps on hook, yo, insert hook in same st, yo, draw lp through, yo, draw through 2 lps on hook, yo, draw through all 3 lps on hook.

For **3-dc cluster (3-dc cl),** yo, insert hook in next st, yo, draw lp through, yo, draw through 2 lps on hook, (yo, insert hook in same st, yo, draw lp through, yo, draw through 2 lps on hook) 2 times, yo, draw through all 4 lps on hook.

PINK EDGING

Row 1: For **foundation,** *ch 5, tr in fifth ch from hook; repeat from * number of times needed to fit across towel, ending with a multiple of 2 lps, **do not turn.**

Row 2: Ch 3, (dc, ch 1, dc, ch 1, dc) around post of first tr, (dc, ch 1, dc, ch 1, dc) around post of each tr across, dc in bottom of last tr, turn.

Row 3: Ch 1, sc in first st, ch 1, sc in next ch sp, (ch 2, sc in next ch-1 sp) across, ch 1, sc in last st, turn.

Row 4: Ch 4, dc in next ch-1 sp, skip next ch-2 sp, *(dc, ch 1, dc, ch 1, dc) in next ch-2 sp, skip next ch-2 sp; repeat from * across to last ch-1 sp, dc in next ch-1 sp, ch 1, dc in last st, turn.

Row 5: Ch 1, sc in first st, sc in next ch sp, (ch 2, sc in next ch sp) across with sc in last st, turn.

Row 6: Ch 2, **shell** *(see Special Stitches)* in next ch sp, (sc in next ch sp, shell in next ch sp) across with sc in last st, **do not turn.** Fasten off.

Row 7: Working on opposite side of foundation, join with sl st in first ch of first ch lp, ch 5, dc in same lp, ch 2, (dc in same ch as next tr, ch 2, dc in next ch lp, ch 2) across with dc in top of last tr, turn.

Row 8: Ch 1, sc in first st, (ch 2, skip next ch sp, sc in next st) across, turn.

Row 9: Ch 1, sc in first st, shell in next ch sp, (sc in next ch sp, shell in next ch sp) across to last ch sp, skip next ch sp, sc in last st. Fasten off.

Weave ribbon through row 7; tack ends to back.

Sew Edging in place across one end of towel.

OFF-WHITE EDGING

Row 1: For **foundation,** *ch 5, tr in fifth ch from hook; repeat from * number of times needed to fit across towel, **do not turn.**

Row 2: Ch 5, dc around post of next tr, ch 2, (dc in same ch as next tr, ch 2, dc around post of next tr, ch 2) across with dc in top of last tr, turn.

Row 3: Ch 1, sc in first st, *ch 2, **3-dc cl** *(see Special Stitches)* in next dc, ch 2, sc in next dc; repeat from * across, turn.

Row 4: Ch 2, dc in same st *(counts as first cl),* ch 2, sc in next cl, ch 2, (3-dc cl in next sc, ch 2, sc in next cl, ch 2) across with **2-dc cl** *(see Special Stitches)* in last sc, turn.

Row 5: Ch 1, sc in first cl, (ch 2, 3-dc cl in next sc, ch 2, sc in next cl) across, turn.

Row 6: *Ch 3, (sl st, ch 3, sl st) in next cl, ch 3, sl st in next sc; repeat from * across, **do not turn.** Fasten off.

Row 7: Working on opposite side of foundation, join with sc in first ch of first ch lp, (ch 3, sc in same lp) 3 times, *sc in next ch lp, (ch 3, sc in same lp) 3 times; repeat from * across to last ch lp, sc in next ch lp, (ch 3, sc in same lp) 2 times, ch 3, sc in last ch of same lp. Fasten off.

Weave ribbon through row 2; tack ends to back.

Sew edging in place across one end of towel. ✿

Wild Rose Doily

DESIGNED BY CAROL ALEXANDER & BRENDA STRATTON
FOR CROCHET TRENDS & TRADITIONS

This simple, yet elegant doily is an irresistible table topper. It's equally as stunning framed as a wall grouping of heirloom photos. However you use it, this doily will be enjoyed by generations.

FINISHED SIZE: 9" across.

MATERIALS: Size 10 crochet cotton thread — 50 yds. each white and rose, 30 yds. shaded rose (variegated) and 15 yds. green; No. 7 steel hook or hook size needed to obtain gauge.

GAUGE: Center flower is 1½" across.

BASIC STITCHES: Ch, sl st, sc, dc.

SPECIAL STITCHES: For **small picot,** ch 2, sc around post of last dc made.

For **large picot,** ch 3, sc around post of last dc made.

DOILY

Rnd 1: With rose, ch 6, sl st in first ch to form ring, ch 1, 16 sc in ring, join with sl st in first sc. *(16 sc made)*

Rnd 2: Ch 7 *(counts as first dc and ch-4),* skip next st, (dc in next st, ch 4, skip next st) around, join with sl st in third ch of ch-7. Fasten off.

Rnd 3: Join white with sl st in any ch-4 sp, ch 3, 3 dc in same sp, ch 10, (4 dc in next ch-4 sp, ch 10) around, join with sl st in top of ch-3.

Rnd 4: Sl st in next st, ch 1, sc in sp between second and third dc of same 4-dc group, (7 dc, ch 5, 7 dc) in next ch-10 sp, *sc in sp between second and third dc of next 4-dc group, (7 dc, ch 5, 7 dc) in next ch-10 sp; repeat from * around, join with sl st in first sc. Fasten off.

Rnd 5: For **leaves,** working in front of last 2 rnds in dc of rnd 2, join green with sl st in any st, ch 3, 2 dc in same st, **large picot** *(see Special Stitches),* (dc, ch 3, sl st) in same st, ch 2, (sl st, ch 3, 2 dc, large picot, dc, ch 3, sl st, ch 2) in each dc around, join with sl st in first ch of ch-3. Fasten off.

Rnd 6: For **flowers,** working in front of leaves around post of dc on rnd 2, join rose with sc around any dc, ch 1, 3 dc around same st, **small picot** *(see Special Stitches)* (2 dc, ch 1, sc) around post of same st, (sc, ch 1, 3 dc, small picot, 2 dc, ch 1, sc) around post of each st around, join with sl st in first sc. Fasten off.

Rnd 7: Join variegated with sc in center ch of any ch-5 on rnd 4, ch 15, (sc in center ch of next ch-5, ch 15) around, join.

Rnd 8: Ch 1, sc in first st, ch 7, sc in next ch sp, ch 7, (sc in same ch sp, ch 7) 2 times, *sc in next st, ch 7, sc in next ch sp, ch 7, (sc in same ch sp, ch 7) 2 times; repeat from * around, join.

Rnds 9-10: Sl st in next 3 chs of next ch-7, ch 1, sc in same ch sp, ch 7, (sc in next ch sp, ch 7) around, join. At end of last rnd, fasten off.

Rnd 11: Join white with sc in first ch sp, ch 11, sc in next ch sp, ch 5, (sc in next ch sp, ch 11, sc in next ch sp, ch 5) around to last 2 ch sps, sc in next ch sp, ch 11, sc in next ch sp, ch 2; to **join,** dc in first sc.

Rnd 12: Ch 1, sc around joining dc, (7 dc, ch 5, 7 dc) in next ch-11 sp, *sc in next ch-5 sp, (7 dc, ch 5, 7 dc) in next ch-11 sp; repeat from * around, join. Fasten off.

Rnd 13: Join pink with sc in any ch sp, 4 sc in same sp, sc in next 7 sts, ch 8, sl st in last sc worked, skip next sc, sc in next 7 sc, *5 sc in next ch sp, sc in next 7 sts, ch 8, sl st in last sc worked, skip next sc, sc in next 7 sts; repeat from * around, join.

Rnd 14: Ch 1, sc in first 2 sts, (*3 sc in next st, sc in next 9 sts, 12 sc in next ch lp, sl st in base of same lp*, sc in next 9 sts) around to last 17 sts; repeat between **, sc in last 7 sts, join. Fasten off. ✿

Colorful Carryall

DESIGNED BY DELORES SPAGNUOLO

You have a case for makeup and a case for money and credit cards. Now you can have a case for crochet hooks, too. This handy holder is made with the star stitch and lots of cheery colors and is big enough to keep all your crochet hooks in order.

FINISHED SIZE: 6" x 7".

MATERIALS: Worsted yarn — 2 oz. white, small amount each red, orange, yellow, lt. green, dk. green, lt. blue, dk. blue, purple and burgundy; polyester fiberfill; tapestry needle; F hook or hook size needed to obtain gauge.

GAUGE: 2 star sts =1"; 3 star st rows = 2".

BASIC STITCHES: Ch, sl st, sc, hdc.

SPECIAL STITCHES: For **beginning star st (beg star st),** ch 3, insert hook in second ch from hook, yo, draw lp through, insert hook in next ch, yo, draw lp through, (insert hook in next st, yo, draw lp through) 2 times, yo, draw through all 5 lps on hook; for **eye,** ch 1.

For **star st** *(see illustration),* insert hook in **eye,** yo, draw lp through, insert hook in same ch or st as last lp of last star st, yo, draw lp through, (insert hook in next ch or st, yo, draw lp through) 2 times, yo, draw through all 5 lps on hook; for **eye,** ch 1.

**Star Stitch
Illustration**

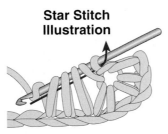

OUTSIDE CASE

Row 1: With burgundy, ch 47, insert hook in second ch from hook, yo, draw lp through, insert hook in next ch, yo, draw lp through, skip next ch, (insert hook in next ch, yo, draw lp through) 2 times, yo, draw through all 5 lps on hook; for **eye,** ch 1; **star st** *(see Special Stitches)* across to last ch, hdc in last ch, turn. *(21 star sts made)*

Row 2: Ch 1, sc in first st, sc in next eye, 2 sc in each eye across, sc in last st changing to purple *(see page 159)* in last st made, turn. *(43 sc)*

Row 3: Beg star st *(see Special Stitches),* star st across to last st, hdc in last st, turn.

Rows 4-17: Following color sequence of dk. blue, lt. blue, dk. green, lt. green, yellow, orange and red, repeat rows 2 and 3 alternately.

Row 18: Repeat row 2, changing to white.

Rnd 19: Working around outer edge, ch 1, sc in each st across, 3 sc in end of each star st across; working on opposite side of starting ch, sc in each ch across, 3 sc in end of each star st across, join with sl st in first sc.

Rnd 20: Working this rnd from to left to right in **front lps** only, ch 1, **reverse sc** *(see page 159)* in each st around, join. Fasten off.

INSIDE CASE

Row 1: With white, ch 25, hdc in third ch from hook, hdc in each ch across, turn. *(24 hdc made)*

Rows 2-12: Ch 2, hdc in next 6 sts, *hdc **front post (fp,** see page 159) around next st, hdc back post **(bp)** around next st; repeat from * 4 more times, hdc in last 7 sts, turn.

Rows 13-14: Ch 2, hdc in each st across, turn.

Rows 15-25: Repeat row 2.

Rnd 26: Working around outer edge, ch 1, sc in each st across, evenly space 43 sc across ends of rows; working on opposite side of starting ch, sc in each ch across, evenly space 43 sc across ends of rows, join.

Holding Inside and Outside Case pieces wrong sides together, working through **back lps** of last rnd on Inside Case and rnd 19 on Outside Case, with white, easing to fit, sl st together.

BUTTON (make 3)

Note: Do not join or turn unless otherwise stated. Mark first st of each rnd.

Rnd 1: With white, ch 2, 5 sc in second ch from hook. *(5 sc made)*

Rnd 2: 2 sc in each st around. *(10)*

Rnd 3: (Sc next 2 sts tog) around, join with sl st in first sc. Leaving 8" for sewing, fasten off.

Stuff; sew opening closed.

Sew Buttons to seam above yellow, dk. green, and dk. blue star st rows on one end of Case.

For **buttonhole lp chain,** with white, ch 50, sl st in second ch from hook, sl st in each ch across. Fasten off.

Sew buttonhole lp chain to opposite side of Case making three buttonhole loops *(see photo).* ✿

Baby Nightcap

DESIGNED BY JANE PEARSON

One of life's most pleasing sights is a little baby taking a sweet nap. It's heartwarming to watch a sleeping newborn open and close her tiny hands, wiggle her pink toes and take small sighing breaths. This cute nightcap makes every naptime cozy.

FINISHED SIZE: Adjusts to fit average newborn's head.

MATERIALS: Sport yarn — 1½ oz. pink and ½ oz. white; 1" white pom-pom; white sewing thread and needle; F hook or hook size needed to obtain gauge.

GAUGE: Rnds 1-3 = 2¾" across.

BASIC STITCHES: Ch, sl st, sc, dc.

CAP

Rnd 1: With pink, ch 4, sl st in first ch to form ring, ch 3, 11 dc in ring, join with sl st in top of ch-3. *(12 dc made)*

Rnds 2-3: Ch 3, dc in same st, 2 dc in each st around, join. *(24, 48)*

Rnd 4: Ch 1, sc in first st, ch 2, (sc in next st, ch 2) around, join with sl st in first sc. *(48 ch-2 sps)*

Rnds 5-14: Sl st in first ch-2 sp, ch 1, sc in same sp, ch 2, (sc in next ch-2 sp, ch 2) around, join.

Rnd 15: Sl st in first ch-2 sp, ch 1, 2 sc in same sp, sc in each of next 3 ch-2 sps, (2 sc in next ch-2 sp, sc in each of next 3 ch-2 sps) around, join. *(60 sc)*

Rnd 16: Working this rnd in **back lps** only, ch 3, dc in each st around, join with sl st in top of ch-3.

Rnd 17: Ch 3, dc in each st around, join. Fasten off.

Rnd 18: Join white with sc in first st, ch 4, (sc in next st, ch 4) around, join with sl st in first sc. Fasten off.

Rnd 19: Working in **remaining lps** of rnd 15, repeat rnd 18.

For **tie,** with white, ch 80. Fasten off. Weave through every other st on rnd 17, pull ends even to fit around head, tie ends into a bow. Sew pom-pom to center of rnd 1. ✿

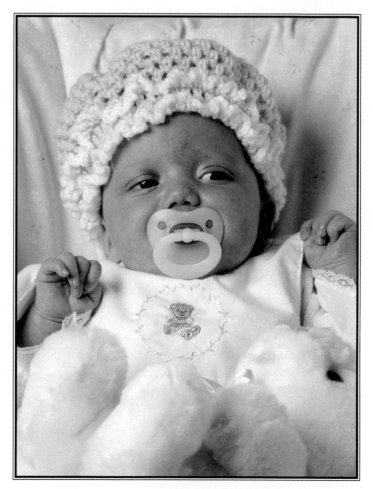

Chapter
Six

119 Striped Wave Afghan
120 Glass Slippers
123 Toe Cozies
125 Doily Hat & Doily
127 Quick Stitch Stocking
128 Playtime Puppets
131 Puff Stitch Pillow
133 Homespun Hat & Scarf
134 Dolly Backpack
136 Sports Carrier

6

Frigg was the goddess of marriage.
She and husband, Odin, watched over
the world. Her day was called Frigedaeg.

Striped Wave Afghan

Designed by Darla Sims

There have been many times over the generations when a need to show our patriotism has been not just a celebratory need, but also an emotional one. Use the red, white and blue colors of our flag to show just how proud you are to be an American.

FINISHED SIZE: 46" x 53".

MATERIALS: Worsted yarn — 15 oz. off-white, 9 oz. each blue and red; I hook or hook size needed to obtain gauge.

GAUGES: 3 dc = 1"; 8 pattern rows = 5".

STITCHES USED: Ch, sl st, sc, dc.

SPECIAL STITCH: For **long double crochet (ldc),** working over next ch sp, yo, insert hook in next st on row before last, yo, draw up long lp, (yo, draw through 2 lps on hook) 2 times.

AFGHAN

Row 1: With off-white, ch 123, dc in fourth ch from hook, dc in next ch, ch 3, skip next 3 chs, (dc in next 5 chs, ch 3, skip next 3 chs) across to last 3 chs, dc in last 3 chs, turn. Fasten off. *(76 dc, 15 ch-3 sps made)*

Row 2: Join blue with sl st in first st, ch 3 *(counts as first dc),* dc in next 2 sts, 3 ldc *(see Special Stitch)* in center ch of next 3 skipped chs on starting ch, (dc in next 5 sts, 3 ldc in center ch of next 3 skipped chs on starting ch) across to last 3 sts on this row, dc in last 3 sts, turn.

Row 3: Ch 3, dc in next 6 sts, ch 3, skip next 3 sts, (dc in next 5 sts, ch 3, skip next 3 sts) across to last 7 sts, dc in last 7 sts, turn. Fasten off. *(79 dc, 14 ch-3 sps)*

Row 4: Join off-white with sl st in first st, ch 3, dc in next 6 sts, 3 ldc in center st of next 3 skipped sts on row before last, (dc in next 5 sts on last row, 3 ldc in center st of next 3 skipped sts on row before last) across to last 7 sts on this row, dc in last 7 sts, turn. *(121 sts)*

Row 5: Ch 3, dc in next 2 sts, ch 3, skip next 3 sts, (dc in next 5 sts, ch 3, skip next 3 sts) across to last 3 sts, dc in last 3 sts, turn. Fasten off. *(76 dc, 15 ch-3 sps)*

Rows 6-7: With red, repeat rows 2 and 3.

Rows 8-9: Repeat rows 4 and 5.

Rows 10-84: Repeat rows 2-9 consecutively, ending with row 4.

Rnd 85: Working in rnds around outer edge, ch 1, 3 sc in first st, sc in each st across to last st, 3 sc in last st; working in ends of rows, sc in first row, 2 sc in each row across; working in starting ch on opposite side of row 1, 3 sc in first ch, sc in each ch across to last ch, 3 sc in last ch, 2 sc in each row across to last row, sc in last row, join with sl st in first sc. Fasten off.

Rnd 86: Join red with sl st in any st, ch 3, dc in each st around with 3 dc in each center corner st, join with sl st in top of ch-3. Fasten off.

Rnd 87: With off-white, repeat rnd 86.

Rnd 88: With blue, repeat rnd 86. **Do not fasten off.**

Rnd 89: Sl st in each st around, join with sl st in joining sl st of last rnd. Fasten off. ✿

Glass Slippers

DESIGNED BY JO ANN MAXWELL

If your fairy tale involves more happily ever after than dancing with royalty at formal balls, you'll appreciate these glass slippers. Even your fairy godmother will tell you these bright beauties are just the thing for a backyard picnic or barbecue.

FINISHED SIZE: Each fits 3" diameter x 6" tall glass.

MATERIALS FOR ALL FOUR: Size 10 crochet cotton thread — 130 yds. each peach, pink, lt. green and yellow, small amount each med. purple, dk. purple, white and dk. green; 3 gold round seed beads; 10 flat assorted ½" buttons; peach sewing thread; sewing needle; craft glue or hot glue gun; No 5 steel hook or hook size needed to obtain gauge.

GAUGE: 8 sts = 1"; 11 hdc rows = 2".

BASIC STITCHES: Ch, sc, hdc, dc, tr.

SPECIAL STITCH: For **picot,** ch 2, sl st in top of last st made.

YELLOW SLIPPER

Rnd 1: With yellow, ch 4, sl st in first ch to form ring, ch 3, 19 dc in ring, join with sl st in top of ch-3. *(20 dc made)*

Rnds 2-3: Ch 3, dc in same st, dc in next st, (2 dc in next st, dc in next st) around, join. *(30, 45)*

Rnd 4: Ch 3, dc in same st, (dc in next st, 2 dc in next st) around, join. *(68)*

Rnd 5: Working this rnd in **back lps** only, ch 2, hdc in each st around, join with sl st in top of ch-2.

Rnds 6-35: Ch 2, hdc in each st around, join.

Rnd 36: Ch 1, sc in each st around, join with sl st in first sc. Fasten off.

Rnd 37: With side of Slipper facing you, working this rnd in **back lps** only, join pink with sc in any st, ch 5, skip next 3 sts, (sc in next st, ch 5, skip next 3 sts) around, join (17 ch sps).

Rnd 38: Ch 1, sc in each of next 2 chs, (sc, ch 4, sc) in next ch, sc in each of next 2 chs, *skip next sc, sc in next 2 chs, (sc, ch 4, sc) in next ch, sc in next 2 chs; repeat from * around, join. Fasten off.

PINK SLIPPER

Rnds 1-36: With pink, work same rnds of Yellow Slipper.

Yellow Pansy

Rnd 1: With med. purple, ch 4, sl st in first ch to form ring, ch 1, (sc in ring, ch 2) 5 times, join with sl st in first sc. Fasten off. *(5 sc, 5 ch sps made)*

Rnd 2: Join yellow with sc in any st, ch 1, *(hdc, ch 1, dc, ch 1) in next ch sp, (tr, ch 1) 5 times in same sp, (dc, ch 1, hdc) in same sp; repeat from *, ch 1, [sc in next st, (hdc, 5 dc, hdc) in next ch sp]; repeat between [ ] 2 more times, join. Fasten off. *(5 petals)*

Row 3: Join white with sl st in first sc, (ch 3, sc in next ch sp) 8 times, (sc in next ch sp, ch 3) 8 times, sl st in next sc leaving remaining sts unworked. Fasten off.

Purple Pansy

With dk. purple for rnd 1 and med. purple for rnd 2, repeat same rnds of Yellow Pansy.

Leaf (make 3)

With lt. green, ch 9, sc in second ch from hook, hdc in next ch, dc in next 5 chs, (dc, ch 1, sl st) in last ch. Fasten off.

Glue Pansies and Leaves to Slipper *(see photo).*

LT. GREEN SLIPPER

Rnds 1-36: With lt. green, work same rnds of Yellow Slipper.

Flower (make 1 pink, 1 yellow, 1 med. purple)

Ch 4, sl st in first ch to form ring, (ch 3, dc in ring, ch 3, sl st in ring) 5 times, ch 3, dc in ring, ch 3, join with sl st in first sl st. Fasten off.

Leaves and Stem (make 3)

With dk. green, ch 11; for **Leaf,** dc in third ch from hook, **picot** *(see Special Stitch),* ch 2, sl st in same ch as last dc made, ch 6, sl st in second ch from hook, sl st in next 4 chs; for **Leaf,** ch 2, (dc, picot, ch 2, sl st) in last sl st made, sl st in remaining chs across ch-11. Fasten off.

Glue Flowers, Leaves and Stems diagonally over Glass Slipper. Glue one bead to center of each Flower.

PEACH SLIPPER

Rnds 1-36: With peach, work same rnds of Yellow Slipper.

Sew buttons evenly spaced around rnds 31-33 of Slipper. ✿

Toe Cozies

DESIGNED BY DIANE SIMPSON

This little piggy went to market, this little piggy stayed home, snug and warm with his new toe cozies! Protect your loved ones' tootsies from chilly floors with these fun-to-make slippers. They work up quickly with two strands of cotton yarn held together.

LADY'S TOE COZIES

FINISHED SIZE: Instructions given are for ladies 9" sole. Changes for 9½" and 10" are in [ ].

MATERIALS: 4-ply 100% cotton — 10 [10½, 11] ozs. fuchsia; 11" square piece batting; tapestry needle; H hook or hook size needed to obtain gauge.

GAUGE: 5 sc = 2"; 4 sc rows = 1½".

BASIC STITCH: Ch, sl st, sc.

SPECIAL STITCH: For **cluster (cl),** yo, insert hook in next st, yo, draw lp through, yo, draw through 2 lps on hook, yo, insert hook in same st, yo, draw lp through, yo, draw through 2 lps on hook, yo, draw through all 3 lps on hook.

NOTE: Use 2 strands same color yarn held together throughout.

SLIPPER (make 2)

Sole (make 2)

Row 1: Starting at **heel,** with fuchsia, ch 7, sc in second ch from hook, sc in each ch across, turn. *(6 sc made)*

Row 2: Ch 1, 2 sc in first st, sc in each st across with 2 sc in last st, turn. *(8)*

Rows 3-11 [3-12, 3-13]: Ch 1, sc in each st across, turn.

Row 12 [13, 14]: Ch 1, 2 sc in first st, sc in each st across, turn. *(9)*

Rows 13-17 [14-18, 15-20]: Repeat row 3.

Row 18 [19, 21]: Ch 1, sc in each st across with sc last 2 sts tog, turn. *(8)*

Row 19 [20, 22]: Repeat row 3.

Row 20 [21, 23]: Repeat row 18 [19, 21]. *(7)*

Rows 21-22 [22-23, 24-25]: Repeat row 3.

Rows 23-24 [24-25, 26-27]: Ch 1, sc first 2 sts tog, sc in each st across with sc last 2 sts tog, turn. Fasten off. *(5, 3)*

Using sole as pattern, cut piece from batting.

Holding 2 sole pieces wrong sides together with batting between, join with sc in any st, sc in each st and in end of each row around with 2 sc in each corner st, join with sl st in first sc. Fasten off.

Top

Row 1: With fuchsia, ch 12, 2 sc in second ch from hook, sc in next 9 chs, 2 sc in last ch, turn. *(13 sc made)*

Row 2: Ch 1, sc in first st, *cl *(see Special Stitch)* in next st, sc in next st; repeat from * across, turn. *(7 sc, 6 cls)*

Row 3: Ch 1, 2 sc in first st, sc in each st across with 2 sc in last st, turn. *(15)*

Row 4: Repeat row 2.

Row 5: Ch 1, sc in each st across, turn.

Row 6: Repeat row 2.

Row 7: Repeat row 5:

Row 8: Ch 1, sc in first 2 sts, (cl in next st, sc in next st) across to last st, sc in last st, turn. *(9 sc, 6 cls)*

Row 9: Repeat row 5.

Row 10: Repeat row 2. *(8 sc, 7 cls)*

Rows 11-12 [11-13, 11-13]: Repeat rows 5 and 8 alternately, ending with row 8 [5, 5]. For **9" sole** only, fasten off.

[Row 14, 14]: Repeat row 2. Fasten off.

Matching ends of row 1 on Top to ends of row 12 [11, 13] on Sole, sew Top around toe and side of Sole.

MAN'S TOE COZIES

SIZE: Instructions given are for man's 9" Sole. Changes for 10" and 11"are in [ ].

continued on page 126

Doily Hat & Doily

DESIGNED BY CAROL ALEXANDER

Here are two decorative accents in one quick-and-easy doily. This set is perfect for an elegant Victorian boudoir or a young girl's room full of frills and lace. These would also make splendid birthday or housewarming gifts.

FINISHED SIZES: Doily is 10" across. Hat is 10" across.

MATERIALS FOR BOTH: 300 yds. aqua size 10 crochet cotton thread; 18" white ⅝" wire-edged ribbon; small 16" floral garland; 4" Styrofoam® ball; liquid fabric stiffener; plastic wrap; rust proof pins; blocking board or Styrofoam®; craft glue or hot glue gun; No. 0 steel hook or hook size needed to obtain gauge.

GAUGE: With **2 strands of thread held together,** rnds 1-5 of Doily and Hat = 2" across.

BASIC STITCHES: Ch, sl st, sc, hdc, dc.

SPECIAL STITCHES: For **beginning cluster (beg cl),** ch 4, *yo 2 times, insert hook in same sp, yo, draw lp through, (yo, draw through 2 lps on hook) 2 times; repeat from *, yo, draw through all 3 lps on hook.

For **cluster (cl),** yo 2 times, insert hook in next ch sp, yo, draw lp through, (yo, draw through 2 lps on hook) 2 times, *yo 2 times, insert hook in same sp, yo, draw lp through, (yo, draw through 2 lps on hook) 2 times; repeat from *, yo, draw through all 4 lps on hook.

NOTE: Hold 2 strands of thread together throughout.

DOILY

Rnd 1: Ch 4, sl st in first ch to form ring, ch 1, 9 sc in ring, join with sl st in first sc. *(9 sc made)*

Rnd 2: Ch 1, 2 sc in each st around, join. *(18)*

Rnd 3: Ch 1, sc in first st, ch 3, skip next 2 sts, (sc in next st, ch 3, skip next 2 sts) around, join. *(6 sc, 6 ch-3 sps)*

Rnd 4: Sl st in first ch sp, ch 1, sc in same sp, ch 3, (sc in next ch sp, ch 3) around, join.

Rnd 5: Sl st in first ch sp, ch 2 *(counts as first hdc),* 4 hdc in same sp, 5 hdc in each ch sp around, join with sl st in top of ch-2. *(30 hdc)*

Rnd 6: Ch 1, sc in first st, ch 3, skip next st, (sc in next st, ch 3, skip next st) around, join with sl st in first sc.

Rnd 7: Repeat rnd 4.

Rnd 8: Sl st in first ch sp, ch 2, 3 hdc in same sp, 4 hdc in each ch sp around, join with sl st in top of ch-2.

Rnd 9: Repeat rnd 6.

Rnd 10: Repeat rnd 4.

Double Crochet Front Strands

Rnd 11: Sl st in first ch sp, ch 3 *(counts as first dc),* (2 dc, ch 3, dc) in same sp, ch 4, dc around front 2 strands of last dc made *(see illustration),* ch 3, 3 dc in same ch sp, sc in next ch sp, *(3 dc, ch 3, dc) in next ch sp, ch 4, dc around front 2 strands of last dc made, ch 3, 3 dc in same ch sp, sc in next ch sp; repeat from * around, join with sl st in top of ch-3.

Rnd 12: Sl st in next 2 sts, sl st in next ch sp, **beg cl** *(see Special Stitches),* (ch 4, **cl**—*see Special Stitch*es in next ch sp) 2 times, *cl in next ch sp, (ch 4, cl in next ch sp) 2 times; repeat from * around, join with sl st in top of beg cl.

Rnd 13: Sl st in first ch sp, ch 1, sc in same sp, ch 3, sc in next cl, ch 3, sc in next ch sp, ch 3, sc in sp between next 2 cls, ch 3, (sc in next ch sp, ch 3, sc in next cl, ch 3, sc in next ch sp, ch 3, sc in sp between next 2 cls, ch 3) around, join with sl st in first sc.

Rnd 14: Repeat rnd 4.

Rnd 15: Sl st in first ch sp, ch 3, (dc, ch 2, 2 dc) in same sp, sc in next ch sp, *(2 dc, ch 2, 2 dc) in next ch sp, sc in next ch sp) around, join with sl st in top of ch-3.

Rnd 16: Sl st in next st, sl st in next ch sp, ch 1, (sc, ch 3, sc) in same sp, ch 3, sc in next sc, ch 3, *(sc, ch 3, sc) in next ch sp, ch 3, sc in next sc, ch 3; repeat from * around, join with sl st in first sc. Fasten off.

HAT
Work same as Doily.

Assembly
1: Cut foam ball in half. Wrap one half in plastic wrap. Apply fabric stiffener to Hat according to manufacturer's instructions. Pin to plastic covered blocking board centered over foam piece. Stretch gently until base of rnd 11 is at bottom edge of foam; pin in place. Stretch remainder of Hat evenly around so Hat measures 10" across. Let dry.

2: Glue garland around rnd 10.

3: Tie ribbon into a bow; cut ends at an angle. Remove one flower from garland. Glue bow to garland where flower was removed. Glue flower to center of bow. ❁

Toe Cozies
continued from page 123

MATERIALS: 4-ply 100% cotton — 6 [7, 8] ozs. gold, 4 [5, 6] ozs. brown; tapestry needle; H hook or hook size needed to obtain gauge.

GAUGE: 5 sc = 2"; 4 sc rows = 1½".

BASIC STITCH: Ch, sl st, sc, hdc, dc.

NOTE: Use 2 strands same color yarn held together throughout.

SLIPPER (make 2)
Sole (make 1 brown and 1 gold)
Rows 1-11 [1-12, 1-13]: Work same rows of Ladies Sole on page 123.

Rows 12-14 [13-15, 14-16]: Repeat row 12 [13, 14] of Ladies Sole, ending with *(11 sts)* in last row.

Rows 15-17 [16-20, 17-22]: Ch 1, sc in each st across, turn.

Rows 18-24 [21-27, 23-29]: Repeat rows 18-24 [19-25, 21-27] of Ladies Sole.

Using Sole as pattern, cut piece from batting.

Holding one brown Sole piece and one gold Sole piece wrong sides together with batting between, join brown with sc in any st, sc in each st and in end of each row around with 2 sc in each corner st, join with sl st in first sc. Fasten off.

Top
Row 1: With gold, ch 25, sc second and third chs from hook tog, sc in each ch across to last 2 chs, sc last 2 chs tog, turn (22).

[Row 2, 2-3]: For **10" and 11" sole** only, ch 1, sc in each st across, turn.

Row 2 [3, 4]: For **all sizes,** ch 2, dc in next st, hdc in next st, sc in each st across to last 3 sts, hdc in next st, dc last 2 sts tog, turn. *(20)*

Row 3 [4, 5]: Ch 1, sc in each st across leaving last st unworked, turn. *(19)*

Row 4 [5, 6]: Ch 1, sc in each st across, turn.

Rows 5-10 [6-11, 7-12]: Repeat rows 2 and 4 [3 and 5, 4 and 6] alternately, ending with *(13 sts)* in last row.

Rows 11-13 [12-14, 13-15]: Ch 1, sc first 2 sts tog, sc in each st across to last 2 sts, sc last 2 sts tog, turn. At end of last row, fasten off. *(11, 9, 7)*

Matching ends of row 1 on Top to sts in joining at ends of row 8 [9, 10] on Sole, with Top facing you, working through both thicknesses, join brown with sc in first st, sc in each st across to opposite end of row 1 on Top. Fasten off.

HEEL
Row 1: With gold Sole facing you, working in joining around heel of Sole, join gold with sc around post of first unworked st, sc **front post (fp,** *see page 159)* around each unworked st across, turn. *(20) [22, 24]*

Row 2: Ch 1, sc in each st across, turn.

Rows 3-7: Ch 1, sc first 2 sts tog, sc in each st across to last 2 sts, sc last 2 sts tog, turn, ending with *(10) [12, 14] sc* in last row.

Row 8: Ch 1, (sc next 2 sts tog) 2 times, sc in next 4 sts, (sc next 2 sts tog) 2 times. Fasten off. *(6) [8, 10]*

Tack ends of row 1 on heel to ends of row 1 on Top. ❁

Quick-Stitch Stocking

DESIGNED BY SANDRA MILLER MAXFIELD

This diminutive stocking fills the bill for yuletide gifts for coworkers, teachers and classmates. Spread holiday cheer by filling them with candy canes and other small treats for smiles all around. They make cute ornaments and stocking stuffers too.

SIZE: 3¾" x 3¾" not including hanging loop.

MATERIALS: Worsted yarn — small amount each red and white; 8" piece strung red sequin trim; craft glue or hot glue gun; H hook or hook size needed to obtain gauge.

GAUGE: 7 hdc sts = 2"; 5 hdc rows = 2".

BASIC STITCHES: Ch, sl st, sc, hdc.

STOCKING SIDE (make 2)

Row 1: Starting at **bottom,** with red, ch 14, hdc in third ch from hook, hdc in each ch across, turn. *(13 hdc made)*

Rows 2-4: Ch 2, hdc in each st across, turn.

Row 5: Ch 2, hdc in next 7 sts leaving remaining sts unworked, turn. *(8)*

Rows 6-7: Ch 2, hdc in each st across, turn.

Row 8: Ch 2, hdc in same st, hdc in each st across with 2 hdc in last st, turn. *(10)*

Row 9: Ch 2, hdc in each st across. Fasten off.

With red, sew sides and bottom together leaving top open.

Trim

Row 1: With white; for **hanging loop,** ch 9, sl st in first ch to form ring, ch 24, sc in second ch from hook, sc in each ch across, turn. *(23 sc made)*

Row 2: Ch 1, sc in first st, (ch 3, sl st in third ch from hook, skip next st, sc in next st) across. Fasten off.

Glue row 1 of Trim around top of Stocking placing hanging loop at back *(see photo)*. Glue sequins around row 1 of Trim. ✿

Playtime Puppets

DESIGNED BY ESTELLA WHITFORD

Children can make rainy-day fun with these playtime puppets and a cardboard box they can cut, tape and shape into a stage. Imagine the adventures awaiting this adorable mouse, bear and dinosaur. For the smaller children, replace button eyes with embroidered eyes.

FINISHED SIZE: Puppets are 10½" tall.

MATERIALS FOR ALL: Worsted yarn — 3½ ozs. each brown, gray, and green, 1 oz. tan, small amount each black, off-white, pink, yellow and blue; 3 pair black 12 mm eyes with washers; polyester fiberfill; three 9" pieces of ½" satin ribbon; heavy duty nylon thread; craft glue or hot glue gun; tapestry needle; H hook or hook size need to obtain gauge.

GAUGE: 7 sc = 2"; 7 sc rows = 2".

BASIC STITCHES: Ch, sc, sl st.

BEAR

Body & Head Side (make 2)

Row 1: With brown, ch 15, sc in second ch from hook, sc in each ch across, turn. *(14 sc made)*

Row 2: Ch 1, 2 sc in first st, sc in each st across with 2 sc in last st, turn. *(16)*

Rows 3-18: Ch 1, sc in each st across, turn.

Rows 19-20: Ch 1, sc first 2 sts tog, sc in each st across with sc last 2 sts tog, turn. *(14, 12)*

Rows 21-22: Repeat row 2. *(14, 16)*

Rows 23-29: Repeat row 3.

Rows 30-33: Repeat row 19, ending with *(8 sts)* in last row. At end of last row, fasten off.

Stomach

Row 1: With tan, ch 9, sc in second ch from hook, sc in each ch across, turn. *(8 sc made)*

Rows 2-3: Repeat row 2 of Body & Head. *(10, 12)*

Rows 4-8: Ch 1, sc in each st across, turn.

Rows 9-10: Repeat row 19 of Body & Head. *(10, 8)* At end of last row, fasten off.

For **front,** center and sew over rows 7-16 on one side of Body & Head.

Paw Side (make 4)

Row 1: With brown, ch 7, sc in second ch from hook, sc in each ch across, turn. *(6 sc made)*

Rows 2-7: Ch 1, sc in each st across, turn.

Rows 8-9: Repeat row 19 of Body & Head. *(4, 2)* At end of last row, fasten off.

Sew one Paw over end of rows 15-20 on each side of each Body & Head piece.

Paw Pad (make 2)

Note: Do not join or turn unless otherwise stated. Mark first st of each rnd.

Rnd 1: With tan, ch 2, 6 sc in second ch from hook. *(6 sc made)*

Rnd 2: 2 sc in each st around, join with sl st in first sc. Fasten off. *(12)*

Sew to front over rows 2-8 of each Paw.

With tan, using French knot *(see page 159)*, embroider 3 **toes** over last row of each Paw.

Muzzle

Rnds 1-2: Repeat same rnds of Paw Pad. *(6, 12)*

Rnd 3: (Sc in next st, 2 sc in next st) around. *(18)*

Rnd 4: (Sc in each of next 2 sts, 2 sc in next st) around. *(24)*

Rnd 5: Sc in each st around. join with sl st in first sc. Fasten off.

Center and sew Muzzle to front over rows 22-29 of Body & Head, stuffing before closing.

With black, using satin stitch and straight stitch *(see page 159)*, embroider **nose and mouth lines** *(see photo)*.

Eye Guard

Row 1: With brown, ch 9, sc in second ch from hook, sc in each ch across, turn. *(8 sc made)*

Rows 2-3: Ch 1, sc in each st across, turn. At end of last row, fasten off.

Attach one pair of eyes over rows 30 and 31 of Body & Head 1" apart. Tack Eye Guard to back side over washers, stuffing lightly before closing.

Ear (make 2 brown, 2 tan)

Row 1: Ch 7, sc in second ch from hook, sc in each ch across, turn. *(6 sc made)*

Row 2: Ch 1, sc in each st across, turn.

Row 3: Ch 1, sc first 2 sts tog, sc in each st across with sc last 2 sts tog, turn. *(4)*

Row 4: Ch 1, sc in first st, sc next 2 sts tog, sc in last st, turn. *(3)*

Row 5: Ch 1, sc next 3 sts tog. Fasten off.

Finishing

1: Holding Body & Head Sides wrong sides together with front facing you, working through both thicknesses, join brown with sc in end of first row, sc in end of each row and in each st around outer edge leaving bottom open for hand.

2: For **Ears,** holding one each color together, working through both thicknesses, sew 2" apart over top of Head.

3: Working around outer edge of one Ear, working through both thicknesses, join brown with sc in end of first row on Ear, sc in end of each row and in each st around. Fasten off. Repeat around opposite Ear.

4: For **hair,** wrap tan around three fingers twelve times, tie separate strand same color yarn around middle of all loops, slip loops off fingers. Cut and trim ends. Tack to top of Head between Ears.

5: Tie one ribbon piece into a bow; tack to front of Body & Head Side below Muzzle.

MOUSE

Body & Head Side (make 2)

With gray, work same as Bear Body & Head Side on page 128.

Stomach

With off-white, work same as Bear Stomach

Paw Side (make 4)

With gray, work same as Bear Paw Side.

With black, using straight stitch, embroider 3 **toenails** over rows 8 and 9 on each front Paw.

Snout

Rnd 1: With gray, ch 2, 6 sc in second ch from hook. *(6 sc made)*

Rnd 2: Sc in each st around.

Rnd 3: (Sc in next st, 2 sc in next st) around. *(9)*

Rnd 4: (Sc in next 2 sts, 2 sc in next st) around. *(12)*

Rnd 5: Sc in each st around.

Rnd 6: (Sc in next 3 sts, 2 sc in next st) around. *(15)*

Rnd 7: (Sc in next 4 sts, 2 sc in next st) around. *(18)*

Rnd 8: Sc in each st around, join with sl st in first sc. Fasten off.

Center and sew Snout over rows 22-28 of Body & Head, stuffing before closing.

For **nose,** with black, repeat rnds 1 and 2 of Snout. At end of last rnd, join with sl st in first sc. Fasten off.

Center and sew to end of Snout.

Eye Guard

With gray, work same as Bear Eye Guard on page 129.

Holding Body & Head Sides wrong sides together with front facing you, working through both thicknesses, join gray with sc in end of first row, sc in end of each row and in each st around outer edge leaving bottom open for hand.

Ear (make 2)

Rnds 1-4: With gray, repeat same rnds of Bear Muzzle, changing to pink *(see page 159)* in last st made of last rnd. *(24)*

Rnd 5: Working this rnd in **back lps** only, sc in each st around.

Rnd 6: (Sc in each of next 2 sts, sc next 2 sts tog) around. *(18)*

Rnd 7: (Sc in next st, sc next 2 sts tog) around. *(12)*

Rnd 8: (Sc next 2 sts tog) around, join with sl st in first sc. Fasten off. Sew opening closed.

Sew Ears to top of Head 2" apart with pink facing you.

Finishing

1: For **whiskers,** cut 6 strands nylon thread each 3" long. Glue 6 whiskers to each side of Head. Let dry.

2: Repeat step 3 of Bear Finishing.

3: For **tail,** with gray, ch 28. Fasten off. Sew over row 10 on back of Body & Head Side.

4: Tie one ribbon piece into a bow; tack to front of Body & Head Side below Muzzle.

DINO

Body & Head Side (make 2)

With green, work same as Bear Body & Head Side on page 128.

Stomach

With yellow, work same as Bear Stomach.

Paw Side (made 4)

With green, work same as Bear Paw Side.

For **toenails,** with black, ch 4, sl st in first ch to form ring, (ch 3, sl st in first ch) 2 times. Fasten off. *(3 toes)*

Sew over last row of Paws. Repeat for opposite Paw.

Muzzle

Rnds 1-3: With green, repeat same rnds of Mouse Snout on page 129.

Rnds 4-7: Sc in each st around. At end of last rnd, join with sl st in first sc. Fasten off.

Center and sew Muzzle over rows 24-29 of Body & Head stuffing before closing.

Mouth

Rnd 1-2: With green, repeat same rnds of Mouse Snout.

Rnds 3-5: Sc in each st around. At end of last rnd, join with sl st in first sc. Fasten off.

Sew Mouth below Muzzle, stuffing before closing.

Tongue

Row 1: With pink, ch 5, sc in second ch from hook, sc in each ch across, turn. *(4 sc made)*

Row 2: Ch 1, sc in each st across, turn.

Row 3: Ch 1, sc in first st, sc next 2 sts tog, sc in last st, turn. *(3)*

Row 4: Ch 1, sc next 3 sts tog. Fasten off. Sew Tongue over top of Mouth.

Eye Guard

With green, work same as Bear Eye Guard.

Finishing

1: Holding Body & Head Sides wrong sides together with front facing you, working through both thicknesses, join green with sc in end of first row, sc in end of each row and in each st around outer edge leaving bottom open for hand.

2: Repeat step 4 of Bear Finishing.

3: With black, using lazy-daisy stitch *(see page 159),* embroider **nostrils** 2" apart over rnd 2 of Muzzle.

4: Tie one ribbon piece into a bow; tack to front of Body & Head Side below Muzzle. ✿

Puff Stitch Pillow

DESIGNED BY ALICE HEIM

Every home can use another accent pillow. Make several of these in understated neutrals, yummy bright colors or pale pastels to cozy up a favorite sofa or easy chair. This pillow is designed to fit a 14" pillow form and includes easy yarn tassels.

FINISHED SIZE: 14" square.

MATERIALS: 6 oz. worsted yarn; 14" square pillow form; tapestry needle; H hook or hook size needed to obtain gauge.

GAUGE: 3 sc sts = 1"; 3 sc rows = 1". 3 dc sts = 1"; 2 dc rows = 1".

BASIC STITCHES: Ch, sl st, sc, dc.

SPECIAL STITCH: For **puff st,** (yo insert hook from right to left around post of next st on row before last, yo, draw through st pulling up long lp) 2 times, yo, pull through 4 lps on hook, yo, pull through 2 lps on hook. Skip next st on last row.

FIRST SIDE

Row 1: Ch 44, sc in second ch from hook, sc in each ch across, turn. *(43 sc made)*

Row 2: Ch 1, sc in each st across, turn.

Row 3: Ch 3, dc in next 2 sts, *****puff st** *(see Special Stitch),* dc in next 3 sts on last row; repeat from * 9 more times, turn. *(10 puff sts)*

Row 4: Ch 3, dc in each st across, turn.

Row 5: Ch 3, (puff st, dc in each of next 3 sts) 10 times, puff st, dc in last st, turn. *(11 puff sts)*

Row 6: Ch 3, dc in each st across, turn.

Rows 7-29: Repeat rows 3-6 consecutively. At end of last row, fasten off.

SECOND SIDE

Row 1: Ch 44, sc in second ch from hook, (dc in next ch, sc in next ch) across, turn. *(43 sts made)*

Row 2: Ch 3, (sc in next dc, dc in next sc) across, turn.

Row 3: Ch 1, sc in first st, (dc in next sc, sc in next dc) across, turn.

continued on page 133

Homespun Hat & Scarf

DESIGNED BY SHIRLEY BROWN

This fuzzy hat and scarf set, featuring interesting nubby yarn, is sure to keep the chill away when winter winds begin to blow. Make it for your favorite teenager or college student, and let her know your warm hugs go with her wherever she goes.

FINISHED SIZES: Hat fits approximately 15"-18" head. Scarf is 6½" x 30".

MATERIALS FOR BOTH: 8 oz. beige multicolor fuzzy boucle yarn; 3" square piece of cardboard; tapestry needle; I hook or hook size needed to obtain gauge.

GAUGE: 13 hdc = 4"; 5 hdc **back lp** rows = 3"; 7 sc **back lp** rows = 2".

BASIC STITCHES: Ch, sl st, sc, hdc.

HAT

Row 1: For **cuff,** ch 30, sc in second ch from hook, sc in each ch across, turn. *(29 sc made)*

Rows 2-52: Working these rows in **back lps** only, ch 1, sc in each st across, turn. At end of last row, matching sts, sl st first and last rows together through **back lps.**

Rnd 53: Working in rnds and in ends of rows, ch 1, sc first 2 rows tog, (sc next 2 rows tog) around, join with sl st in first sc. *(26 sc)*

Rnd 54: For **crown,** working in **both lps,** ch 1, sc in each st around, join.

Rnd 55: Ch 1, sc in first 2 sts, (sc next 2 sts tog, sc in next st) around, join. *(18)*

Rnd 56: Ch 1, sc in each st around, join.

Rnd 57: Ch 1, sc first 2 sts tog, (sc next 2 sts tog) around, join. *(9)*

Rnd 58: Ch 1, sc in first st, (sc next 2 sts tog) around, join. Leaving 6" end for weaving, fasten off.

Weave end through sts of last rnd; pull tight to gather. Secure. Fold Cuff up.

Pom-Pom

Wrap yarn around cardboard 75 times, slide loops off cardboard. Tie separate strand tightly around middle of all loops. Cut loops. Trim.

Tie to top of Hat.

SCARF

Row 1: Ch 20, hdc in second ch from hook, hdc in each ch across, turn. *(19 hdc made)*

Rows 2-50: Working these rows in **back lps** only, ch 1, hdc in each st across, turn. At end of last row, fasten off. ✿

Puff Stitch Pillow

continued from page 131

Repeat rows 2 and 3 alternately until piece is same size as First Side. At end of last row, fasten off.

Hold Sides wrong sides together, working through both thicknesses, easing to fit, sc together inserting pillow form before closing.

Tassel (make 4)

Cut 26 strands of yarn each 4" long. With all strands held together, tie separate strand around center. Fold strands in half, tie separate strand around folded strands 1" from fold. Trim. Hide ends inside Tassel.

Sew one Tassel to each corner of Pillow. ✿

Dolly Backpack

DESIGNED BY MARY S. OTTINGER

For the little girl who won't leave the house without taking her doll along, this backpack carries dolly in style. It's the perfect addition to a gift of a new doll for a birthday or when Mommy and Daddy bring little brother or sister home from the hospital.

FINISHED SIZE: 8" x 13".

MATERIALS: Worsted yarn — 5 oz. desired color; 4 white ⅞" shank buttons; 20" matching ¾" ribbon; matching sewing thread; sewing and tapestry needles; H hook or hook size needed to obtain gauge.

GAUGE: 7 hdc = 2"; 3 hdc rows = 1".

BASIC STITCHES: Ch, sl st, sc, hdc.

BACKPACK

Row 1: Starting at **top front,** ch 28, hdc in third ch from hook, hdc in each ch across, turn. *(27 hdc made)*

Rows 2-25: Ch 2, hdc in each st across, turn.

Rows 26-36: Ch 2, hdc next 2 sts tog, hdc in each st across to last 2 sts, hdc last 2 sts tog, turn, ending with *(5 sts)* in last row.

Row 37: For **crotch,** repeat row 2.

Rows 38-46: For **back,** ch 2, hdc in same st, hdc in each st across to last st, 2 hdc in last st, turn, ending with *(23 sts)* in last row.

Rows 47-48: Ch 5, hdc in third ch from hook, hdc in each of next 2 chs, hdc in each st across, turn, ending with *(31 hdc)* in last row.

Rows 49-57: Repeat row 2. At end of last row. Fasten off.

Trim

Working across one leg opening, join with sc in end of row 27 on left side, sc in end of each row across to row 47; holding front and back wrong sides together, matching rows 48-57 over rows 17-26, with back towards you, working through both thicknesses, sc in end of row 48, sc in end of next 9 rows; working on front only, sc in end of each row across; working in starting ch on opposite side of row 1, 3 sc in first ch, sc in each ch across to last ch, 3 sc in last ch, sc in end of next 16 rows; working through both thicknesses of front and back, sc in end of next 10 rows; working around other leg opening, sc in end of each row around, join with sl st in next sc. Fasten off.

BACK STRAPS

Row 1: With back facing you, ch 30, working in center 5 sts on Trim, join with sc in first st, sc in next 4 sts, ch 31, turn.

Row 2: Sc in second ch from hook, sc in each ch and in each st across, turn. *(65 sc)*

Row 3: Ch 1, sc in first st; for **buttonhole,** ch 3, skip next 3 sts; sc in each st across to last 4 sts; for **buttonhole,** ch 3, skip next 3 sts; sc in last st, turn.

Row 4: Ch 1, sc in first st, 3 sc in next ch sp, sc in each st across to last ch sp, 3 sc in last ch sp, sc in last st. Fasten off.

FRONT STRAP (make 2)

Row 1: Ch 44, hdc in third ch from hook, hdc in each ch across, turn. *(43 hdc made)*

Row 2: Ch 2, hdc in each st across to last 10 sts; for **buttonhole,** ch 3, skip next 3 sts; hdc in each of next 3 sts; for **buttonhole,** ch 3, skip next 3 sts; hdc in last st, turn.

Row 3: Ch 2, 3 hdc in each ch sp and hdc in each st across. Fasten off.

FINISHING

1: With wrong side of front facing you, sew one button to each side of front directly above back.

2: Sew ends of Front Straps without buttonholes to each side of row 1 on wrong side. Sew one button to same end of each Strap.

3: Bring Front Straps over front and crisscross over child's chest, button to buttons above back. Place doll in pack; button Back Straps to buttons on shoulders.

4: Tie ribbon into a bow; sew to center back below Back Straps. ✿

Sports Carrier

DESIGNED BY JENNY KING

This sporty carrier is a handy and fashionable helper for anyone who enjoys camping or spending time at the beach. It's lightweight, colorful and ideal for taking along toiletries, change of clothes and towel when trekking to the bathhouse.

FINISHED SIZE: 20½" long not including Strap.

MATERIALS: 4 oz. variegated 100% cotton sport yarn; F hook or hook size needed to obtain gauge.

GAUGE: 9 sc = 2"; rnds 1 and 2 of Carrier = 1½" across.

BASIC STITCHES: Ch, sl st, sc, dc.

CARRIER

Rnd 1: Ch 4, sl st in first ch to form ring, ch 1, 15 sc in ring, join with sl st in first sc. *(15 sc made)*

Rnd 2: Ch 3 *(counts as first dc),* dc in same st, 2 dc in each st around, join with sl st in top of ch-3. *(30 dc)*

Rnd 3: Ch 1, sc in first st, (ch 5, sc in next st) around; to **join,** ch 2, dc in first sc. *(30 ch sps made)*

Rnds 4-51: Ch 1, sc around joining dc, (ch 5, sc in next ch sp) around, join as before.

Rnd 52: Ch 1, sc around joining dc, ch 5, (sc in next ch sp, ch 5) around, join with sl st in first sc.

Rnd 53: Sl st in first ch sp, ch 1, 5 sc in same sp, 5 sc in each ch sp around, join. Fasten off.

STRAP

Ch to measure 78", 2 sc in second ch from hook, sc in each ch across to last ch, 3 sc in last ch; working on opposite side of ch, sc in each ch across, sc in same ch as first sc, join with sl st in first sc. Fasten off.

Weave Strap through ch sps of rnd 52, bring across back and weave one end through center of rnd 1 and out through one ch sp of rnd 3. Pull Strap so both sides are same length across back of Carrier; tie ends together. ✿

Chapter Seven

139 Bridal Set
142 Puttin' on the Ritz
144 Mini Angels
147 Cool Crochet Poncho
148 Hat Pincushion
151 Li'l Cowpokes
153 Currents Afghan
154 Centerpieces

7

The Roman god, Saturn, ruled over the farmlands, controlling the weather. His day is Saturni dies, Latin for "day of Saturn."

Bridal Set

*Little pieces of finery can be
necessary and sentimental additions
to the splendor of a wedding day.
And after the wedding, these
accessories become family heirlooms.*

HEADPIECE

DESIGNED BY BRENDA STRATTON

FINISHED SIZE: 1⅜" wide not including flowers.

MATERIALS: 100 yds. white/pearl size 10 crochet cotton thread; 22½" *(or length to fit snugly around head)* clear iridescent 7 mm strung beads; 2 sprays of white bridal flowers with leaves and beads; white sewing thread; hook and eye closure; sewing needle; No. 7 steel hook or hook size needed to obtain gauge.

GAUGE: Rnds 1 and 2 = ¾" across.

BASIC STITCHES: Ch, sl st, sc, dc.

SPECIAL STITCHES: For **beginning horizontal cluster (beg hcl),** sc in same ch sp, ch 3, (yo, insert hook from front to back around post of last sc made, yo, draw lp through, yo, draw through 2 lps on hook) 2 times, yo, draw through all 3 lps on hook.

For **horizontal cluster (hcl),** sc in next ch sp, ch 3, (yo, insert hook from front to back around post of last sc made, yo, draw lp through, yo, draw through 2 lps on hook) 2 times, yo, draw through all 3 lps on hook.

HEADPIECE

Rnd 1: Working in sps between even-number of strung beads, join with sc in sp between first 2 beads, sc in same sp, *(ch 1, 2 sc in sp between next 2 beads) across, ch 4*; working on opposite side of beads, 2 sc in sp between first 2 beads; repeat between **, join with sl st in first sc.

Rnd 2: Sl st in next st, sl st in next ch-1 sp, ch 1, **beg hcl** *(see Special Stitches),* **hcl** *(see Special Stitches)* in each ch-1 sp around with 5 sc in each ch-4 sp, join with sl st in first sc of beg hcl.

Rnd 3: Sl st in next ch-3 sp of same hcl, ch 4 *(counts as first dc and ch-1 sp),* dc in same sp, (ch 1, dc in same sp) 2 times, sl st in next ch sp, [*dc in next ch sp, (ch 1, dc in same sp) 3 times, sl st in next ch sp*; repeat between ** across to 5 sc group on next end, sc in next sc, (2 sc in next sc, sc in next sc) 2 times]; repeat between [ ], join with sl st in third ch of ch-4. Fasten off.

Sew hook and eye to ends of Headpiece.

Sew or glue one floral spray about 4" from each end of Headpiece.

Optional: A veil may be attached to Headpiece between floral sprays.

PURSE
DESIGNED BY CAROL ALEXANDER

FINISHED SIZE: 5" tall not including handles.

MATERIALS: 200 yds. white/pearl size 10 crochet cotton thread; 27" white 1/4" satin ribbon; small white wedding floral spray; white sewing thread; sewing and tapestry needles; No. 7 steel hook or hook size needed to obtain gauge.

GAUGE: Rnds 1-3 = 2" across.

BASIC STITCHES: Ch, sl st, sc, hdc, dc.

SPECIAL STITCHES: For **beginning shell (beg shell),** ch 3, 4 dc in same st or sp.

For **shell,** 5 dc in next st or ch sp.

For **beginning V st (beg V st),** ch 4 (counts as first dc and ch-1 sp), dc in same st.

For **V st (V-st),** (dc, ch 1, dc) in next st.

For **picot,** ch 2, sc around post of last dc made.

PURSE

Rnd 1: Ch 4, sl st in first ch to form ring, ch 3 *(counts as first dc),* 15 dc in ring, join with sl st in top of ch-3. *(16 dc made)*

Rnd 2: Ch 3, dc in same st, 2 dc in each st around, join. *(32)*

Rnd 3: Beg V st *(see Special Stitches),* skip next st, ***V st** (see Special Stitches)* in next st, skip next st; repeat from * around, join with sl st in third ch of ch-4. *(16 V sts)*

Rnd 4: Sl st in next ch sp, ch 3, dc in same sp, 2 dc in sp between next 2 dc, (2 dc in next ch sp, 2 dc in sp between next 2 dc) around, join. *(64 dc)*

Rnd 5: Ch 3, dc in next 2 sts, 2 dc in next st, (dc in next 3 sts, 2 dc in next st) around, join. *(80)*

Rnd 6: Repeat rnd 3. *(40 V sts)*

Rnd 7: Sl st in next ch sp, ch 3, dc in same sp, dc in sp between next 2 dc, (2 dc in next ch sp, dc in sp between next 2 dc) around, join. *(120 dc)*

Rnd 8: Ch 3, dc in next 12 sts, dc next 2 sts tog, (dc in next 13 sts, dc next 2 sts tog) around, join. *(112)*

Rnd 9: Beg V st, skip next 3 sts, **shell** *(see Special Stitches)* in next st, skip next 3 sts, (V st in next st, skip next 3 sts, shell in next st, skip next 3 sts) around, join with sl st in third ch of ch-4. *(14 V sts, 14 shells)*

Rnd 10: Sl st in first ch sp, **beg shell** *(see Special Stitches),* V st in third dc of next shell, (shell in ch sp of next V st, V st in third dc of next shell) around, join with sl st in top of ch-3.

Rnd 11: Ch 3, dc in next 4 sts, (*dc in sp between last shell and next V st, dc in next V st, dc in sp between last V st and next shell*, dc in next 5 sts) 13 times; repeat between **, join. *(112 dc)*

Rnd 12: Ch 3, dc in each st around, join.

Rnds 13-23: Repeat rnds 9-12 consecutively, ending with rnd 11.

Rnd 24: Ch 5 *(counts as first dc and ch-2 sp),* skip next 3 sts, (dc in next st, ch 2, skip next 2 sts) around, join with sl st in third ch of ch-5. *(37 dc, 37 ch-2 sps)*

Rnd 25: (Sl st, ch 3, dc) in first ch sp, **picot** *(see Special Stitches),* (dc, ch 3, sl st) in same sp, (sl st, ch 3, dc, picot, dc, ch 3, sl st) in each ch sp around, join with sl st in first sl st. Fasten off.

For **handle (make 2),** ch 100, hdc in third ch from hook, hdc in each ch across. Fasten off.

Sew ends of one handle together on inside of Purse over rnd 22. Repeat with other handle on opposite side.

Starting with ch sp between handles, weave ribbon through ch sps of rnd 24. Pull ends to gather; tie ends into a bow.

Sew floral spray to center front of Purse.

HANDKERCHIEF EDGING
DESIGNED BY BRENDA STRATTON

FINISHED SIZE: Edging is 1" wide.
MATERIALS: 225 yds. white size 10 crochet cotton thread; 11" square white hemmed cotton handkerchief; $2\frac{3}{4}$ yds. lt. blue $\frac{1}{8}$" satin ribbon; four lt. blue $\frac{3}{8}$" satin ribbon roses with leaves; white sewing thread; sewing needle or sewing machine; tapestry needle; No. 7 steel hook or hook size needed to obtain gauge.
GAUGE: 4 dc rows of Foundation = 1".
BASIC STITCHES: Ch, sl st, sc, dc, tr.

FOUNDATION
Row 1: Ch 3, dc in third ch from hook, **do not turn.** *(one dc, 2 chs made)*
Rows 2-176: Ch 2, dc in sp between first ch-2 and next dc, **do not turn.** *(one dc, 2 chs)* At end of last row, turn, **do not fasten off.**

EDGING
Rnd 1: Working in ch-2 sps across Foundation, ch 1, 2 sc in each ch-2 sp across, join with sl st in first sc. Fasten off. Sew ends of Foundation together. *(352 sc made)*
Rnd 2: Working around post of dc sts on opposite side of Foundation, join with sl st around first dc, ch 5 *(counts as first dc and ch-2 sp),* dc around same dc, ch 1, sc around next dc, ch 1, *(dc, ch 2, dc) around next dc, ch 1, sc around next dc, ch 1; repeat from * around, join with sl st in third ch of ch-5. *(88 ch-2 sps)*
Rnd 3: Sl st in first ch-2 sp, ch 1, sc in same sp, *skip next 2 ch-1 sps, tr in next ch-2 sp, (ch 1, tr in same sp) 5 times, skip next 2 ch-1 sps, *sc in next ch-2 sp, skip next 2 ch-1 sps, tr in next ch-2 sp, (ch 1, tr in same sp) 5 times, skip next 2 ch-1 sps; repeat from * around, join with sl st in first sc. Fasten off.

FINISHING
1: Easing around each corner so Edging lays flat, machine or hand sew sts on row 1 of Edging to handkerchief. Sew ends of Edging together.

2: Cut four pieces ribbon each 24" long. Working on each side between corners, weave one piece through Foundation on each side. Pull ends even; tie into a bow at each corner.

3: Sew one ribbon rose to center of each bow.

GARTER
DESIGNED BY BRENDA STRATTON

FINISHED SIZE: $1\frac{1}{2}$" wide.
MATERIALS: 225 yds. white size 10 crochet cotton thread; length of lt. blue $\frac{1}{4}$" satin ribbon to fit around thigh plus 23"; lt. blue $\frac{3}{8}$" satin ribbon rose with leaves; lt. blue sewing thread; sewing needle; No. 7 steel hook or hook size needed to obtain gauge.
GAUGE: One shell and 5 chs = $\frac{3}{4}$"; 4 shell rows = $1\frac{1}{2}$".
BASIC STITCHES: Ch, sl st, sc, dc, tr.
SPECIAL STITCHES: For **shell**, (2 dc, ch 2, 2 dc) in next ch sp.

For **scallop**, tr in next row, (ch 1, tr in same row) 5 times.

GARTER
Row 1: Ch 4, sl st in first ch to from ring, ch 5, **shell** *(see Special Stitches)* in ring, turn. *(one shell, 5 chs made)*
Rows 2-55: Ch 5, shell in ch sp of next shell, turn.
Row 56: Ch 5, sl st in next shell; working in ends of rows, **scallop** *(see Special Stitches)* in ch-5 sp on next row, (sc in next row, scallop in ch-5 sp on next row) across to last row, skip last row, sc in beginning ring of row 1, turn.
Row 57: Ch 1, sl st in first 2 sts, sc in next ch sp, (ch 2, sc in next ch sp) across to last tr of last scallop, sl st in last tr. Fasten off.

FINISHING
Cut length of ribbon long enough to fit around thigh plus an additional 14" for bow. Weave ribbon through ch-5 sps on straight edge of Garter. Gather Garter as desired. Tie ends into a bow.

Tie 9" piece of ribbon into a bow; sew to shell at center of row 27. Sew ribbon rose to center of bow. ✿

Puttin' on the Ritz

DESIGNED BY PRISCILLA COLE

*Even if you're not a ruffles-and-frills type of lady, it's nice to add some
glamour and glitz when you're going out on the town. This dressy, tailored look has plenty
of flair to make your entrance memorable. Set includes bow tie and cummerbund.*

CUMMERBUND

FINISHED SIZE: 3¾" wide.
MATERIALS: 100% cotton worsted yarn — 3 oz. black; interlocking belt buckle; G hook or hook size needed to obtain gauge.
GAUGE: 7 sc and 7 ch lps = 3¾".
BASIC STITCHES: Ch, sl st, sc.

CUMMERBUND

Row 1: Work 11 sc over one half of belt buckle (*see page 159*), turn. (*11 sc made*)

Row 2: Ch 1, sc in first st, (ch 3, skip next st, sc in next st) across, turn. (*6 sc, 5 ch sps*)

Row 3: Ch 1, sc in first st, ch 3, (sc in next ch sp, ch 3) 5 times, sc in last st, turn. (*7 sc, 6 ch sps*)

Row 4: Ch 4, (sc in next ch sp, ch 3) 6 times, sc in last st, turn. (*7 sc, 7 ch sps*)

Row 5: Ch 4, sc in next ch sp, (ch 3, sc in next ch sp) across, turn.

Repeat row 5, ending with odd-numbered row, until Cummerbund measures 2" less than waist measurement while comfortably stretched.

Next 2 Rows: Sl st in first ch sp, ch 1, sc in same sp, (ch 3, sc in next ch sp) across, turn, ending with (*6 sc and 5 ch sps*) in last row.

Last Row: Sl st in first ch sp, ch 1; working over second half of belt buckle, 2 sc in same sp and in each ch sp across. Fasten off.

BOW TIE

FINISHED SIZE: 2" x 4¾".
MATERIALS: Size 10 brilliant crochet cotton — 65 yds. black; clip on bow tie clip; tapestry needle; No. 4 steel hook or hook size needed to obtain gauge.
GAUGE: 8 sc = 1"; 9 sc rows = 1".
BASIC STITCHES: Ch, sl st, sc.

BOW TIE

Side (make 2)

Row 1: Ch 37, sc in second ch from hook, sc in each ch across, turn. (*36 sc made*)

Rows 2-14: Ch 1, sc in each st across, turn. At end of last row, **do not turn.**

Rnd 15: Ch 1; working form left to right, **reverse sc** (*see page 159*) in each st and in end of each row around with 3 reverse sc in each corner, join with sl st in first sc. Fasten off.

CENTER PIECE

Row 1: Ch 17, sc in second ch from hook, sc in each ch across, turn. (*16 sc made*)

Rows 2-4: Ch 1, sc in each st across, turn. At end of last row, **do not turn.**

Rnd 5: Repeat rnd 15 of Side.

Finishing

Sew clip to back of one Side. Holding Side pieces together with clip at back, wrap Center Piece around center and sew ends of rows together in back. ✿

Mini Angels

DESIGNED BY SUE CHILDRESS

*Delicate wings give visual flight to a message of hope and love.
Whether as tree ornaments, package trims or brooches, these messages of peace
are always welcome. Carry an angel on your shoulder by pinning one to your lapel.*

FINISHED SIZE: Large Angel is 4" x 4¾".
Small Angel is 3" x 3¼".

**MATERIALS FOR ONE OF EACH
SIZE:** Size 10 crochet cotton thread — 75
yds. white; 12" metallic cord or satin ribbon;
tapestry needle; No. 8 steel hook or hook size
needed to obtain gauge.

GAUGE: Rnds 1-3 = ¾" across; 4 shell
rows = 1½".

BASIC STITCHES: Ch, sl st,
sc, hdc, dc.

SPECIAL STITCHES: For
shell, (2 dc, ch 2, 2 dc) in next st
or sp.

For **beginning shell (beg shell),** ch
3, (dc, ch 2, 2 dc) in same st or sp.

For **picot,** ch 3, sl st in top of last
st made.

NOTES: Do not join or turn
unless otherwise stated. Mark first
st of each rnd.

Ch-3 at beginning of each row
counts as first dc.

Angels may ruffle until blocked.

LARGE ANGEL

Rnd 1: Starting at **head,** ch 2, 4 sc
in second ch from hook. *(4 sc made)*

Rnds 2-3: 2 sc in each st around.
(8, 16)

Row 4: Working in rows, ch 1,
hdc in same st as last st on rnd 3,
hdc in next st leaving remaining sts
unworked, **turn.** *(2 hdc)*

Row 5: Ch 4, (dc, ch 1, dc) in first st, (ch 1,
dc) 3 times in last st, turn. *(6 dc, 5 ch sps)*

Row 6: Ch 3, 3 dc in each ch sp and dc in
each dc across, turn. *(21 dc)*

Row 7: Ch 3, dc in each st across, turn.

Row 8: Ch 3, dc in same st, 2 dc in each st
across, turn. *(42)*

Row 9: Ch 3, dc in next 9 sts, sc in next st, ch

2, *skip next st, **shell** *(see Special Stitches)* in next st; repeat from * 8 more times, ch 2, skip next st, sc in next st, dc in next 10 sts, skip last st, **do not turn.** *(20 dc, 9 shells, 2 sc)*

Row 10: Working across top of wings and around head, in ends of rows and in sts, (ch 3, sc in next row) 5 times, 2 sc in each st around head, (sc in next row, ch 3) 5 times, sl st in top of last row, **do not turn.**

Row 11: For **first wing,** working in first 10 dc on row 9, ch 3, 3 dc in next st, ch 3, (sc in next st, ch 3, 3 dc in next st) 4 times, ch 3, sc in same st, **turn.**

Row 12: Ch 3, sc in center dc of first 3-dc group, (ch 3, sc in next sc, ch 3, sc in center dc of next 3-dc group) 4 times, ch 3, sl st in top of last st. Fasten off.

Row 11: For **second wing,** working in last 10 dc on row 9, join with sl st in last st, repeat same row of first wing.

Row 12: Repeat same row of first wing.

Skirt

Row 1: With wrong side of shells on row 9 facing you, join with sl st in ch sp of second shell, **beg shell** *(see Special Stitches),* shell in ch sp of next 6 shells leaving last shell unworked, turn. *(7 shells)*

Rows 2-3: Sl st in next st, sl st in next ch sp, beg shell, shell in each shell across, turn.

Row 4: Sl st in next st, sl st in next ch sp, ch 3, (2 dc, picot, 3 dc, picot, 3 dc) in same sp, *sc in next shell, (3 dc, picot, 3 dc, picot, 3 dc) in next shell; repeat from * across. Fasten off.

Block to shape *(see photo);* weave cord or ribbon through ch sps of row 5, or through sts of shells on row 9. Pull to gather slightly if desired; tie ends into a bow and trim.

SMALL ANGEL

Rnds/Rows 1-6: Repeat same rnds/rows of Large Angel.

Row 7: For **first wing,** ch 3, 2 dc in same st, 3 dc in each of next 4 sts leaving remaining sts unworked, turn. *(15)*

Row 8: (Ch 3, sc in next st) 13 times leaving last st unworked, **do not turn.**

Row 9: Working in ends of rows and in sts around head, ch 3, (sc in next row, ch 3) 3 times, sc around post of next hdc on row 4, 2 sc in each st around head, sc around post of next hdc on row 4, (ch 3, sc in next row) 2 times, **do not turn.**

Row 7: For **second wing,** working in first 5 sts on opposite side of row 6, repeat same row of first wing.

Rnd 8: (Ch 3, sc in next st) across, ch 3, sl st in last sc on row 9. Fasten off.

Skirt

Row 1: Working in unworked sts of row 6, with right side facing you, skip first 2 sts, join with sl st in next st, **beg shell** *(see Special Stitches),* *skip next st, **shell** *(see Special Stitches)* in next st; repeat from * 2 more times leaving last 2 sts unworked, turn. *(4 shells)*

Rows 2-3: Sl st in next st, sl st in next ch sp, beg shell, shell in each shell across, turn.

Row 4: Ch 3, sc in next shell, ch 3, (sc in next sp between shells, ch 3, sc in next shell, ch 3) across, sc in last dc of last shell. Fasten off.

Block to shape; add ribbon if desired. ✿

Cool Crochet Poncho

DESIGNED BY ELIZABETH ANN WHITE

*This is a quick-and-easy fashion treat that can be made in no time
and served as a scrumptious addition to any wardrobe.
This versatile piece of clothing is suitable for casual or dressier looks.*

FINISHED SIZE: Adult one size fits all.

MATERIALS: 5,060 yds. sport yarn; No. 0 steel hook or hook size needed to obtain gauge.

GAUGE: 2 shells and one ch-1 sp = 1½"; 2 shell rows = 1".

BASIC STITCHES: Ch, sl st, dc.

SPECIAL STITCHES: For **shell**, 3 dc in next ch sp.

For **beginning shell (beg shell),** sl st in next 2 sts, (sl st, ch 3, 2 dc) in first ch sp.

For **double shell (dbl shell),** (3 dc, ch 2, 3 dc) in next ch-2 sp.

PONCHO

For **foundation,** (ch 4, dc in fourth ch from hook) 40 times; being careful not to twist, join with sl st in first ch of first ch-4. *(40 ch sps made)*

Rnd 1: Sl st in first ch sp, (ch 3, 2 dc) in same sp *(first shell made),* ch 1, ***shell** *(see Special Stitches)* in next ch sp, ch 1; repeat from * 3 more times, **dbl shell** *(see Special Stitches)* in next ch sp, ch 1, [(shell in next ch sp, ch 1) 9 times, dbl shell in next ch sp, ch 1]; repeat between [ ] 2 more times, (shell in next ch sp, ch 1) 4 times, join with sl st in top of ch-3. *(40 ch-1 sps, 36 shells, 4 dbl shells)*

Rnds 2-4: Beg shell *(see Special Stitches),* ch 1, (shell, ch 1) in each ch-1 sp around with (dbl shell, ch 1) in each corner ch-2 sp, join, ending with *(52 ch-1 sps, 48 shells and 4 dbl shells)* in last rnd.

Rnd 5: Beg shell, ch 1, (shell in next ch sp, ch 1) 4 times, dbl shell in next ch sp, ch 1, (shell in next ch sp, ch 1) 13 times, (shell, ch 1) in next corner ch-2 sp, (shell in next ch sp, ch 1)

13 times, dbl shell in next ch sp, ch 1, (shell in next ch sp, ch 1) 13 times, (shell, ch 1) in next corner ch-2 sp, (shell in next ch sp, ch 1) 8 times, join. *(56 ch-1 sps, 54 shells, 2 dbl shells)*

Rnds 6-26: Beg shell, ch 1, (shell, ch 1) in each ch-1 sp around with (dbl shell, ch 1) in each corner ch-2 sp, join. At end of last rnd, fasten off.

FRINGE

For **each Fringe,** cut six strands each 29" long. Holding all strands together, fold in half, insert hook in ch sp, draw fold through, draw all loose ends through fold, tighten. Trim ends.

Fringe in each ch sp across bottom of Poncho. Separating strands evenly on each Fringe, tie another knot about 1½" below first one *(see illustrations).* ✿

KNOTTED FRINGE

First row of knots

Second row of knots

Hat Pincushion

DESIGNED BY JERI STEPHENS

Even if sewing is not your cup of tea, you'll have no trouble finding a place for this adorable tiny hat pincushion. Keep it near your mending area to hold pins, needles and safety pins. It would also make a wonderful display holder for antique hatpins.

FINISHED SIZE: 4½" across.

MATERIALS: Size 10 crochet cotton thread — 100 yds. pink; 18" ecru 1" organza ribbon; 7" cream 3 mm strung pearl beads; two 1½" silk flowers; polyester fiberfill; craft glue or hot glue gun; tapestry needle; No. 12 steel hook or hook size needed to obtain gauge.

GAUGE: 6 sc = ½"; 7 sc rows = ½". Rnds 1-5 of Top = 1" across.

BASIC STITCHES: Ch, sl st, sc.

SPECIAL STITCHES: For **beginning cluster (beg cl),** ch 3, (yo, insert hook in same st, yo, draw lp through, yo, draw through 2 lps oh hook) 2 times, yo, draw through all 3 lps on hook.

For **cluster (cl),** yo, insert hook in next st, yo, draw lp through, yo, draw through 2 lps on hook, (yo, insert hook in same st, yo, draw lp through, yo, draw through 2 lps on hook) 2 times, yo, draw through all 4 lps on hook.

TOP

Rnd 1: Ch 5, sl st in first ch to form ring, ch 1, 10 sc in ring, join with sl st in first sc. *(10 sc made)*

Rnd 2: Ch 1, 2 sc in each st around, join. *(20)*

Rnd 3: Ch 1, sc in first st, 2 sc in next st, (sc in next st, 2 sc in next st) around, join. *(30)*

Rnd 4: Ch 1, sc in each st around, join.

Rnd 5: Ch 1, sc in first 2 sts, 2 sc in next st, (sc in next 2 sts, 2 sc in next st) around, join. *(40)*

Rnd 6: Repeat rnd 4.

Rnd 7: Ch 1, sc in first 3 sts, 2 sc in next st, (sc in next 3 sts, 2 sc in next st) around, join. *(50)*

Rnd 8: Repeat rnd 4.

Rnd 9: Ch 1, sc in first 4 sts, 2 sc in next st, (sc in next 4 sts, 2 sc in next st) around, join. *(60)*

Rnd 10: Repeat rnd 4.

Rnd 11: Ch 1, sc in first 5 sts, 2 sc in next st, (sc in next 5 sts, 2 sc in next st) around, join. *(70)*

Rnd 12: Repeat rnd 4.

Rnd 13: Ch 1, sc in first 6 sts, 2 sc in next st, (sc in next 6 sts, 2 sc in next st) around, join. *(80)*

Rnds 14-24: Ch 1, sc in each st around, join.

Rnd 25: Repeat rnd 3. *(120)*

Rnd 26: Beg cl *(see Special Stitches),* ch 1, skip next st, *cl (see Special Stitches) in next st, ch 1, skip next st; repeat from * around, join with sl st in top of beg cl. *(60 cls, 60 ch sps)*

Rnd 27: Sl st in first ch sp, beg cl, ch 1, (cl in next ch sp, ch 1) around, join.

Rnd 28: Sl st in first ch sp, ch 1, sc in same sp, (ch 5, skip next ch sp, sc in next ch sp) around to last ch sp, skip last ch sp; to **join,** ch 2, dc in first sc. *(30 sc, 30 ch sps)*

Rnd 29: Ch 1, sc around joining dc, 9 dc in next ch sp, (sc in next ch sp, 9 dc in next ch sp) around, join with sl st in first sc.

Rnd 30: Ch 1, sc in first st, (ch 4, skip next st, sc in next st) 2 times, ch 4, (sc, ch 6, sc) in next st, ch 4, sc in next st, *(ch 4, skip next st, sc in next st) 4 times, ch 4, (sc, ch 6, sc) in next st, ch 4, sc in next st; repeat from * around to last 3 sts, ch 4, skip next st, sc in next st, ch 4, skip last st, join. Fasten off.

BASE

Rnds 1-10: Repeat same rnds of Top.

Rnd 11: Ch 1, sc in first 2 sts, 2 sc in next st, (sc in next 2 sts, 2 sc in next st) around, join. *(80)*

Rnds 12-13: Ch 1, sc in each st around, join. Fasten off.

Finishing

Sew rnd 24 of Top to last rnd of Base, stuffing Top firmly before closing.

Tie organza ribbon into a bow around Top of Hat. Fold strung beads in half to form loop. Glue bead loop and 2 silk flowers to bow. ✿

Li'l Cowpokes

DESIGNED BY SUE CHILDRESS

*Your little buckaroo and cowgirl will be ready to rope
that next bottle of milk while dressed in their western gear.
Just teach them to say, "Yippee-tay-yi-yay, get along little dogie."*

FINISHED SIZES & GAUGE: 0-3 mos.
E hook, 5 dc sts = 1"; 5 dc rows = 2". **3-6
mos.** F hook, 9 dc sts = 2"; 9 dc rows = 4". **9-
12 mos.** G hook, 4 dc sts = 1"; 2 dc rows = 1".

MATERIALS: Nubby sport yarn — 3 [3½,
4] oz. aqua for boy or pink for girl; 18½"
[20½", 23"] white 2" fringe; 6 white 1⅛" star
appliques for boy; 4 pink 1¼" flower
appliqués for girl; white sewing thread; sewing
and tapestry needles; hook needed to obtain
gauge and size given above.

BASIC STITCHES: Ch, sl st, sc, hdc, dc, tr.

VEST

Row 1: Starting at **neckline,** with aqua for
boy or pink for girl, ch 51, sc in second ch from
hook, sc in next 9 chs, 3 sc in next ch, sc in next
7 chs, 3 sc in next ch, sc in next 12 chs, 3 sc in
next ch, sc in next 7 chs, 3 sc in next ch, sc in
last 10 chs, turn. *(58 sc made)*

Row 2: Ch 1, sc in each st across with 3 sc in
each center corner st, turn. *(66)*

Row 3: Ch 3, dc in each st across with (2 dc,
ch 2, 2 dc) in each center corner st, turn. *(78 dc,
4 ch sps)*

Rows 4-6: Ch 3, dc in each st across with (2
dc, ch 2, 2 dc) in each corner ch sp, turn, ending with *(126 dc and 4 ch sps)* in last row.

Row 7: For **front,** ch 3, dc in next 19 sts, dc
in next ch sp; for **armhole opening,** ch 6, skip
next 27 sts; for **back,** dc in next ch sp, dc in
next 32 sts, dc in next ch sp; for **armhole opening,** ch 6, skip next 27 sts; for **front,** dc in next
ch sp, dc in last 20 sts, turn. *(76 dc, 2 ch-6 sps)*

Row 8: Ch 3, dc in each st and in each ch
across, turn. *(88)*

Row 9-18: Ch 3, dc in each st across, turn.

Row 19: Sl st in first 4 sts, sc in next st, *hdc
in each of next 2 sts, dc in each of next 2 sts, (2
dc, 2 tr, 2 dc) in next st, dc in each of next 2 sts,
hdc in each of next 2 sts*, sc in next 60 sts;
repeat between **, sc in next st, sl st in last 4
sts, **do not turn.**

Rnd 20: Working around outer edge, ch 1, 2
sc in end of each dc row and sc in end of each
sc row around with 3 sc in each corner st and
skipping each inside corner st on neck edge,
join with sl st in first sc. Fasten off.

For **armhole trim,** join with sc in center ch
on one underarm, sc in each st and 2 sc in end
of each row around, join. Fasten off.

Repeat on other armhole.

BOOT (make 2)

Rnd 1: Starting at **sole,** with aqua for boy or
pink for girl, ch 6, hdc in second ch from hook,
hdc in next 3 chs, 5 dc in last ch; working on
opposite side of ch, hdc in next 3 chs, 2 hdc in
last ch, join with sl st in first hdc. *(14 hdc made)*

Rnd 2: Ch 1, 2 sc in first st, sc in next 4 sts,
3 dc in each of next 3 sts, sc in last 6 sts, 2 sc in
joining sl st, join with sl st in first sc. *(23 sts)*

Rnd 3: Ch 2, hdc in same st, hdc in next 9 sts,
2 hdc in each of next 3 sts, hdc in last 10 sts, hdc
in joining sl st, join with sl st in top of ch-2. *(28)*

Rnd 4: Ch 2, hdc in same st, hdc in next 11
sts, 2 dc in each of next 4 sts, hdc in last 12 sts,
hdc in joining sl st, join. *(34 sts)*

Rnds 5-6: Ch 2, **back post (bp,** see page
159) around each st around.

Rnd 7: Ch 2, bp around next 14 sts, (skip
next st, bp around next st) 3 times, bp around
last 13 sts, join. *(31)*

continued on page 153

Currents Afghan

Designed by Maggie Weldon

Have you sat on the beach at sunset and noticed the play of light as it is reflected in the waves? These hues seem to flow from pale pinks to pulsating purples and into blackened shadows. The colors always give me such a sense of peace and tranquility.

FINISHED SIZE: 37" x 60" not including Fringe.

MATERIALS: Fuzzy chunky yarn — 18 oz. black, 14 oz. each purple, fuchsia and teal; H hook or hook size needed to obtain gauge.

GAUGE: 13 sc = 4"; 7 sc rows = 2".

BASIC STITCHES: Ch, sc.

AFGHAN

Note: Leave 7" end when joining or fastening off for Fringe.

Row 1: With black, ch 197, sc in second ch from hook, (ch 2, skip next 2 chs, sc in next ch) across, turn. *(66 sc, 65 ch-2 sps made)*

Row 2: Ch 1, sc in first st, (2 sc in next ch sp, sc in next st) across, turn. Fasten off.

Row 3: Join fuchsia with sc in first st, (ch 2, skip next 2 sts, sc in next st) across, turn.

Row 4: Repeat row 2.

Rows 5-130: Working in color sequence of teal, purple, black and fuchsia, repeat rows 3 and 4 alternately, ending with black.

FRINGE

For **each Fringe,** cut 4 strands each 14" long. With all 4 strands held together, fold in half, insert hook in end of row, draw fold through, draw all loose ends including 7" end through fold, tighten, trim.

Using color to match stripe, Fringe in end of first row of each stripe across each short end. ❀

Li'l Cowpokes

continued from page 151

Rnd 8: Ch 2, bp around next 11 sts, (skip next st, bp around next st) 4 times, bp around last 11 sts, join. *(27)*

Rnd 9: Ch 3, dc in next 10 sts, (dc next 2 sts tog) 3 times, dc in last 10 sts, join with sl st in top of ch-3. *(24)*

Rnds 10-12: Ch 3, dc in each st around, join.

Rnd 13: *sc in next st, hdc in next 2 sts, dc in next 2 sts, (2 dc, 2 tr, 2 dc) in next st, dc in next 2 sts, hdc in next 2 sts, sc in next st*, sl st in next st; repeat between **, join with sl st in joining sl st of last rnd.

Rnd 14: Ch 1, sc in each st around, join. Fasten off.

FINISHING

1: For **lapels,** tack corner of either Vest front to row 4 on Vest. *(see photo)*

2: Sew fringe to row 8 of Vest; trim excess.

3: For boy sew one star appliqué to top of fringe, ½" from each edge of Vest.

4: For boy sew one star appliqué over front of rows 17-19 on Vest above each curved edge.

5: For boy, sew one star appliqué over rows 9-11 to outside of each Boot below curved edge.

6: For girl, sew one flower appliqué to each front of Vest over rows 4-6.

7: For girl, sew one flower appliqué over rows 9-11 on outside of each Boot below curved edge. ❀

Centerpieces

DESIGNED BY MAGGIE PETSCH

*It's a gift of love to take along a host or hostess gift when visiting during the holidays.
These small glass centerpieces hold yuletide scenes and are perfect for sharing
Christmas friendship and joy. They're also lovely office accent gifts for coworkers.*

CORSAGE CENTERPIECE

FINISHED SIZE: Fits 4" tall bowl with
2¾" opening.

MATERIALS: 225 yds. white size 10 crochet cotton thread; gold blending filament;
2¾" circle of white felt; 2¾" circle of plastic
canvas or cardboard; small artificial sprig of
Christmas greenery; one artificial sprig of
holly berries; one small craft gift
box; one small craft apple; 8" red
⅝" grosgrain ribbon; 10" red mini
star garland; 4" tall fishbowl with
2¾" opening; white craft glue; tapestry needle; No. 7 steel hook or
hook size needed to obtain gauge.

GAUGE: Rnds 1-9 of Base &
Sides = 2".

BASIC STITCHES: Ch, sl st,
sc, tr.

SPECIAL STITCHES: For
triple treble crochet (ttr), yo 4
times, insert hook in next ch, yo,
draw lp through, (yo, draw through
2 lps on hook) 5 times.

For **quadruple treble crochet
(qtr),** yo 6 times, insert hook in next
ch, yo, draw lp through, (yo, draw
through 2 lps on hook) 7 times.

For **front post stitch (fp),** yo,
insert hook from right to left
around post of st on designated rnd,
yo, draw lp through, (yo, draw
through 2 lps on hook) 2 times.
Skip next st on last rnd behind fp.

NOTES: Glue felt circle to
inside bottom of bowl.

Cut "V" in each end of ribbon.

Glue ribbon, greenery, apple, gift box and
holly berries to felt as desired.

Work with one strand crochet cotton and
one strand blending filament held together
throughout.

BASE & SIDES

Rnd 1: Starting at **Base,** ch 2, 6 sc in second ch

from hook, join with sl st in first sc. *(6 sc made)*

Rnd 2: Ch 1, 2 sc in each st around, join. *(12)*

Rnd 3: Ch 1, sc in first st, 2 sc in next st, (sc in next st, 2 sc in next st) around, join. *(18)*

Rnd 4: Ch 1, 2 sc in first st, sc in next 2 sts, (2 sc in next st, sc in next 2 sts) around, join. *(24)*

Rnd 5: Ch 1, sc in first st, 2 sc in next st, (sc in next 3 sts, 2 sc in next st) around to last 2 sts, sc in last 2 sts, join. *(30)*

Rnd 6: Ch 1, sc in first 3 sts, 2 sc in next st, (sc in next 4 sts, 2 sc in next st) around to last st, sc in last st, join. *(36)*

Rnd 7: Ch 1, 2 sc in first st, sc in next 5 sts, (2 sc in next st, sc in next 5 sts) around, join. *(42)*

Rnd 8: Ch 1, sc in first 4 sts, 2 sc in next st, (sc in next 6 sts, 2 sc in next st) around to last 2 sts, sc in last 2 sts, join. *(48)*

Rnd 9: Ch 1, sc in first 6 sts, 2 sc in next st,

(sc in next 7 sts, 2 sc in next st) around to last st, sc in last st, join. *(54)*

Rnd 10: Ch 1, sc in first 3 sts, 2 sc in next st, (sc in next 8 sts, 2 sc in next st) around to last 5 sts, sc in last 5 sts, join. *(60)*

Rnd 11: Ch 1, sc in first 9 sts, 2 sc in next st, (sc in next 9 sts, 2 sc in next st) around, join. *(66)*

Rnd 12: For **Sides**, ch 14 *(counts as first ttr and ch-9 sp)*, skip next 5 sts, **ttr** *(see Special Stitches)* in next st, (ch 9, skip next 5 sts, ttr in next st) around to last 5 sts, ch 4; to **join**, ttr in fifth ch of ch-14. *(11 ttr, 11 ch-9 sps)*

Rnd 13: Ch 18 *(counts as first ttr and ch-13 sp)*, ttr in fifth ch of next ch-9, (ch 13, ttr in fifth ch of next ch-9) around, ch 6; to **join, qtr** *(see Special Stitches)* in fifth ch of ch-18.

Rnd 14: Ch 20 *(counts as first ttr and ch-15 sp)*, ttr in seventh ch of next ch-13, (ch 15, ttr in seventh ch of next ch-13) around, ch 8; to **join,** qtr in fifth ch of ch-20.

Rnd 15: Ch 14 *(counts as first ttr and ch-9 sp)*, (ttr in eighth ch of next ch-15, ch-9) around; slip cover over bowl, join with sl st in fifth ch of ch-14.

Rnd 16: Ch 4 *(counts as first tr)*, 7 tr in each ch sp around, join with sl st in top of ch-4. Fasten off. *(78 tr)*

LID TOP

Rnds 1-3: Repeat same rnds of Base & Sides.

Rnd 4: Ch 1, 2 sc in first st, sc in next st, **fp** *(see Special Stitches)* around first st on rnd 1, (2 sc in next st on last rnd, sc in next st, fp around next st on rnd 1) around, join with sl st in first sc. *(24 sts)*

Rnds 5-6: Repeat same rnds of Base & Sides.

Rnd 7: Ch 1, 2 sc in first st, sc in next 4 sts, fp around next fp on rnd 4, (2 sc in next st on last rnd, sc in next 4 sts, fp around next fp on rnd 4) around, join. *(42)*

Rnds 8-9: Repeat same rnds of Base & Sides.

Rnd 10: Ch 1, 2 sc in first st, sc in next 7 sts, fp around next fp on rnd 7, (2 sc in next st on last rnd, sc in next 7 sts, fp around next fp on rnd 7) around, join. *(60)*

Rnd 11: Repeat same rnds of Base & Sides.

Rnd 12: Ch 1, sc in first 4 sts, 2 sc in next st, (sc in next 10 sts, 2 sc in next st) around to last 6 sts, sc in last 6 sts, join with sl st in first sc. *(72)*

Rnd 13: Ch 1, 2 sc in first st, sc in next 10 sts, fp around next fp on rnd 10, (2 sc in next st on last rnd, sc in next 10 sts, fp around next fp on rnd 10) around, join. Fasten off. *(78)*

LID BOTTOM

Rnds 1-12: Repeat same rnds of Base & Sides.

Rnd 13: Ch 1, sc in first 11 sts, 2 sc in next st, (sc in next 11 sts, 2 sc in next st) around, join. *(78)*

Rnd 14: Holding Lid Top and Bottom wrong sides together, with cardboard or plastic canvas circle between, with Lid Top towards you, working through both thicknesses in **back lps,** ch 1, sc in each st around, join with sl st in first sc.

Rnd 15: Ch 1; working from left to right, **reverse sc** *(see page 159)* in each st around, join. Fasten off.

Sew sts on last rnd of Sides to remaining lps of rnd 13 on Lid Bottom.

FINISHING

Cut one star from garland. Glue to center of Lid Top. Cut six pieces of three stars each. Glue each piece vertically between each vertical fp stripe.

SILENT NIGHT CENTERPIECE

FINISHED SIZE: Fits 4" tall bowl with 2¾" opening.

MATERIALS: 150 yds. lt. blue size 10 crochet cotton thread; blue metallic blending filament; white sewing thread; 2¾" circle of white felt; 2¾" circle of plastic canvas or cardboard; 1⅛" white star bead; miniature nativity figures; 10" gold mini star garland; 4" tall fishbowl with 2¾" opening; white craft glue; sewing and tapestry needles; No. 7 steel hook or hook size needed to obtain gauge.

GAUGE: Rnds 1-9 of Base & Sides = 2".

BASIC STITCHES: Ch, sl st, sc, tr.

SPECIAL STITCHES: For **trible treble crochet (ttr),** yo 4 times, insert hook in next ch, yo, draw lp through, (yo, draw through 2 lps on hook) 5 times.

For **quadruple treble crochet (qtr),** yo 6 times, insert hook in next ch, yo, draw lp through, (yo, draw through 2 lps on hook) 7 times.

For **front post stitch (fp),** yo, insert hook from right to left around post of st on designated rnd, yo, draw lp through, (yo, draw through 2 lps on hook) 2 times. Skip next st on last rnd behind fp.

NOTES: Glue felt circle to inside bottom of bowl.

With tweezers, glue nativity figures to felt as desired.

Use one strand crochet cotton and one strand blending filament held together throughout.

BASE & SIDES

Work same as Corsage Centerpiece Base & Sides.

LID TOP

Work same as Corsage Centerpiece Lid Top.

Thread sewing thread through top of star. Allowing star to hang down about ½", sew to center bottom of Lid Top.

LID BOTTOM AND FINISHING

Work same as Corsage Centerpiece Lid Bottom and Finishing. ✿

General Instructions

Yarn & Hooks

Always use the weight of yarn specified in the pattern so you can be assured of achieving the proper gauge. It is best to purchase extra of each color needed to allow for differences in tension and dyes.

The hook size stated in the pattern is to be used as a guide. Always work a swatch of the stitch pattern with the suggested hook size. If you find your gauge is smaller or larger than what is specified, choose a different size hook.

Gauge

Gauge is measured by counting the number of rows or stitches per inch. Each of the patterns featured in this book will have a gauge listed. Gauge for some small motifs or flowers is given as an overall measurement. Proper gauge must be attained for the project to come out the size stated and to prevent ruffling and puckering.

Make a swatch in the stitch indicated in the gauge section of the instructions. Lay the swatch flat and measure the stitches. If you have more stitches per inch than specified in the pattern, your gauge is too tight and you need a larger hook. Fewer stitches per inch indicates a gauge that is too loose. In this case, choose a smaller hook size. Next, check the number of rows. If necessary, adjust your row gauge slightly by pulling the loops down a little tighter on your hook, or by pulling the loops up slightly to extend them.

Once you've attained the proper gauge, you're ready to start your project. Remember to check your gauge periodically to avoid problems later.

Pattern Repeat Symbols

Written crochet instructions typically include symbols such as parentheses, asterisks and brackets. In some patterns a diamond or bullet (dot) may be added.

( ) Parentheses enclose instructions which are to be worked again later or the number of times indicated after the parentheses. For example, "(2 dc in next st, skip next st) 5 times" means to follow the instructions within the parentheses a total of five times. If no number appears after the parentheses, you will be instructed when to repeat further into the pattern. Parentheses may also be used to enclose a group of stitches which should be worked in one space or stitch. For example, "(2 dc, ch 2, 2 dc) in next st" means to work all the stitches within the parentheses in the next stitch.

* Asterisks may be used alone or in pairs, usually in combination with parentheses. If used in pairs, the instructions enclosed within asterisks will be followed by instructions for repeating. These repeat instructions may appear later in the pattern or immediately after the last asterisk. For example, "*Dc in next 4 sts, (2 dc, ch 2, 2 dc) in corner sp*, dc in next 4 sts; repeat between ** 2 more times" means to work through the instructions up to the word "repeat," then repeat only the instructions that are enclosed within the asterisks twice.

If used alone an asterisk marks the beginning of instructions which are to be repeated. Work through the instructions from the beginning, then repeat only the portion after the * up to the word "repeat"; then follow any remaining instructions. If a number of times is given, work through the instructions one time, repeat the number of times stated, then follow the remainder of the instructions.

[ ] Brackets, ◊ diamonds and • bullets are used in the same manner as asterisks. Follow the specific instructions given when repeating.

Finishing

Patterns that require assembly will suggest a tapestry needle in the materials. This should be a #16, #18 or #26 blunt-tipped tapestry needle. When stitching pieces together, be careful to keep the seams flat so pieces do not pucker.

Hiding loose ends is never a fun task, but if done correctly, may mean the difference between an item looking great for years or one that quickly shows signs of wear. Always leave 6-8" of yarn when beginning or ending. Thread the loose end into your tapestry needle and carefully weave through the back of several stitches. Then, weave in the opposite direction, going through different strands. Gently pull the end and clip, allowing the end to pull up under the stitches.

If your project needs blocking, a light steam pressing works well. Lay your project on a large table or on the floor, depending on the size, shaping and smoothing by hand as much as possible. Adjust your steam iron to the permanent press setting, then hold slightly above the stitches, allowing the steam to penetrate the thread. Do not rest the iron on the item. Gently pull and smooth the stitches into shape, spray lightly with starch and allow to dry completely.

Stiffening

There are many liquid products on the market made specifically for stiffening doilies and other soft items. For best results, carefully read the manufacturer's instructions on the product you select before beginning.

Forms for shaping can be many things. Styrofoam® shapes and plastic margarine tubs work well for items such as bowls and baskets. Glass or plastic drinking glasses are used for vase-type items. If you cannot find an item with the dimensions given in the pattern to use as a form, any similarly sized item can

be shaped by adding layers of plastic wrap. Place the dry crochet piece over the form to check the fit, remembering that it will stretch when wet.

For shaping flat pieces, corrugated cardboard, Styrofoam® or a cutting board designed for sewing may be used. Be sure to cover all surfaces of forms or blocking board with clear plastic wrap, securing with cellophane tape.

If you have not used fabric stiffener before, you may wish to practice on a small swatch before stiffening the actual item. For proper saturation when using conventional stiffeners, work liquid thoroughly into the crochet piece and let stand for about 15 minutes. Then, squeeze out excess stiffener and blot with paper towels. Continue to blot while shaping to remove as much stiffener as possible. Stretch over form, shape and pin with rust-proof pins; allow to dry, then unpin.

Stitch Guide

Chain (ch)
Yo, draw hook through lp.

Slip Stitch (sl st)
Insert hook in st, yo, draw through st and lp on hook.

Single Crochet (sc)
Insert hook in st (a), yo, draw lp through, yo, draw through both lps on hook (b).

a

b

Standard Stitch Abbreviations

ch(s)	chain(s)
dc	double crochet
dtr	double treble crochet
hdc	half double crochet
lp(s)	loop(s)
rnd(s)	round(s)
sc	single crochet
sl st	slip stitch
sp(s)	space(s)
st(s)	stitch(es)
tog	together
tr	treble crochet
tr tr/ttr	triple treble crochet
yo	yarn over

The patterns in this book are written using American crochet stitch terminology. For our international customers, hook sizes, stitches and yarn definitions should be converted as follows:

But, as with all patterns, test your gauge (tension) to be sure.

US	= UK
sl st (slip stitch)	= sc (single crochet)
sc (single crochet)	= dc (double crochet)
hdc (half double crochet)	= htr (half treble crochet)
dc (double crochet)	= tr (treble crochet)
tr (treble crochet)	= dtr (double treble crochet)
dtr (double treble crochet)	= ttr (triple treble crochet)
skip	= miss

Thread/Yarns
Bedspread Weight	= No.10 Cotton or Virtuoso
Sport Weight	= 4 Ply or thin DK
Worsted Weight	= Thick DK or Aran

Measurements
1"	=	2.54 cm
1 yd.	=	.9144 m
1 oz.	=	28.35 g

Crochet Hooks
Metric	US	Metric	US
.60mm	14	3.00mm	D/3
.75mm	12	3.50mm	E/4
1.00mm	10	4.00mm	F/5
1.50mm	6	4.50mm	G/6
1.75mm	5	5.00mm	H/8
2.00mm	B/1	5.50mm	I/9
2.50mm	C/2	6.00mm	J/10

Half Double Crochet (hdc)

Yo, insert hook in st (a), yo, draw lp through (b), yo, draw through all 3 lps on hook (c).

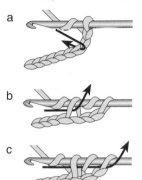

Double Crochet (dc)

Yo, insert hook in st, yo, draw lp through, (yo, draw through 2 lps on hook) 2 times.

Treble Crochet (tr)

Yo 2 times, insert hook in st, yo, draw lp through, (yo, draw through 2 lps on hook) 3 times.

Double Treble Crochet (dtr)

Yo 3 times, insert hook in st, yo, draw lp through, (yo, draw through 2 lps on hook) 4 times.

Straight Stitch

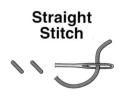

Front Loop/ Back Loop

(front lp/back lp)

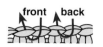

Reverse Single Crochet (reverse sc)

Working from left to right, insert hook in next st to the right (a), yo, draw through st, complete as sc (b).

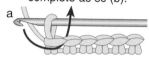

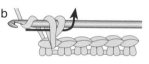

Single Crochet Color Change (sc color change)

Drop first color; yo with 2nd color, draw through last 2 lps of st.

Front Post/Back Post Stitches (fp/bp)

Yo, insert hook from front to back or back to front around post of st on indicated row; complete as stated in pattern.

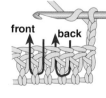

Satin Stitch

Lazy Daisy Stitch

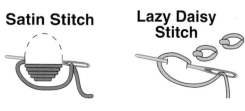

Single Crochet next 2 stitches together (sc next 2 sts tog)

Draw up lp in each of next 2 sts, yo, draw through all 3 lps on hook.

Half Double Crochet next 2 stitches together (hdc next 2 sts tog)

(Yo, insert hook in next st, yo, draw lp through) 2 times, yo, draw through all 5 lps on hook.

Double Crochet next 2 stitches together (dc next 2 sts tog)

(Yo, insert hook in next st, yo, draw lp through, yo, draw through 2 lps on hook) 2 times, yo, draw through all 3 lps on hook.

Sc Over Ring

French Knot (2-wrap)

Index

Alexander, Carol 31, 112, 125, 139
An Annie Original Design 88
Augostine, Denise 90
Autumn Doily 90
Baby Night Cap 116
Bath Duo 98
Black & White Afghan 95
Bridal Set 139
Bright Basics 76
Brown, Shirley 133
Centerpieces 154
Chamberlain, Lena 42
Childress, Sue 24, 54, 84, 144, 151
Christmas Shell Afghan 51
Cole, Priscilla 142
Colorful Carryall 114
Cool Crochet Poncho 147
Cool Water Bottle Holder 66
Cotton Candy 62
Country Dining 14
Cro-Tat™ Snowflakes 105
Cro-Tat™ Jar Topper 64
Currents Afghan 153
Diagonal Dishcloth 44
Doily & Bowl Cover 70
Doily Hat & Doily 125
Doily Sachet 53
Dolly Backpack 134
Drake, Dot 21
Earring Jackets 23
Eaves, Ellen Anderson 76
Elegant Pastels 79
Eng, Katherine 12, 51, 81
Fans & Lace 40
Fanton, Darla 44
Fentress, Sandra 98
Field, Liz 57
Fielder, Erma 64, 105
Floor Doily 88

Floral Doily 31
Flower Girl Basket 12
Foot Warmers 42
Gale, Norma J. 70
Glass Slippers 120
Hat Pincushion 148
Hatfield, Jan 8
Hatfield, Sharon 35
Hawke, Kyleigh C. 86, 103
Headband and Mittens 58
Heim, Alice 131
Heirloom Tablecloth 10
Helpful Holders 84
Herrin, Janie 32
Hildebrand, Tammy 79
Homespun Hat & Scarf 133
Hooded Scarf 75
King, Jenny 136
Kitchen Extras 54
Lace Tissue Holder 47
Lacy Bib and Bottle 26
Lacy Bookmarks 38
Lacy Towel Edgings 110
LaFlamme, Lucille 101
Li'l Cowpokes 151
Little Sweetie 24
Marrs, Dee 52
Maxfield, Sandra Miller 127
Maxwell, Jo Ann 120
McCaughin, Terri 23, 48
McClain, Jennifer 14, 110
Mini Angels 144
Nagy, Maria 56
On The Double Shawl 7
Ottinger, Mary S. 134
Padded Hangers 8
Pastel Bookmarks 103
Patterson, Shirley 58
Peach Parfait 101
Pearson, Jane 116
Petsch, Maggie 154

Photo Album 56
Pillow Toppers 81
Pineapple Doily 18
Pixie Christmas Stocking 35
Playtime Puppets 128
Ponytail Ruffles 48
Present Pillow 73
Puff Stitch Pillow 131
Puppy Poncho 57
Puttin' on the Ritz 142
Quick Stitch Stocking 127
Rabier, Josie 53
Sass, Jocelyn 40
Scrubby Pad 32
Serenade Doily 21
Sewing Helper 36
Simply Beautiful Bibs 86
Simpson, Diane 123
Sims, Darla 7, 95, 119
Spagnuolo, Delores 114
Sports Carrier 136
Stephens, Jeri 148
Stratton, Brenda 112, 139
Striped Chair Pad 96
Striped Wave Afghan 119
Sunderman, Vida 10
Sweet Baby Hat 68
Teague Treece, Judy 18
Teapot Tidee 52
Toe Cozies 123
Victorian Snuggler 16
Weldon, Maggie 16, 153
White, Elizabeth Ann 26, 66, 73, 75, 147
Whitford, Estella 128
Wigington, Kathy 62, 96
Wilcox, Michele 68
Wild Rose Doily 112
Willson, Margret 38, 47
Yorston, Debra 36